BUSINESS EXPERT SYSTEMS

The Irwin Series in Information and Decision Sciences

Consulting Editors

Robert B. Fetter
Yale University

Claude McMillan
University of Colorado

BUSINESS EXPERT SYSTEMS

Clyde W. Holsapple
Associate Professor of Management
Purdue University

Andrew B. Whinston
Professor of Management, Economics, and Computer Science
Purdue University

Illustrations by Jon Kerry

1987
IRWIN
Homewood, Illinois   60430

We recognize that certain terms in this book are trademarks, and we have made every effort to print these throughout the text with the capitalization and punctuation used by the holder of the trademark.

ISBN 0-256-05544-0

Library of Congress Catalog Card No. 86–81649

Printed in the United States of America

1 2 3 4 5 6 7 8 9 0 K 4 3 2 1 0 9 8 7

Dedicated to the memory of our invaluable coresearcher and very good friend Robert H. Bonczek (1951–1985)

Preface

Not so long ago, a founding father of the artificial intelligence (AI) movement, Nobel laureate Herbert Simon, remarked

> A few years from now, a single book will be too small to even sketch out the uses of AI techniques in management.*

Today these techniques are rapidly emerging as important contributors to effective management. One of the greatest growth areas lies in the use of expert systems for supporting managerial decision processes. Expert system techniques, a major branch of the AI field, have only recently begun to be applied to business problems. This book explores the potential of business expert systems and explains how to transform that potential into reality. It is designed to engender an in-depth understanding of business expert systems from the standpoints of what they are, how they can be developed, how they work, how they can be used, and what their significance is for modern organizations.

Business Expert Systems is appropriate for business school students in either an undergraduate or graduate level course. A reasonable degree of familiarity with both management and business computing basics (e.g., data management and spreadsheets) is a recommended prerequisite. However, an extensive background in programming or other elements of computer science is unnecessary. No prior training in any aspect of artificial intelligence is assumed. To maximize the book's relevance and practical value to business students we have taken an applied tone, carefully avoiding technicalities and abstractions that are not immediately relevant to building and using business expert systems. Although such abstractions may be intellectually interesting to some,

---

*Taken from the foreword to *Foundations of Decision Support Systems* by R. H. Bonczek, C. W. Holsapple, and A. B. Whinston (New York: Academic Press, 1981).

we find that they are best reserved for follow-up coursework, at which point they will be less formidable and better appreciated.

Our purpose in this book is to make business expert systems as real as possible to business students. For both undergraduate and graduate students (including executive MBAs), we have found the level and scope of coverage to be suitable for a one semester course, while still allowing time for student projects in business application areas of the students' own choosing. Of course, instructors are free to supplement the book with more abstract and highly specialized technical material.

We have also been careful to avoid letting this book become just another general survey of the expert system field. We believe that the title is quite descriptive and consider *Business* to be an essential ingredient in the title. For this reason, we intentionally avoid topics such as infectious blood diseases, geological analysis, classification schemes for animals, ways of getting to a theater, Sherlock Holmes cases, and other problems dealt with in traditional books about expert systems. Rather than a few fleeting references to business applications of expert system technology, *Business Expert Systems* is entirely devoted to providing an in-depth examination of such applications. However, even though it has a definite business orientation, this book is also worthwhile for readers dealing with certain nonbusiness applications (e.g., engineering) and those with a general interest in the expert system field.

From a pedagogical standpoint, our experience has shown that there are two keys to highly productive learning experiences concerning business expert systems: (1) selection of a real-world application problem that is sufficiently rich to illustrate all important aspects of business expert system construction and usage, yet sufficiently easy to understand by students with diverse business training and experience; and (2) selection of a real-world AI software environment that is sufficiently versatile to illustrate the construction and usage of a business expert system for the chosen application, yet sufficiently easy to understand by students with fairly minimal levels of computer exposure. These two keys have had a fundamental influence on this book's content and style. They allow us to avoid the discontinuity and relative superficiality (or size explosion) that typically result from skipping from one application to another or from one piece of software to another. The result is a more efficient and effective instructional experience.

The ongoing business application example used throughout this book is concerned with the problem of establishing sales quotas. As each new expert system concept or technique is introduced, it is illustrated and reinforced within the context of this example. The sales quota application is familiar enough to be readily grasped by business readers. At the same time, it is rich enough to provide a source for the realistic examples used to illustrate each new point as it is introduced. The ongoing elaborations and variations to this business application lend an important sense of continuity to the presentation and are suggestive of features that readers may want to incorporate into their own business expert systems.

Though the sales quota example is sufficiently comprehensive to illustrate all of the major business expert system topics, we believe it is useful for students to see other applications of the concepts and techniques covered by this example. Rather than a passive approach of having students read about other applications, we have had good success with an active approach in which students devise their own business expert systems in areas that are of particular interest to them. We find that such projects form a very interesting basis for both individual learning and shared classroom discussion. This book's content is, in our experience, a sufficient foundation for such projects.

The AI software environment used throughout this book is Guru.®* As our examination of the expert system for setting sales quotas unfolds, we show how it can actually be developed and consulted within the Guru environment.** This will enable the reader to readily grasp the ideas, principles, techniques, and terminology that are essential for understanding the application of expert system technology to business. Guru is a commercially available AI environment for building and using business expert systems. It is used by governments and corporations (from those that are small to some of the very largest) for implementing a wide range of business expert systems. In our opinion, its flexibility, power, and convenience combine to make Guru a valuable guide for understanding the world of business expert system possibilities.

It is worth noting that selection of the quota application and the Guru development tool do not limit the value and applicability of this book for an introductory course about business expert systems. The selection of the quota advice application does not mean that a student will be unable to apply what is learned to other business application areas. Its intention and effect is to illustrate, not to restrict. It provides patterns that can be applied elsewhere. Similarly, the selection of Guru as the development tool does not mean that a student will be unable to apply what is learned when it comes to using other tools (subject to their capabilities, of course). Again, the intention and effect is to illustrate, not to restrict.

---

*Guru is a registered trademark of Micro Data Base Systems, Inc.

**All examples have been implemented on an IBM microcomputer using Guru. There are several photos showing actual multicolor screens generated by Guru on a PGS color monitor. Figures containing printed output from Guru were produced on an inexpensive IBM graphics printer. More expensive printers or plotters would yield output that is visually much more refined and colorful.

Business Expert Systems is organized into four major parts:

Part I. Setting the Stage for Business Expert Systems

Part II. Business Expert Systems: Basic Concepts

Part III. Building a Business Expert System

Part IV. What to Look for: Today and Tomorrow

Part I introduces you to the world of artificial intelligence. The emphasis is on reasoning systems, from the seminal work of Simon and Newell, through the classic expert systems. Tracing the evolution of business computing, it becomes clear how expert system technology is a revolutionary, yet natural, next step in harnessing the power of computers for business. Successful expert systems for real business problem solving were not in widespread use in 1985. Part I concludes by explaining why this was so and why it is now in the process of changing.

Part II explains the basic concepts of business expert systems. It draws a clear distinction between the expert systems and the tools with which they are built. The three elements of an expert system (its user interface, inference engine, and rule set) are described. The notion of a rule as a means for capturing a fragment of reasoning expertise is examined. This is followed by a description of how an inference engine can reason with a set of rules in order to solve problems. Methods for reasoning with various kinds of uncertainty are discussed. Finally, the possibilities for requesting an expert system consultation by invoking its inference engine are explored. All of these basic concepts are illustrated with the ongoing example of a business expert system that provides sales quota advice.

Part III presents a number of advanced expert system concepts that are of primary interest to expert system developers. These practitioner topics include rule specification strategies, exercising control over an inference engine's reasoning behavior, comparisons of certainty algebras, and techniques for fuzzy variable manipulation. Part IV begins with a summary of what should be considered when choosing a tool for expert system development. It concludes with a vision of tomorrow's knowledge-based organizations in which artificially intelligent application systems for decision support will play a prominent role. A glossary is also provided for quick reference to common terms.

In closing, we express our thanks to the many practicing managers and management school students whose participation in our coursework and seminars has played an important role in the evolution of *Business Expert Systems*. The sales quota case study is based, in part, on useful suggestions provided by Kristina Ferguson. The book has benefited from the constructive comments provided by Dr. Ron Adelsman, Dr. Robert Johnson, Steve Thompson, and Mickey Williamson during the final preparation of the manuscript. We are also appreciative of Kathy Smith's diligent and tireless typing efforts and of Kathey Freeman's photographic, typing, and indexing assistance.

The general atmosphere of the Management Information Research Center (MIRC) in Purdue University's Krannert Graduate School of Management was particularly conducive to the development of the insights and perspectives presented in this book. MIRC has received generous corporate support from IBM, GE, and others. Mr. Francis G. (Buck) Rodgers, Vice President of Marketing, and Mr. Charles Bowen, Director of Plans and Program Administration, both at IBM, have supported our MIRC program in many ways, and we wish to thank them. We are also grateful to Dr. Gary Koehler and Dr. Mike Gagle (and his technical staff) of Micro Data Base Systems, Inc. for providing the Guru software used to develop the examples shown in this book.

Clyde W. Holsapple
Andrew B. Whinston

Contents

Chapter Five: Reasoning with Rules   73

The Advisor Rule Set. Challenge of the Unknown Variables: *Three Approaches to Knowing. Customizing the User Interface.* Beyond User Interaction—The Power of Integration: *Data Base Management within a Rule Set. Spreadsheets within a Rule Set. Procedural Modeling within a Rule Set. Consultation within a Rule Set. Graphics within a Rule Set. Integrated Knowledge Acquisition.* Rule-Based Reasoning. Reasoning with Rules—Forward Reasoning: *An Example of Forward Reasoning.* Presenting the Results of a Consultation. Reasoning with Rules—Reverse Reasoning: *General Description of Reverse Reasoning. Controlling the Reasoning Flow. An Example of Reverse Reasoning.*

Chapter Six: Dealing with Uncertainty   105

Certainty Factors. The Certainty of a Premise: *Joint Certainty for a Premise. Confirmative Certainty for a Premise.* The Certainty of a Variable's Value: *Reporting the Certainty Factor of a Variable's Value. Capturing a User's Uncertainty.* The Certainty of a Rule Action: *Passing an Action's Certainty along to a Variable. Different Certainties for Different Actions in a Conclusion. Variable Degrees of Certainty.* Firing Multiple Rules for the Same Variable Value: *Replacement versus Additive Assignments. Confirming a Variable's Value.* Fuzzy Variables: *Reasoning with Fuzzy Variables. Reporting the Values and Certainties of a Fuzzy Variable.* Threshold of the Unknown.

Chapter Seven: Invoking an Inference Engine   125

The Consultation Environment: *The Consultation Context. Environment Controls. Knowledge Security.* Methods for Requesting a Consultation: *Command Invocation of the Inference Engine. Menu-Guided Invocation of the Inference Engine. Natural Language Invocation of the Inference Engine. Customized User Interfaces for Invoking the Inference Engine. Artificially Intelligent Application Systems.* The Explanation Abilities: *Explanations during a Consultation. Explanations after a Consultation.*

PART III: BUILDING A BUSINESS EXPERT SYSTEM   149

Chapter Eight: Developing a Rule Set   151

Expert System Opportunities. An Aside for Programmers. Seizing an Expert System Opportunity: *Objectives. Planning.* The Development Process. Study and Problem Definition. Rule Set Specification: *Discovering*

Chapter Thirteen: Knowledge-Based Organizations   301

Knowledge Workers: *Technological Advances. Training. Cooperation.* Infrastructure. Management of a Knowledge-Based Organization. Realization of Knowledge-Based Organizations.

Part I

SETTING THE STAGE FOR BUSINESS EXPERT SYSTEMS

We'd be out on a ledge, too, if it weren't for the expert systems.

Chapter One

The World of Artificial Intelligence

Although artificial intelligence (AI) has scarcely touched today's managers, it will begin to have dramatic and widespread impacts on their activities over the next few years. Looking farther out, to the end of the century, practical fruits from the past 30 years of AI research will be commonplace. The application of artificial intelligence techniques will play a major role in reshaping traditional notions of what organizations are, how they are managed, and how decisions are made. All of this presents a major challenge and an important opportunity to today's managers and organizations. Though the transition will not be without growing pains, it will lead to tremendous increases in the productivity of managers and organizations. Those organizations in the forefront of applying AI methods to aid in management will have distinct competitive advantages over those that lag.

Perhaps the largest AI payoff will come in the realm of expert systems. These are systems that employ AI reasoning techniques in order to offer expert advice about problems posed by their users. An expert system makes use of expertise that has been gathered from a human expert about how to solve a specific type of problem or class of related problems. The potential benefits of such systems range from the distribution and omnipresence of expertise to the formalization and preservation of an organization's reasoning knowledge. The commonly cited obstacles of long development times, high development costs, difficult development tools, and isolation from the mainstream of data processing are vanishing because of a new kind of tool for expert system development.

Before exploring the realm of expert systems in detail, it is worthwhile to step back and view the broader field of artificial intelligence. This introductory chapter provides a brief overview of the AI field from its beginnings up to the very latest major development: a software environment that blends AI techniques with the mainstream of management information processing methods.

WHAT IS ARTIFICIAL INTELLIGENCE?

Strive

Artificial intelligence endeavors to make machines such as computers capable of displaying intelligent behavior. This means behavior that would reasonably be regarded as intelligent if it were observed in humans. Two cornerstones of intelligence are the ability to understand natural language and the ability to reason. These, in turn, represent two principal areas of research in the AI field. This research has led to the discovery of practical techniques for building software that enables computers to understand natural language and to solve problems by reasoning. It is important to understand that these techniques do not pretend to employ the same internal mechanisms as a human in carrying out such activities. However, they do produce results that are more or less comparable to what would be expected of a human.

NATURAL LANGUAGE SYSTEMS

The central AI objective of natural language processing is to allow humans to interact with computers in their own natural language, rather than a computer language. The user of a natural language system does not need to learn or remember any special language before asking for desired information. Talking to the computer is just about like talking to a human assistant. The only difference is that requests are typed out on a keyboard rather than spoken—and even this difference may disappear as further advances in voice recognition occur.

When conversing with a natural language system, you do not need to be concerned about adhering to a rigid computer language syntax. Everyday words, sentences, and even sentence fragments are just fine. Just as in a human conversation, you may make a request that is not fully understood. It might contain a new word whose meaning is unknown, a word that is known to have multiple meanings, a word that you have inadvertently misused, and so forth. Just as in a human conversation, the natural language system will interact with you to clarify the request. It is able to learn the meanings of new terms as you introduce them into the conversation. It then understands all future references to those terms. This is a handy way for customizing the system's vocabulary to include your own favorite terms, jargon, and abbreviations.

Some natural language systems are able to detect typing or spelling errors in a request and automatically correct them for you. For instance, if you inadvertently typed lsit rather than list, the system would surmise that you really meant to enter list. As a courtesy, you would be asked whether this interpretation is correct. Alternatively, you may want to define lsit to be a new term in the system's vocabulary.

Just as in a human conversation, a natural language system is able to understand a request in the context of the requests that preceded it. For instance, you might ask:

```
Who is in New York?
```

The system might respond by asking you whether you mean New York state or city. After indicating that you are referring to the city, the system will respond with a listing of employees who are based in New York City. Next, you might ask:

```
What are their salaries?
```

The system will respond with a two-column report showing names of New York City employees in one column and their respective salaries in the second column. If you then decide that you want to see this information shown as a pie graph, your next request might be:

```
Plot them in a pie.
```

The result is a pie graph showing the relative salary percentages for New York City employees. If you next wanted to see the same information portrayed as a bar graph, you might say:

```
Graph it as bars.
```

The same information that was formerly shown as a pie is now shown in a bar graph.

Today, the most widespread use of natural language processing is for retrieving information from data files or data bases. In the course of understanding a request, the natural language system builds a comparable retrieval command in the language that can be processed by a particular file or data base management system. The resultant command is then executed by the file or data base management software in order to actually retrieve the desired information and present it to the user. In this way, the user is insulated from any need to know about how the file or data base is organized. Some of the more advanced natural language systems are also able to handle requests for data modification, numeric computations, statistical analyses, graphics generation, model execution, and even expert system consultation.

A first-rate natural language system can increase the productivity of both managers and data processing professionals. It allows managers who are only occasional or casual computer users to *directly* get answers to ad hoc information needs. Without such a system, the manager must either go to the data processing staff (if it exists) for help, or learn how to use the data base management system's query language or menu interface (if it exists). Neither is a particularly satisfying strategy: The first ends up overloading the data processing staff, which is expensive and time consuming, while the second forces the manager to learn a new language and use it enough so that it does not have to be relearned from time to time. The natural language solution frees the data processing staff to work on application systems for high-volume, repetitive tasks and frees the manager to concentrate on decision making rather than computerese.

Table 1–1 summarizes some of the natural language systems that are commercially available today. They are operable on micro, mini, and mainframe computers. For the most part, computer size is not a major determinant of how sophisticated or extensive a natural language system's capabilities are. In addition to file management systems, natural language interfaces have been successfully developed for nearly all major types of data base management systems. This includes the ancient hierarchical approach to data base management, as well as the more popular relational and CODASYL* approaches.

Most natural language systems are stand-alone in nature, functioning as add-on utility programs for file or data base management systems. However, in a couple of cases, natural language processing has been entirely integrated as part of a single program that carries out data base management, statistics, graphics, spreadsheet, and other kinds of processing. This integration is an important step toward a more versatile generation of natural language systems, capable of understanding requests for procedural modeling and computer- based reasoning [4].

REASONING SYSTEMS: AN OVERVIEW

The quest for computer systems that can reason about facts and assertions in order to solve problems lies at the heart of the AI field. In general, reasoning systems have three major parts or subsystems:

- A *knowledge system* that holds facts and assertions about some problem area.

- A *language system* for stating specific problems to be solved.

- A *problem-processing system* that draws on the content of the knowledge system in order to solve problems stated with the language system.

---

*Conference on Data Systems Languages network data model.

TABLE 1-1 Commercial natural language systems

Natural language system	Vendor	Host machine	Type	Data sources	Graphics supported
Clout	Microrim	Micro	Stand-alone	R:base	None
Guru®	MDBS, Inc.	Mini, micro	Integral	Guru data bases	Bar, pie, line, etc.
INTELLECT	Artificial Intelligence Corporation	Mainframe	Stand-alone	IDMS, ADABAS, Vsam, FOCUS	Bar
K-Chat	MDBS, Inc.	Mini, micro	Integral	KnowledgeMan data bases	Bar, pie, line, etc.
RAMIS II English	Mathematica Products Group, Inc.	Mainframe	Stand-alone	RAMIS II	None
THEMIS	Frey Associates	Mini	Stand-alone	Datatrieve, DBMS-32	None

Research into the nature of reasoning systems has been concerned with developing increasingly powerful and flexible techniques for building these three subsystems.

Although it is commonplace in AI literature to see the term *data base* used when referring to a knowledge system, we shall avoid using it in this way. The approaches that AI researchers have invented for representing knowledge in a knowledge system include array structures, semantic networks, property hierarchies, various list structures, and predicate calculus expression sets. While all of these are interesting and have their uses, they have little to do with the data base management systems in widespread use today. Nor do you need to understand them in order to build or use a business expert system. We shall reserve the term *data base* for referring to the body of data managed by a data base management system. As discussed later, AI knowledge representation methods can be effectively combined with the data base methods that are so familiar to today's data processing professional. This is a key for the merging of AI reasoning systems into the field of business computing.

Of the three subsystems, the language system has received the least attention. The facilities that a reasoning system furnishes for stating a problem to be solved or a goal to be achieved tend to be quite rudimentary. They could conceivably allow natural language statements for specifying a problem. However, they typically involve prompting a user to provide values for a set of parameters. The values that a user provides effectively define the problem that is to be handled by the reasoning system.

Suppose, for instance, that a reasoning system is built to solve the problem of how much an individual should invest in growth stocks. Its knowledge system would contain various facts about the present status of the stock market and assertions about how an individual should invest under various circumstances. The user of this system would state a specific problem by typing in answers to a predetermined series of questions regarding the nature of the individual (e.g., assets, income level, age, and dependents). These answers characterize a particular individual and therefore constitute a particular problem statement. Some reasoning systems would then incorporate this problem into the knowledge system for the duration of the reasoning process. Other reasoning systems would not consider the problem statement to be part of the knowledge system. In either case, the problem-processing system would now proceed to reason with the knowledge system contents in order to solve the investment problem of a particular individual.

AI research into reasoning systems has concentrated on the problem-processing system, because that is what actually does the reasoning about facts and assertions held in a knowledge system. For a specific problem, the objective is to examine the *relevant* facts and assertions in a *sequence* that results in deriving or discovering a solution to the problem. At various steps in a reasoning process, the problem processor may need to ask the user for further information or clarification of problems being considered.

Just as in human reasoning, it is important for the problem processor to be able to differentiate between knowledge that is relevant and that which is irrelevant to the specific problem at hand. It is also important to consider the relevant knowledge in a logical sequence, rather than with random browsing or jumping to conclusions. Otherwise, the problem "solution" may be unsound or may take a very long time to derive. AI researchers and logicians have devised many strategies for deciding what knowledge to examine next at each step in a reasoning process.

In general, the reasoning strategies fall into two broad categories: forward reasoning and reverse reasoning. Forward reasoning begins with the basic knowledge about the problem area. This knowledge is examined in a particular sequence, with the problem processor keeping track of the implications of examined fragments of knowledge each step of the way. This proceeds until the implications are discovered to provide a solution to the specific problem being processed. Reverse reasoning, on the other hand, begins with the original problem statement. This problem is decomposed into subproblems, which are in turn broken into further subproblems, and so forth. The idea is that a small subproblem is likely to be easier to solve than a large problem. That is, it may be solved by simply looking up a relevant fact or assertion in the knowledge system. By solving all (or even some) of a problem's subproblems, the problem itself can then be easily solved.

Interestingly, one of the earliest centers for research into reasoning systems back in the mid-1950s was a management school: the Graduate School of Industrial Administration at the Carnegie Institute of Technology (now, Carnegie-Mellon University). Though artificial intelligence is often regarded as a field within the area of computer science, not a single computer science department existed at the time that Carnegie's Herbert Simon and Allen Newell began their investigations into the nature of reasoning systems.* Though a very small number of management schools have conducted ongoing reasoning systems research, the vast majority have been inactive from both the research and teaching standpoints. There are signs that this situation is changing, since effective reasoning is a major facet of management.

Together with J. C. Shaw of the RAND Corporation, Newell and Simon developed the Logic Theorist in 1956 [16]. This system used reverse reasoning to solve problems (i.e., prove theorems) in proposi-

---

*The first computer science department was established at Purdue University in the early 1960s.

tional calculus, with a small set of axioms as its initial knowledge system. In 1957 they began a much more ambitious project that was to extend over the next decade. This was the landmark General Problem Solver (GPS) [8,17]. Unlike the Logic Theorist, GPS was not specifically targeted toward solving propositional calculus problems—or problems in any other specific area. Instead, it endeavored to embody general reasoning methods that were applicable to a wide range of problem areas. In other words, it attempted to specify a general approach to problem solving.

The intent of GPS was to furnish a problem-processing system whose software never had to change, regardless of the problem area being addressed. This was accomplished by storing all problem-specific knowledge, including reasoning knowledge peculiar to a problem area, in the knowledge system rather than weaving it into the problem processor software. Thus, by changing the content of its knowledge system, GPS was capable of solving problems in diverse areas including propositional calculus, symbolic integration, resolution theorem proving, and various puzzles (e.g., tower of Hanoi, missionaries and cannibals).

A specific problem would be described to GPS in terms of an existing, initial situation and a desired, goal situation. The knowledge system contained operators (reasoning knowledge), each allowing the problem processor to determine that one situation can be reached from another, given situation. To solve a problem, the problem-processing system searches through the operators to discover a sequence of operators—a flow of logic—that can lead from the initial situation, through various intermediate situations, to the goal. By establishing this flow of reasoning, the problem is solved. Such searches are governed by heuristics—problem-solving processes that are generally effective, yet do not completely ensure that a solution will be found.

While GPS itself turned out to have limited generality in terms of the breadth and depth of problems it actually solved, the principles it embodied were significant [18]. Reasoning systems research is greatly indebted to the trailblazing work of Simon and Newell for insights into the nature of reasoning and for the guiding spirit it provided to other researchers during the formative years of the field. Their former students have themselves gone on to make important contributions in the area of reasoning systems.

By the early 1970s a major new thrust was underway. This involved the creation of reasoning systems that concentrated on solving difficult problems in very narrow problem areas. There was an emphasis on real-life problems such as diagnosing diseases, assessing the chemical structures of unknown molecules, and applied mathematical analysis. Because these systems are able to solve problems that would otherwise require the services of experts in their respective problem areas, they have come to be known as expert systems. Work on the earliest of these, DENDRAL, began in the mid-1960s [12]. In the late 1970s a flurry of expert systems burst upon the scene.

A sampling of representative expert systems appears in Table 1–2. The most important thing to note about these expert systems is that *they do work.* This is indisputable. They solve practical problems that would otherwise require the services of human experts. Today, many of them are routinely used for providing expert advice. As of 1985, however, few (if any) notable expert systems have been built to solve managerial or business problems.

Unlike the General Problem Solver, the problem processors of expert systems were not designed to be general. They were custom built to be operable for very specific problem areas. Reasoning methods peculiar to a specific problem area were incorporated into an expert systems' problem-processing software. Thus the problem-processing system of DENDRAL is not suited for diagnosing bacterial blood infections. Conversely, the MYCIN problem processor is not sufficiently general to undertake molecular analysis. The implementers of expert systems each built their own problem-processing software from scratch, usually using special programming languages such as LISP, a language that is over 25 years old, and oriented toward processing collections of related lists of symbols. The time required to implement each of these expert systems normally amounted to many worker-years of effort. Implementation was expensive and required AI specialists rather than mainstream data processing professionals.

TABLE 1–2   Representative expert systems

Expert system	Problem area
DENDRAL [13]	Determines the chemical structures of unidentified molecules.
MACSYMA [14]	Solves differential and integral calculus problems in applied mathematics.
MYCIN [20]	Diagnoses and prescribes treatments for bacterial blood infections.
INTERNIST, CADUCEUS [19]	Diagnoses internal medical ailments.
CASNET [22]	Diagnoses glaucoma and recommends therapies.
PUFF [12]	Diagnoses lung dysfunctions.
SACON [2]	Advises how to analyze mechanical structures.
PROSPECTOR [6]	Determines the major types of ore deposits present in a geological site.
CRYSALIS [7]	Determines the protein structures of unidentified molecules from electron density maps.
R1, XCON [15]	Determines an appropriate computer system configuration for a customer's needs.

The effectiveness of expert systems having been proven, attention began to turn toward the invention of general-purpose tools for building expert systems more quickly and inexpensively. This was perhaps the central AI challenge as the 1980s began—a challenge that had to be met before expert systems could come into widespread use. Considerable progress has been made. Through their experiences in implementing expert systems, AI researchers noted certain commonalities across problem areas and began to design problem processors whose reasoning mechanisms were independent of the problem areas being addressed, and in which all problem-specific reasoning knowledge could be held in the knowledge system.

One of the earliest such tools was EMYCIN—a somewhat general problem processor patterned after MYCIN's problem-processing system [21]. As such, it is oriented toward certain kinds of diagnosis problems and it is restricted to operating on MYCIN-style knowledge systems. There are many real-world problem areas whose reasoning knowledge is not amenable to being represented in this kind of knowledge system. Nevertheless, for someone faced with the task of developing an expert system whose problem area closely resembles that of MYCIN, EMYCIN would be a useful tool. Because it provides a ready-made problem processor for reverse reasoning, there is no need to program a new problem processor for the expert system, and the developer can concentrate on filling the knowledge system with problem-specific reasoning knowledge. Tools such as EMYCIN are sometimes called "expert systems shells."

Considerably more general tools for developing expert systems are the OPS5 [15] and ROSIE [9] interpreters. These are problem processors that use forward reasoning to solve problems. To build an expert system with such tools, the developer creates a program consisting of statements describing a flow of reasoning to be followed when solving a problem. Though this involves considerably less effort than programming an expert system from scratch in the LISP or PROLOG languages, it does not offer many of the built-in conveniences available with tools such as EMYCIN. On the other hand, tools such as OPS5 are helpful in developing expert systems that do not naturally fit into the confines of more specialized tools like EMYCIN.

In the last couple of years, several serious tools for building expert systems have become available commercially. Though there are interesting differences among them, as a group they have tended to follow the EMYCIN rather than OPS5 philosophy. These systems include KEE, KES, M.1, ART, Personal Consultant, TIMM, and RuleMaster. The appearance of such tools represented an important step beyond commercial LISP and PROLOG interpreters. However, none of them show evidence of having been designed with the intent of building business expert systems. They are quite isolated from the mainstream of management information systems and business data processing.

There is no technical reason why this alienation should exist. Conceptually, they complement each other quite nicely [4]. However, software companies serving the mainstream data processing community apparently lack the research and development skills to deliver expert system development tools. Conversely, creators of the commercial tools cited above have no appreciable track record in creating data base management, spreadsheet, and other widely used software tools.

The situation has changed recently with the introduction of Guru®, a new kind of software tool that integrates expert system technology with mainstream data processing methods. The Guru system is based on concepts introduced by Bonczek, Holsapple, and Whinston for devising artificially intelligent decision support systems [4]. Unlike the conventional expert system development tools, Guru is not a stand-alone system (see Table 1–3). Some of the earlier tools furnished data import or export facilities for transferring data between expert systems and external software packages: This compatibility is also provided by Guru. However, Guru actually incorporates full-scale data base management, spreadsheet, structured programming language, business graphics, text processing, and other capabilities into a single, unified environment for expert system development and business computing.

The implications are many and far-reaching. Most important, artificial reasoning will take its rightful place in the mainstream of the data processing world, blending the new with the familiar. No longer will expert system construction be relegated to the exclusive domain of a few specialists who are keen on programming with LISP or developing isolated systems with stand-alone tools. Because of this new kind of tool, the incorporation of reasoning abilities into management information systems and decision support systems will shortly become routine, if not indispensable. The nature and impacts of this breakthrough in practical expert systems for management are explored in detail throughout the remainder of this book.

OTHER AI INVESTIGATIONS

Expert systems and software for natural language processing will dominate the AI marketplace for the foreseeable future, with expert system sales in the United States expected to lead the way, topping $1 billion by 1990.* Nevertheless, there are other AI investigations of importance. These include the topics of automatic programming, learning, knowledge representation, and pattern recognition. All of these are related (potentially, at least) to the topic of expert systems.

Automatic programming is concerned with mechanisms for automatically generating a program that will carry out some prescribed task [3]. The idea is that a person who is not a programmer can describe the

---

*DM Data, Inc., Scottsdale, Arizona.

TABLE 1-3 Expert system development tools

Tool	Type	Vendor	Host machine requirements	Cost
KEE	Stand-alone	IntelliCorp	Symbolics (and other) LISP machines	$60,000
KES	Stand-alone	Software A&E, Inc.	Symbolics (and other) LISP machines, IBM® XT™, VAX 11/780	$4,000–$23,500
M.1	Stand-alone	Teknowledge	IBM Personal Computer, XT™, AT™ (PC-DOS™)	$10,000
ART	Stand-alone	Inference Corp.	Symbolics (and other) LISP machines, VAX 11/780 (equipped with VAX-LISP)	$50,000
Personal Consultant	Stand-alone	Texas Instruments Incorporated	TI Professional Computer (768K RAM)	$3,000
TIMM	Stand-alone	General Research Corp.	IBM XT, VAX 11/780	$9,500–$39,500
RuleMaster	Stand-alone	Radian Corp.	UNIX™ operating system	$5,000–$15,000
Guru	Integral	MDBS, Inc.	IBM Personal Computer, XT, AT (PC-DOS) 16-bit machines with MS-DOS®, VAX 11/780	$2,995–$30,000

Note: Host machine requirements and prices subject to change.

nature of a desired task. This description specifies the characteristics and behavior that the program should exhibit, but does not need to specify how to actually build the program. The description is input to automatic programming software, which actually builds a program that can accomplish the task that was described.

An example of an automatic program generator used in managerial settings is the RDL Analyzer [5]. This software generates C language programs that are capable of producing varied reports for end users. A generated program contains all input and output logic necessary for interacting with the end user, all computational logic for needed calculations, all access logic for retrieving desired data from a data base, and all formatting logic for controlling the layout of reports produced. Thus, the automatic program generator is able to create programs comparable to those of a human programmer. It would not be surprising to see expert system techniques increasingly employed for the purpose of automatic program generation in the near future. In a related vein, systems analysis and data base design activities are also susceptible to these techniques [11].

Incorporating the ability to learn into a software system is another subject of AI investigation. A good natural language system is able to interact with its user to learn the meaning of an unfamiliar term, adding it to the vocabulary so it will be understood in future conversation. Tools for developing expert systems normally allow incremental additions and changes to the reasoning knowledge stored in a knowledge system, allowing an expert system developer to "teach" the system over time. But, of course, there is much more to learning than the accumulation of facts. There are the issues of learning from experience, learning by examples, and learning by analogy. There is the issue of modifying the basic behavior (i.e., the program) that acts on stored knowledge, as well as behavioral changes based on changes to the stored knowledge. Expert system techniques may make an important contribution here, allowing a program to become an expert learner. Automatic programming is also important for creating programs that learn by changing themselves. Though AI progress on the topic of learning has been minimal to date, it certainly deserves further investigation.

The effective management of knowledge is an essential ingredient of intelligent behavior. Thus, the exploration of methods for representing knowledge is an important AI research topic. As might be expected, there is no single knowledge representation method that is best for all types of knowledge or for all problem areas. The prevalent method for representing reasoning knowledge in an expert system is to use "productions." Newell and Simon introduced this approach in the models of human thinking that they developed [18]. A production is simply a rule. It says that if a particular situation exists, then a particular conclusion can be drawn; or if certain conditions are satisfied, then a certain action can be produced.

In an expert system, the reasoning knowledge that pertains to a given problem area is typically represented as a collection of rules. This usage of the everyday notion of a rule has a considerable intuitive appeal. As discussed in later chapters, the flexibility that an expert system development tool provides for stating rules is an important determinant of the tool's convenience and power.

Another topic of AI investigations is concerned with pattern recognition, including both visual and audio patterns. The ability to exhibit intelligent behavior in relation to one's surroundings depends in part on the ability to perceive those surroundings. To the extent that a computer system's perception is limited to sensing keystrokes or mouse movements, the end user is somewhat burdened relative to normal interhuman communication. Pattern recognition research aims to ease this burden [10]. As progress is made, we move closer to systems (expert systems, for instance) that will be driven by spoken words and visual images. In addition, progress in pattern recognition has had and will continue to have an important impact on the entire field of robotics.

CONCLUSION

Like human intelligence, artificial intelligence has many aspects [1]. One of the most significant is the ability to reason. The AI quest for reasoning systems has matured to the point where computers are able to display expert behavior. To assist in the construction of these expert systems, several software tools are now being offered commercially. Until recently, these were stand-alone tools that had little in common with the mainstream of management information processing. Their use for practical managerial expert systems has been correspondingly negligible.

All of this is changing because of a fundamentally new kind of development tool that obliterates the traditional barrier between expert system software and familiar business software. As the following chapter explains, this is a major step forward in the progression of business software. The application of this new, integrated approach to expert systems for management can change the very nature of decision-making processes, managerial practices, and an organization itself. The succeeding chapters are designed to acquaint you with the possibilities, challenges, and opportunities of expert systems.

EXERCISES

1. Describe several aspects of human intelligence.
2. How does a natural language differ from a command language?

3. What kinds of factors should be considered when assessing the capabilities of a natural language?

4. How do various natural language systems such as those in Table 1–1 fare with respect to these factors?

5. What are some potential drawbacks of a natural language interface?

6. Describe the three subsystems of a reasoning system.

7. What are the advantages of keeping all application-specific reasoning knowledge separate from the software that uses that knowledge?

8. Explain the difference between an expert system shell and an expert system.

9. What are the three main classes of tools available for developing expert systems?

10. Give three examples of rules that might govern human reasoning in the course of solving a business problem.

References

1 Barr, A., and E. A. Feigenbaum, eds. *The Handbook of Artificial Intelligence*, vols. 1–3. Los Altos, Calif.: William Kaufmann, 1982.

2 Bennett, J. S., and R. S. Englemore. "SACON: A Knowledge-Based Consultant for Structural Analysis." *International Joint Conferences on Artificial Intelligence 6*, 1979.

3 Bierman, A. W. "Approaches to Automatic Programming." In *Advances in Computers*, vol. 15, ed. M. Rubinoff and M. C. Yovits. New York: Academic Press, 1976.

4 Bonczek, R. H.; C. W. Holsapple; and A. B. Whinston. *Foundations of Decision Support Systems*. New York: Academic Press, 1981.

5 _____. *Micro Database Management—Practical Techniques for Application Development*. New York: Academic Press, 1984.

6 Duda, R. O.; J. G. Gaschnig; and P. E. Hart. "Model Design in the PROSPECTOR Consultant System for Mineral Exploration." In *Expert Systems in the Micro-Electronic Age*, ed. D. Michie. Edinburgh: Edinburgh University Press, 1979.

7 Engelmore, R. E., and A. Terry. "Structure and Function of the CRYSALIS System." *International Joint Conference on Artificial Intelligence 6*, 1979.

8 Ernst, G. W., and A. Newell. *GPS: A Case Study in Generality and Problem Solving*. New York: Academic Press, 1969.

9   Fain, J.; D. Gorlin; F. Hayes-Roth; S. J. Rosenschein; H. Sowizral; and D. Waterman. *The ROSIE Language Reference Manual.* Santa Monica, Calif.: Rand Corporation, 1981.

10. Fu, K. S., and A. B. Whinston, eds. *Pattern Recognition: Theory and Applications.* Noordhoff International Publishing Co.: Layden, The Netherlands, 1977.

11   Holsapple, C. W.; S. Shen; and A. B. Whinston. "A Consulting System for Data Base Design." *International Journal of Information Systems* 7, no. 3, 1982.

12   Kunz, J. C.; R. J. Fallat; D. H. McClung; J. J. Osborne; R. A. Votteri; H. P. Nii; J. S. Aikens; L. M. Fagan; and E. A. Feigenbaum. "A Physiological Rule-Based System for Interpreting Pulmonary Function Test Results." Stanford, Calif.: Stanford University, HPP-78-19, Computer Science Department, 1978.

13   Lindsay, R. K.; B. G. Buchanan; E. A. Feigenbaum; and J. Lederberg. *Applications of Artificial Intelligence for Chemical Inference: The DENDRAL Project.* New York: McGraw-Hill, 1980.

14   Martin, W. A., and R. J. Fateman. "The MACSYMA System." *Proceedings of the Second Symposium on Symbolic and Algebraic Manipulation,* Los Angeles, Calif., 1971.

15   McDermott, J. "R1: The Formative Years." *AI Magazine* 2, no. 2, 1981.

16   Newell, A.; J. C. Shaw; and H. A. Simon. "Empirical Explorations with the Logic Theory Machine: A Case History in Heuristics." In *Computers and Thought,* ed. E. A. Feigenbaum and J. A. Feldman. New York: McGraw-Hill, 1963.

17   Newell, A., and H. A. Simon. "GPS: A Program that Simulates Human Thought." In *Computers and Thought,* ed. E. A. Feigenbaum and J. A. Feldman. New York: McGraw-Hill, 1963.

18   _____. *Human Problem Solving.* Englewood Cliffs, N.J.: Prentice-Hall, 1972.

19   Pople, H. E., Jr.; R. D. Myers; and R. A. Miller. "DIALOG: A Model of Diagnostic Logic for Internal Medicine." *International Joint Conferences on Artificial Intelligence* 4, 1975.

20   Shortliffe, E. H. *Computer-Based Medical Consultation: MYCIN.* New York: Elsevier, 1976.

21   Van Melle, W. "A Domain-Independent Production Rule System for Consultation Programs." *International Joint Conferences on Artificial Intelligence* 6, 1979.

22   Weiss, S. M.; C. A. Kulikowski; and A. Safir. "A Model-Based Consultation System for the Long-Term Management of Glaucoma." *International Joint Conferences on Artificial Intelligence* 5, 1978.

Chapter Two

Business Computing— from Record-Keeping to Expert Systems

In the previous chapter, we stated that expert systems will revolutionize the nature of organizations and management. They will do so by being assimilated into the mainstream of business computing. This will result in a fundamental reorientation of the business-computing field [10]. It will affect all types of businesses—manufacturing, agriculture, commerce, banking, construction, services, government, and so on.

To appreciate how business computing will be changed by expert system technology, it is useful to review the state of business computing today—the major developments that have brought us to the present point and the major kinds of software currently in use. This chapter provides a perspective on such developments as record-keeping, decision support systems, and software integration. It also identifies the principal kinds of business software tools. Against this background view, it becomes clear how expert system technology can be blended into the business-computing mainstream.

RECORD-KEEPING

Computers have already had a significant impact on organizations and society. By automating the task of record-keeping, they have facilitated new ways of operating companies, encouraged the birth and dramatic growth of certain industries, and affected the ways in which organizations interact with each other. The tremendous growth in airline passenger travel, the multitude of banking services, and the explosion in financial market trading volumes would have been impossible without automated record-keeping. This development has enabled an organization to store, maintain, and retrieve masses of knowledge about itself and its environment, as a basis for ongoing operations.

The software implemented for record-keeping is commonly called a management information system (MIS). If used exclusively for accounting, an MIS might be called an accounting information system. If used only for marketing, an MIS might be called a marketing information system, and so forth. Such systems provide information that management uses in controlling the operations of an organization. Data processing departments that build and maintain management information systems are pervasive throughout medium-sized and large organizations. What was 20 years ago viewed as a breakthrough in organizational productivity is today taken for granted as an absolute essential. Even the smallest of organizations are now automating their record-keeping with inexpensive microcomputers. Lacking their own data processing staffs, they frequently use generic or custom-built management information systems purchased from external sources.

Advances in record-keeping abilities have resulted from the evolution of tools for building management information systems, as well as the relentless onslaught of increasingly powerful computer hardware. The earliest record-keeping tools were file management systems. Practically all programming languages used for business computing had built-in file management capabilities. There were also file management systems that could be used as extensions to programming languages for more advanced record-keeping. Other file managers were self-contained, not needing to operate within a host programming language. File management systems are still used today, especially in record-keeping applications where only a few types of records exist.

By the mid-1960s, the inadequacies of file management had become well known [8]. In response to these shortcomings a new kind of record-keeping tool began to appear: data base management systems. A data base management system (DBMS) is an implementation of one of the major data models. A data model has two aspects: (1) a method for representing various types of records and their interrelationships, and (2) one or more languages for accessing data organized according to this representation method.

The earliest data models were the hierarchical and shallow-network, which appeared in the last half of the 1960s. Because of the severe limitations they place on data organization, no important new hierarchical or shallow-network DBMSs have been introduced in nearly a decade (the last being FOCUS in the mid-70s). These limitations were significantly relaxed by the relational and CODASYL-network data models, both of which appeared in 1970–71. As the basis for many DBMSs that have been used for many years, the CODASYL model has enjoyed widespread acceptance among data processing professionals. The most famous implementation of this data model is IDMS, which Cullinet acquired from B. F. Goodrich in the early 1970s. Commercial implementations of the relational model were much slower to arrive on the scene. First appearing in the late 1970s, they are now accepted tools for handling modest record-keeping applications that do not involve many types of records or intricate interrecord relationships.

While the CODASYL-network and relational approaches were definite improvements over earlier data models, even they imposed a variety of troubling restrictions on the developers of management information systems. These were overcome by the postrelational (alias, extended-network) data model introduced in the late 1970s. The central theme of this model is to give the developer a way to directly represent all naturally occurring real-world relationships, while preserving the strengths of the relational and CODASYL models [13]. In so doing, it turned out that the postrelational model led to performance gains as well. Interestingly, the first postrelational implementation (MDBS I in 1979) was also the first viable DBMS to exist for microcomputers. Its descendant, MDBS III, is arguably the most sophisticated DBMS in existence today [8].

Leading implementations of each of the major data models are summarized in Table 2–1. Before leaving the topic of data base management, a word about terminology is in order. In the microcomputer world, there are many file managers that are routinely promoted as "relational data base" managers (even some spreadsheets are called

TABLE 2–1 Implementations of the major data models

Data model	Data base management system	Vendor
Hierarchical	DL/1, IMS	IBM
	System 2000	Intel
	RAMIS II	Martin Marrietta
	FOCUS	IBI
Shallow-network	TOTAL	Cincom
	Image	HP
CODASYL-network	IDMS	Cullinet
	IDS II	Honeywell
	DMS 1100	Sperry Rand Corp.
	DG DBMS	Data General
	Prime DBMS	Prime
Relational	SQL/DS, DB2	IBM
	Oracle	Oracle
	Ingres	RTI
	KnowledgeMan	MDBS
	Guru	MDBS
	CA Universe	Computer Associates
Postrelational	MDBS III	MDBS

DBMSs). These are easy to spot. For instance, their documentation often uses the terms "file" and "data base" interchangeably. Of course, a data base is something quite different than a file. In this book, the term *data base* is used in the classic technical sense in which a DBMS must adhere to one of the major data models.

By automating record-keeping activities for large volumes of information, management information systems play an important role in modern organizations. However, beyond supplying management with timely standardized reports about an organization's environment, these systems make little direct contribution to actual decision-making activities. To increase the value of computers to management, a new class of software began to emerge in the 1970s: decision support systems.

DECISION SUPPORT

The essence of management is decision making, for the purpose of determining what course of action will be taken. Up-to-date knowledge about the environment in which a decision will be made is a necessary ingredient for good decision making. In addition, the decision maker must be able to analyze, evaluate, and reason with this knowledge in appropriate ways. A decision support system is software that helps the decision maker address these issues [7].

Researchers in the various disciplines of management (e.g., operations research, finance, applied economics) have devised quantitative techniques and algorithms to assist decision makers. These techniques and algorithms are commonly referred to as models. They can be used to analyze knowledge about the environment in order to generate new facts, expectations, or beliefs as a basis for decision making. A model is procedural knowledge—a sequence of one or more steps that specify how to generate new knowledge from existing knowledge about the environment. Examples of common models include linear regression, optimization algorithms, inventory control procedures, rate of return computations, and so forth.

Like a management information system, a decision support system (DSS) has record-keeping capabilities. Though these capabilities are often more modest than those of an MIS, there is no reason why they must be so. Beyond record-keeping, a DSS has the following traits:

- It can carry out analyses by fitting environmental knowledge into models.

- It furnishes users with powerful, convenient languages for problem solving.

- It can be used to support comparatively unstructured decision activities.

In a decision support system, models take the form of programs or functions that can be executed by the DSS. This execution occurs in response to a user's query. The language for stating the query should not require computer expertise on the part of a user. It should support queries for ad hoc retrieval, as well as ad hoc analysis. The ability to make ad hoc (i.e., nonroutine, nonstandard) requests is important for supporting unstructured decision-making processes.

The classic structure of a decision support system is shown in Figure 2-1 [4]. Notice that a DSS has three major parts or subsystems: a language system, a knowledge system, and a problem-processing system. A language system is the collection of all linguistic facilities provided by a DSS. These facilities allow a decision maker to issue requests to the DSS and to reply to any requests the DSS may make of the decision maker. The knowledge system of a DSS consists of knowledge about the decision maker's environment, perhaps some procedural knowledge, and some knowledge derived from analyzing the environment via models. The problem-processing system lies at the core of a DSS. It is able to understand a user's request as stated with the language system and access the knowledge system contents in order to satisfy a user's request for retrieval or analysis.

In the 1970s, decision support systems tended to be built from scratch with programming languages such as COBOL or FORTRAN. Their procedural modeling knowledge was typically incorporated into their problem processors rather than their knowledge systems. Toward the end of the decade, the principle of a generalized problem-processing system (GPPS) was introduced [4,11]. A generalized problem processor is a single invariant problem processor that is operable for a broad range of decision support applications—from market forecasting and resource allocation to operations management and financial analysis.

The software of a GPPS *never* changes regardless of the decision support application for which it is used. This is possible because there is

FIGURE 2-1   DSS structure

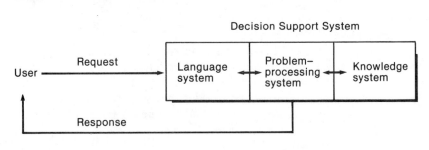

no application-specific knowledge incorporated into the GPPS software. If the problem processor of a DSS is general, then all application-specific knowledge is stored in the knowledge system. This includes environment knowledge, procedural knowledge, derived knowledge, linguistic knowledge,* and other kinds of knowledge [12]. A DSS based on a generalized problem processor can be transformed into a DSS for some other decision support application by exchanging one knowledge system for another. Such a DSS can be extended by simply modifying its knowledge system contents. The advantages that a GPPS offers for rapid, inexpensive development and maintenance of decision support systems are obvious.

Today there are many commercial tools available for building decision support systems for financial applications. These include Execucom's IFPS, Ferox's Encore!, MPS's IDSS, and Conshare's System W. While these have been useful tools, none of them is a GPPS. Their knowledge representation and processing facilities are specifically oriented to financial applications rather than a broad range of application areas. Popular spreadsheet programs such as Lotus® 1-2-3® have a somewhat broader orientation. They too can serve as problem-processing systems for various kinds of decision support applications—namely those whose knowledge systems can be represented as spreadsheets. However, there is a multitude of decision support applications for which the spreadsheet method of knowledge representation and processing by itself is inconvenient, inadequate, or infeasible.

THE QUEST FOR GENERALITY

The key to problem processor generality is the ability to handle many different knowledge representation methods [4,14]. The knowledge system of one DSS may involve knowledge represented in text files, spreadsheets, and relational data tables. The knowledge representation methods of another DSS's knowledge system might include structured programs, postrelational data bases, spreadsheets, and graphics images. If these two decision support systems are to have the same problem processor, that problem processor must be able to work with all of the various representation methods that can be employed across the universe of knowledge systems.

A particular type of knowledge is susceptible to being represented in various ways. Environment knowledge might be represented in text files, a data base, a spreadsheet, and so on. Procedural knowledge can be represented as programs, as formulas in a spreadsheet, and so on. Clearly, no single representation method is superior to all others in all situations. This is why it is necessary that a GPPS be able to accommo-

---

*Application-specific knowledge about the DSS's language system.

date knowledge systems that utilize all of these various representation methods.

For each knowledge representation method that can be used in a knowledge system, a GPPS must possess a corresponding knowledge-processing ability. If a GPPS's knowledge system can include text files, data bases, programs, and spreadsheets, then the GPPS software must be able to process text files, access data bases, execute programs, and manipulate spreadsheets. Important knowledge-processing abilities that should be possessed by any GPPS include:

Data base management

Spreadsheet processing

Statistical analysis

Ad hoc inquiry

Program execution

Business graphics

General-purpose text processing

Calculator functions

Remote communications

Forms management

With such a tool, developers of decision support systems would have enormous latitude. Any of the GPPS knowledge-processing abilities could be used or ignored as desired within a specific DSS, as dictated by its knowledge system contents.

There was a major hurdle that had to be overcome before the idea of a GPPS could turn into reality: how to effectively combine so many knowledge-processing abilities into a *single* invariant program. The knowledge-processing abilities had to be combined in such a way that each individual ability could be used without the others. For instance, a DSS developer creating a knowledge system should not be forced to represent knowledge in a spreadsheet in order to make use of non-spreadsheet-processing abilities. The developer should be able to use a data base method of representing knowledge without being required to use a spreadsheet method, and vice versa.

While this independence of knowledge-processing abilities is essential, it does not imply that a GPPS is merely a hodgepodge of separate components. Such segregation would not permit multiple abilities to work together simultaneously. It would require switching back and forth among various components. Instead, the component abilities of a GPPS had to be combined in such a way that several of them could be exercised in a single operation. The traditional barriers that separated various knowledge representation and processing methods had to be removed for a GPPS to become a reality [15].

This conception of a GPPS presented a host of challenging questions to the business-computing community. Why should there be any rigid separation between spreadsheets and data bases? Shouldn't a spreadsheet cell be able to access data held in a data base? Shouldn't a query be able to simultaneously access knowledge held in a spreadsheet and a data base? Shouldn't the values of data base fields be able to be dynamically determined by a spreadsheet computation? Why should knowledge represented in a textual fashion be separate? In the midst of editing some text, shouldn't a user be allowed to make data base and spreadsheet references to incorporate knowledge from these sources into the text—either immediately, or on a dynamic basis as the text is printed? Why should a programming language be separate? Shouldn't spreadsheet cells and data base fields be available as variables in the procedural knowledge captured by a program? Shouldn't it be possible to define a spreadsheet cell in terms of an entire program?

This is a small sampling of what becomes possible with a GPPS. A full exploration of such possibilities could easily fill an entire book. For further examples, see Holsapple and Whinston [15]. The main points to keep in mind here are:

1. A GPPS must have a broad range of knowledge-processing capabilities for working with a broad range of knowledge representation methods.

2. The knowledge-processing abilities or components of a GPPS must be able to operate independently of each other.

3. The components must be blended together into a single program in such a way that there are no barriers among them and their abilities can be used together in a single operation.

Interestingly, this blending resembles what goes on within human consciousness. A bit of introspection makes it clear that our own minds have multiple kinds of knowledge-processing abilities that can be exercised independently or together. For instance, in arriving at a decision without computer support, the human decision maker might access knowledge about the environment from memory or from a co-worker, analyze it with various mental models, sketch out graphs of the results, reanalyze the situation with altered environment assumptions, and write a report that shows the decision.

Clearly, a decision process can involve a broad range of knowledge-processing activities. This same mental processing tool can be applied to diverse decision problems and its component capabilities can work separately or together. The goal of a GPPS is to supplement the innate human tool with an analogous computer-based tool. In early 1983, the first commercial software based on the idea of a GPPS appeared. This generalized problem processor is called KnowledgeMan (the knowledge manager) [1,19]. A significantly enhanced version, KnowledgeMan/2, has recently become available [18]. Broadly speaking, KnowledgeMan is often classified as an integrated software system. However, as explained below, it is fundamentally different than ordinary "integrated" software.

INTEGRATED SOFTWARE

The notion of integrated software was popularized by the Lotus 1-2-3 spreadsheet program. This program has had a very important impact on the business computing world. It helped fuel the boom of 16-bit business microcomputers in the early 1980s, just as the VisiCalc® spreadsheet did for 8-bit micros a few years earlier. 1-2-3 and its descendants (e.g., Symphony®, Framework™) follow a nested approach to integration.

The theory of software integration has identified three distinct styles of integration [16,17]. Before briefly describing each, it is important to point out that integration means something quite different than compatibility. If one program can read a file of data output by another program, then the two programs are compatible. If two programs are able to access the same file, then they are compatible programs. However, their respective functionalities are not coordinated with each other—they are not integrated.

One obvious approach to integration is to begin with a group of compatible stand-alone programs and add some software for coordinating their activities—for integrating them. Such integrating software is called an operating environment. Examples of generic operating environments include DesQ, Gem, TopView, and Windows. Others have been designed to work with only a specific collection of programs. An operating environment allows a user to select any of the programs for execution, switch to any other program as desired, and later resume working with the former program at the point where its execution was interrupted. At any moment, the user is directly interacting with only one program, though other programs may be completing processing tasks that were started before switching away from them. Oftentimes, each program is assigned to its own window on the screen to help keep track of which programs are available for resumption. The facilities of two separate programs cannot be used together in a single operation.

A user can transfer data between two programs by creating intermediate data transfer files each time a transfer is needed. For small amounts of data the user may be able to use what is called a "cut and paste" process. While working with one program, the user identifies some of its data that are to be "cut out" for transfer. After switching to another program, the user identifies where the "cut out" data are to be "pasted in" for use within this second program. Because the other two integration styles do not involve switching among separate programs, their users do not have to bother with intermediate data transfer files or laborious cutting and pasting operations.

The nested (sometimes called inclusive) style of integration nests one or more secondary components within a dominant component. In 1-2-3, for instance, the dominant component is a spreadsheet processor. The secondary components are a rudimentary graph generator and a pseudo–file management capability. Though this latter capability is sometimes loosely called "data base management," it is not even at the level of stand-alone file managers such as pfs:File or dBASE®—much less at the level of a real data base management system. Users of this capability should realize that data base management is immensely more powerful, flexible, and convenient. Because of the nesting, all processing must be accomplished through the spreadsheet. It is impossible to use a secondary component by itself.

Another difficulty with the nested integration approach is that the capabilities and capacities of the secondary components are restricted by the dominant component. This weakness has led various commentators to predict the demise of integrated software's popularity in favor of collections of stand-alone programs. The claim is that as users become more skilled, they need and demand the greater functionality that can be delivered by stand-alone programs rather than restricted secondary components. While this claim has merit with respect to nested integration, it ignores the fact that this problem is solved by a different style of integration—without incurring the inconveniences and inefficiences of trying to coordinate separate programs.

This third major style of integration is aptly called synergistic integration [14]. The term *synergy* refers to the integration of multiple components in such a way that no component restricts any other and the total effect of the system is much greater than the sum of its components' individual effects. If an integrated software package is synergistic, any of its component abilities (spreadsheet, data management, etc.) can be used without even knowing about the existence of the others. In no way does any component restrict or interfere with any other component. On the other hand, there are no barriers between components. Data management, spreadsheet, programming language, and other components blend into each other in such a way that there are really no clear dividing lines between them . . . and why should there be?

It is this blending that yields a whole that is greater than the sum of its parts. Data bases, spreadsheets, program variables, and so on can all be referenced in a single operation. The concept of data base management is effectively expanded to encompass spreadsheet processing: data base management operations can reference spreadsheets. From a different perspective, the concept of spreadsheet processing is effectively expanded to encompass data base management: spreadsheet operations can reference data bases. Similar relationships exist for each component pair, triplet, and so on.

All of this is more than just a symmetric, elegant, aesthetically pleasing concept. It enables components to individually be as extensive as they are in stand-alone programs, while supporting many kinds of processing that are not possible with the two more limited integration styles, with so-called fourth generation languages, or with stand-alone programs. The result is greater convenience and productivity, without

sacrificing functionality. In fact, there is actually a gain in functionality. In time, synergistic software may very well make traditional stand-alone programs obsolete. Why, for instance, would a prudent person willingly choose to use a stand-alone data management package rather than synergistic software whose data management component is by itself on at least a par with the stand-alone capabilities—particularly when the stand-alone package is more expensive?

Perhaps the most important impact of synergistic software integration is that it has made generalized problem processors possible. As in the case of KnowledgeMan, a GPPS can be implemented by synergistically integrating a large number of traditionally separate knowledge-processing abilities. This integration style also provides an important clue as to how to go about bringing expert system techniques into the mainstream of business computing.

BUSINESS EXPERT SYSTEMS—OBSTACLES

It is into this business-computing climate of management information systems, decision support systems, and integrated software that expert system technology must be absorbed. In order for business expert systems to be created and used on a widespread basis, there must be development tools that are well adapted to this climate. To understand what is needed in the way of tools for business expert systems, it is useful to examine the obstacles inherent in the conventional expert system development tools cited in Chapter 1.

The source. Without exception, conventional tools for developing expert systems have been designed and implemented by companies with no appreciable experience in creating software for business computing—spreadsheet processors, data base management systems, text processors, business graphics generators, and so on. Conversely, most creators of successful business software apparently lack the research and development skills or interest to deliver expert system development tools to their customers. As they develop their AI skills or interests, business software companies will be well suited for producing expert system development tools that fit into the business-computing world.

Alien. A common complaint of corporate and government data processing professionals is that expert system development requires specialized training in the use of tools that are alien to the business-computing world. Conventional tools often require the use of exotic languages (LISP, PROLOG, OPS5, etc.) or peculiar memory structures such as frame hierarchies. This isolation of tools from the business-computing mainstream contributes to their relative lack of use.

Unnumeric. Many potential expert system applications for business are inherently numerical. Many conventional tools have quite limited, if any, number-handling capabilities. Those with appreciable numeric abilities still tend to be modest relative to the numeric operators and functions that are commonplace in business computing. Even text string–handling abilities such as concatenation and substring manipulation are often close to nonexistent in conventional tools.

Special hardware. Some of the conventional tools are becoming available on popular micro and mini computers. However, some of the most advanced conventional tools are still operable only with special, expensive hardware. This is hardware that does not support any familiar business software.

Inflexible. The facilities for representing reasoning knowledge with conventional tools are extremely inflexible. The expressive power that they offer to expert system developers pales in comparison to what is today possible. The result of these impoverished approaches to representing reasoning knowledge is a proliferation of reasoning rules. Rather than concisely representing expertise as a set of 50 rules, 500 rules might be required. This rapidly becomes an unruly situation: It requires more developer effort and skill to specify and maintain the 500 rules and it also detracts from the performance of the resultant expert system.

Narrow reasoning. Conventional expert system development tools offer no (or few) built-in controls for governing the general processors' innate reasoning activities. The result is a tool that may reason well for some expert system activities, but not for others. For instance, the needed approach to reasoning about uncertainty may be very different in one context than it is in another.

Stand-alone. Without exception, conventional expert system development tools are stand-alone in nature. They can be used to build expert systems—and nothing more. The conventional tool supports only one kind of knowledge-processing activity: reasoning. While this is a very interesting and useful kind of knowledge processing, there are many other kinds of knowledge processing that are also important. In view of the limited focus of conventional tools, it is curious that expert system developers have come to be called "knowledge engineers" and the reasoning expertise of an expert system is often referred to as a "knowledge base." Of course, anyone familiar with business computing realizes that it is intimately involved with many approaches to representing and processing knowledge. Aside from the trivial notion of file importing, conventional tools entirely ignore the existence of these many knowledge management methods that are so important for business computing.

Critics of expert system practicality frequently point out that expert system development is an expensive proposition—requiring long development times (e.g., many worker-years) and developers who are AI experts. This has been true principally because of the kinds of development tools that have been available—tools that do not address the foregoing obstacles. As a result, expert system development is arduous, especially for the uninitiated. Tools that rise above these obstacles can go a long way toward dispelling the aura of mystery or confusion that so often surrounds the topic of expert systems. Such tools mean that expert system development is no longer such a lengthy, costly, and elitist activity.

BUSINESS EXPERT SYSTEMS—SOLUTIONS

Can the obstacles to fulfilling expert system potential for business be surmounted? The answer is an emphatic *yes*. In fact, they have already been overcome by Guru [20], a revolutionary new kind of tool that is today readily available for expert system development. The tool is revolutionary from both an AI perspective and a business-computing perspective. It dramatically extends the conventional AI notions of knowledge representation and processing to embrace well-known business-computing methods. Conversely, it can be viewed as an incorporation of traditionally alien AI techniques into a single business problem-solving environment, taking a quantum leap beyond prior business-computing methods.

To understand the nature and significance of this new tool, it is worthwhile to see how it came into being. The new tool is the natural and inevitable fruit of the reasoning systems research traced in Chapter 1 and the business-computing developments already summarized in this chapter. The fact that an expert system fits the classic structure of a DSS has long been recognized [3]. An expert system is a special kind of DSS whose problem processor performs reasoning tasks, whose language system is a mechanism for requesting consultation and explanation, and whose knowledge system consists of application-specific reasoning expertise. However, because of their narrow focus, conventional expert system development tools fall far short of the generalized problem processor ideal.

The theoretical concept of an artificially intelligent GPPS was introduced many years ago [3,4,11]. This research argued that artificial intelligence techniques could reasonably be integrated with other knowledge representation and processing techniques, all within the scope of a generalized problem-processing system. For instance, data base management and AI methods of knowledge representation could by synergistically integrated to capitalize on their respective complementary strengths [2,5,6]. AI methods for representing and processing reasoning knowledge were shown to be especially useful for handling metaknowledge [4]. In DSS theory, metaknowledge is knowledge about how to use other knowledge concerning the environment, procedural models, linguistics, and so forth. It enables a problem processor to reason about how to use other kinds of knowledge in order to satisfy a user's request. This is crucial for the existence of a GPPS that can be used to develop artificially intelligent decision support systems.

The key to transforming all of these concepts and theories about an intelligent GPPS into a practical tool was the mastery of synergistic software integration. This occurred with the appearance of Knowledge-Man, which made it clear that a large-scale GPPS is not only possible but also extremely valuable for DSS development. KnowledgeMan accommodates all familiar business-computing approaches to knowledge representation and processing in a synergistic fashion. This practical mastery of the technology of synergy, coupled with many years of fundamental research concerning the integration of reasoning system abilities into a GPPS, has resulted in a tool that overcomes all of the previously cited obstacles to business expert systems.

The first implementation of this new kind of tool is called Guru [9]. By the synergistic integration of expert system development capabilities with all the familiar business-computing approaches, Guru surmounts every one of the previously cited obstacles to business expert systems.

The source. Here is the first example of an expert system development tool implemented by a company devoted to business software. Over the years, this company—MDBS, Inc.—has become well known among serious elements of the business-computing world for its sophisticated data base management tools, integrated decision support tools, and large-scale customized application systems for record-keeping and decision support. This is an ideal base for launching an expert system development tool especially designed for the business community and designed according to the theoretical principles of a generalized problem-processing system.

Familiar. This new kind of development tool provides familiar surroundings to today's users of business software tools. Spreadsheet users find a spreadsheet here, too. DBMS users can step right into Guru's relational (SQL—IBM's Structured Query Language) or more advanced postrelational data base management capabilities. Programmers can use the built-in structured programming language. Users of business graphics packages will find comparable facilities here, and so on. The new-generation expert system development tool offers a multitude of familiar entry points, from which users can comfortably ease into expert system development. When creating an expert system with Guru, a spreadsheet cell is still a cell, a data base field is still a field, a variable is still a variable, a screen I/O form is still a form, and so on. All the customary knowledge representation methods are always available.

With this tool, you are always free to use as little or as much of its expert system development capabilities as you desire. You can start out simply and progress into the more advanced features at your own pace. The old necessities of learning LISP or PROLOG, complex memory structures or other alien prerequisites are absent. With a tool such as Guru, expert system development is well within the grasp of today's competent DBMS users, spreadsheet template builders, COBOL or BASIC programmers, application system developers, and so forth. It most certainly is now readily accessible to business-computing professionals in government and corporations.

Numeric. All number-handling abilities that are normally expected of familiar business software tools are now available to expert system developers as well. These include numeric operators for addition, subtraction, multiplication, division, exponentiation, and modulo. Numeric functions include absolute value, square root, logarithms, trigonometric functions, and random number generation. Statistics generation is supported, including means and standard deviations. There is even a general-purpose root finder for solving rate of return and differential calculus problems. Any of these numeric abilities can be used for building expert systems. Text string processing can be important for business applications. Built-in string-handling mechanisms include string concatenation, case conversion, substring matching, substring extraction, and substring pattern replacement.

Everyday computers. Because expert system development facilities are now integrated with familiar business-computing capabilities, they are operable on a variety of ordinary business computers. In the case of Guru, these include the popular IBM Personal Computer, XT, and AT microcomputers, 16-bit microcomputers with the MS-DOS operating system, on up to the VAX 11/780 series. Multiuser versions of Guru are available for operating systems like UNIX and for various local area networks such as Novell's Netware and IBM's PC Net.

Flexibility. The synergistic integration gives rise to an unprecedented degree of knowledge representation flexibility. This translates into faster and less expensive expert system development. It can also lead to more efficient expert system operation due to a more concise representation of reasoning knowledge. There is another consequence that is just as important as this increased productivity and efficiency. The dramatically expanded flexibility means that it is now possible to build expert systems with advanced capabilities not even dreamed of with conventional tools. These are *expert systems that can themselves* carry out real data base management, build and use spreadsheets, execute analytical models, generate business graphics and statistics, produce text, communicate with remote computers, and so on—all according to the application-specific reasoning expertise held in their knowledge systems.

Control. In many areas of business computing, the existence of controls for modifying software behavior and for performance tuning is taken for granted. This carries over into the new-generation expert system development tool. For instance, Guru has over 100 built-in controls. Such control is important when it is remembered that a single tool is being applied to a wide variety of business expert systems. The ability to adjust its behavior and tune its performance to meet the situation at hand is a major reason why a tool such as Guru is both general-purpose and viable. Developers are free to use as few or as many of the built-in controls as desired.

Integration. The synergistic integration of expert system development technology with business-computing technology eliminates the many problems inherent in stand-alone tools, without sacrificing functionality. Indeed, the integrated tool's synergy yields a greater functionality than a collection of stand-alone programs. It enables any familiar business-computing capabilities to be exercised both within an expert system and independent of an expert system, according to user needs. Conversely, it enables an expert system to be directly used within a spreadsheet cell's definition, so that the cell's value is determined by consulting an expert system. Expert system consultations can be embedded wherever desired within analytical models and application programs. They can be requested to generate new text in the midst of interactive text processing, to derive a data source for subsequent graphing, to determine the content of a printed form, to set conditions for relational SQL queries, and so forth.

By overcoming the major obstacles to business expert systems, this new kind of tool constitutes a major advance in *practical* artificial intelligence. It also marks the opening of a significant new direction in the continuing evolution of business computing. In a more global sense, it is ushering in the era of knowledge-based organizations as discussed in the final chapter of this book. The intervening chapters explore business expert system development and usage in considerable depth. In the absence of any alternative standard for describing business expert system development, Guru will be used to illustrate the possibilities that exist today.

CONCLUSION

Advances in business computing have changed the way in which organizations operate. They will continue to do so with the next big advance—business expert systems. LISP, PROLOG, OPS5, and conventional expert system development tools will not be significant factors in this advance. The obstacles that they impose have been (and still are) too severe to encourage widespread use of expert systems for addressing either small or large-scale business applications.

The solution lies in a new kind of development tool that is based on the DSS concept of a generalized problem-processing system having integral reasoning capabilities. The practical technique of synergistic software integration turned the theoretical concept into a working reality. This breakthrough effectively merges expert system technology into the business-computing mainstream, allowing business expert system development to be less elitist, less time consuming, and less costly.

EXERCISES

1. Explain how a management information system differs from a decision support system.
2. What are the two major aspects of a data model?
3. Identify the five major data models.
4. What is a procedural model?
5. Describe the notion of a generalized problem processor.
6. List some of the different kinds of knowledge-processing abilities that a GPPS could possess.
7. How does software integration differ from software compatibility?
8. Identify three distinct styles of software integration.
9. Cite some of the advantages of a synergistic approach to integration.
10. Explain the kinds of processing that are available when there is a synergistic integration of programming and spreadsheet capabilities.
11. What characteristics of conventional expert system development tools have inhibited the widespread creation and use of business expert systems?
12. Describe how expert system capabilities can be incorporated into a decision support system.
13. Someone claims that expert system technology cannot be widely applied to business problem solving because human decision makers exercise intuitive and creative faculties. Explain the fallacy of such a claim.

References

1 Aarons, R. N. "Wising Up with KnowledgeMan." *PC* 3, no. 4, 1984.

2 Bonczek, R. H.; C. W. Holsapple; and A. B. Whinston. "The Integration of Data Base Management and Problem Resolution." *International Journal of Information Systems* 4, no. 2, 1979.

3 _____. "Future Directions for Developing Decision Support Systems." *Decision Sciences* 11, no. 4, October 1980.

4 _____. *Foundations of Decision Support Systems*, New York: Academic Press, 1981.

5 _____. "A Generalized Decision Support System Using Predicate Calculus and Network Data Base Management." *Operations Research* 29, no. 2, 1981.

6 _____. "Specifications of Modeling Knowledge in Decision Support Systems." In *Processes and Tools for Decision Support*, ed. H. G. Sol. Amsterdam: North-Holland, 1983.

7 _____. "Developments in Decision Support Systems." In *Advances in Computers*, ed. M. Yovits. New York: Academic Press, 1984.

8 _____. *Micro Database Management—Practical Techniques for Application Development.* New York: Academic Press, 1984.

9 *Guru Reference Manual*, vols. 1–2. Lafayette, Ind.: MDBS, Inc., 1985.

10 Holsapple, C. W. "The Knowledge Revolution." *Knowledge Matters* 2, no. 3, 1986.

11 Holsapple, C. W. "Framework for a Generalized Intelligent Decision Support System." Doctoral dissertation, Krannert Graduate School of Management, Purdue University, 1977.

12 _____. "The Knowledge System for a Generalized Problem Processor." Working paper, Department of Business Administration, University of Illinois, 1981.

13 _____. "A Perspective on Data Models." *PC Tech Journal* 2, no. 1, 1984.

14 _____. "Synergistic Software Integration for Microcomputers." *Systems and Software* 3, no. 2, 1984.

15 Holsapple, C. W., and A. B. Whinston. "Software Tools for Knowledge Fusion." *ComputerWorld* (In Depth) 17, no. 15, 1983.

16 _____. "Aspects of Integrated Software." *Proceedings of the National Computer Conference*, Las Vegas, 1984.

17 _____. "The Nature of Software Integration." *InfoAge*, October 1984.

18 *KnowledgeMan Reference Manual*, version 2. Lafayette, Ind.: MDBS, Inc., 1985.

19 Walker, J. W. "KnowledgeMan." *Byte* 9, no. 2, 1984.

20 Williamson, M. "In Guru, the Business World Finally Has Its First, True AI-Based Micro Package," *PC Week* 3, nos. 11–14, 1986.

Part II

BUSINESS EXPERT SYSTEMS: BASIC CONCEPTS

So this is what it means to explore an expert's line of reasoning.

Now that we have the expert system, I have more time to be creative.

Chapter Three

Getting Acquainted with Expert Systems

With the appearance of tools specifically designed for developing business expert systems, managers and business-computing professionals can no longer regard the topic of expert systems as an intellectual curiosity or the domain of a select few. To do so is to be left in the wake of a tremendous advance in decision-making productivity. The advance will be led by those who most quickly grasp the nature and significance of expert systems for business. The possible applications are virtually endless, including both small and large expert systems in such problem areas as:

Establishing sales quotas

Conducting trainee orientations

Recommending acquisition strategies

Generating project proposals

Planning advertising spot layouts

Job shop scheduling

Facilities maintenance

Selection of forecasting models

Determining credit limits

Selecting transport routes

Providing investment counseling

Analyzing market timing situations

Offering job-costing advice

Assessing job qualifications

Performance evaluation

Requirements planning

Application of discounting policies

Responding to customer inquiries

In short, any repository of problem-solving expertise that exists in an organization is a candidate for expert system development—be it secretarial expertise or knowledge about solving strategic management problems. This chapter begins with an overview of expert system structure and development. It then introduces an application scenario concerned with establishing sales quotas. This application area is typical of business problems that are candidates for expert system development. The application scenario serves as a basis for expert system examples in the chapters that follow. As you read through these chapters, the many benefits of expert systems for business will become evident. This chapter provides a preview of these benefits and concludes with a discussion of the implications of expert systems for an organization's competitive strategy.

EXPERT SYSTEM STRUCTURE

An expert system has three primary aspects: a user interface, an inference engine, and stored expertise (see Figure 3–1). When consulting an expert system, a user states a problem and then interacts with the system via its user interface. This interaction can occur both during the reasoning process and after the reasoning is concluded. An expert system's inference engine is the problem processor software that actually carries out the reasoning needed to solve a problem. In so doing, it draws on the stored reasoning expertise about the problem area. In addition, it may interact with the user to find out further details about the nature of the problem being solved. When the problem is solved, the inference engine reports the solution to the user and is able to explain its line of reasoning in reaching that solution.

The stored expertise about a problem area can be represented as a rule set.* A rule set contains a collection of rules, each of which captures some piece of knowledge about how to reason in the specific problem area addressed by the expert system. Even though it deals with the representation of reasoning knowledge only, a rule set is often called a "knowledge base" by the AI community. As suggested earlier, the much richer notion of an integrated knowledge system supports not only this representation of reasoning knowledge, but many other types of knowledge representation as well (see Figure 3–2). The *knowledge base* term is avoided here to prevent confusion of its narrow connotations with the more significant idea of knowledge integration. In a business expert system, the inference engine is not restricted to rule set processing, but is able to handle many other kinds of knowledge representation as well.

---

*Though rules provide a particularly convenient and practical approach to representing reasoning expertise, there are other methods. For instance, expertise could be represented in pieces of text, in program logic, as collections of predicates [2], in frame-oriented structures [8], as semantic nets [4], and so on. Such alternatives are not examined here.

FIGURE 3–1   Structure of a conventional expert system

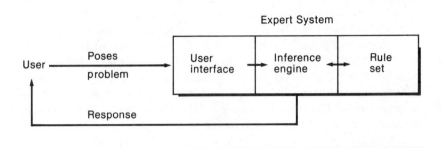

FIGURE 3–2   Structure of a business expert system

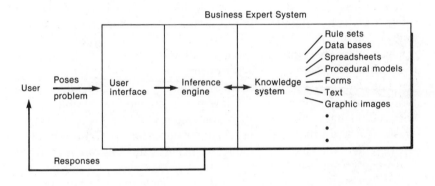

DEVELOPMENT TOOLS

An expert system development tool usually consists of two modules: a rule set manager and an inference engine. The rule set manager is software for building, maintaining, and compiling rule sets pertaining to various problem areas. Building a rule set consists of specifying its rules and various knowledge about the usage of those rules. Rule set maintenance involves changing this specification as new reasoning expertise becomes known.

After a rule set is built or changed, the developer uses the rule set manager to compile it. The compilation activity checks the validity of the rule set and reports any errors to the developer. If the rule set specification is valid, then a new version of the rule set is generated. This com-

piled version of the rule set is what the inference engine actually draws
on during a reasoning process: It consumes less computer memory than
the original source version and it also allows the inference engine to
solve problems much more rapidly than would be possible if only a
source version of the rule set were available for processing.

The second module of an expert system development tool consists
of an inference engine that can reason with any rule set that has been
built and compiled via the rule set management software.* Such an inference engine is therefore general with respect to the rule sets that can
be specified with its rule set manager. This reduces the activity of creating an expert system to that of building and compiling its rule set.

Some inference engines work with a single, rigid user interface.
With the exception of furnishing content for prompts presented to a
user, these give the developer little control over the nature of user interfaces. Regardless of the problem area addressed by an expert system, its
user interface is essentially the same as those of all other expert systems
that use the inference engine. The developer is normally left without
such niceties as control over prompt positionings, use of form-oriented
interaction, color and intensity selection, customized menus for user input, and so on. Such flexibility is, however, provided by tools that integrate an inference engine component with the screen and form management capabilities so familiar in the business-computing realm.

The power of a tool's inference engine is very much related to the
kinds of rules it can process. A low-power engine is only able to run
with rudimentary rules. A high-power engine is able to process both sophisticated and primitive rules. Another important aspect of an inference engine is the kind of reasoning it can perform. This can be forward
reasoning (often called "forward chaining"), reverse reasoning (often
called "backward chaining"), or both. An engine that can run in either
direction at the developer's discretion clearly offers more versatility for
expert system development and usage.

Another important issue for evaluating a development tool's inference engine is its ability to deal with uncertainty. There are many kinds
of uncertainties that may need to be factored into human decision processes. Inference engines differ in terms of the kinds of uncertainties
they handle and the control they give over how these uncertainties are
factored into a reasoning process.

The environment within which an inference engine can run is also
significant. The inference engine of a stand-alone tool is an isolated program that can be executed from the operating system. In contrast, an integrated tool's inference engine can be invoked wherever desired within
a business-computing environment—interactively, within a spread-

---

*Some rule set managers do not support the compilation feature. Their in-
ference engines can only interpret source versions of rule sets.

Screen 1. Text-Processing Screen for Creating the
            ADVISOR Rule Set

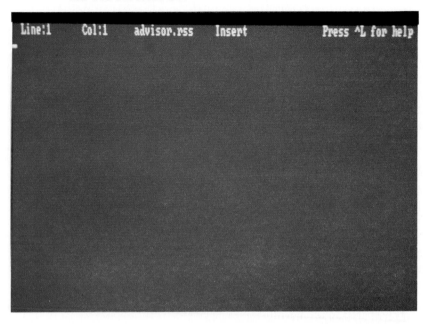

Screen 2. Text-Processing Screen after Entering
            Rules R1 and R2

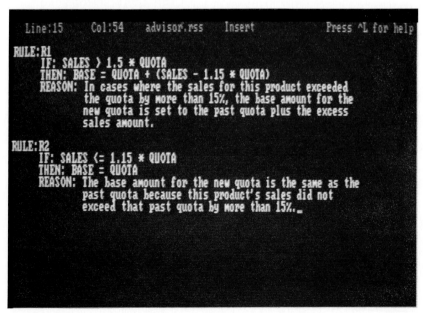

Screen 3. Main Menu of Options for Rule Set
            Management

Screen 4. Creating Rule R1

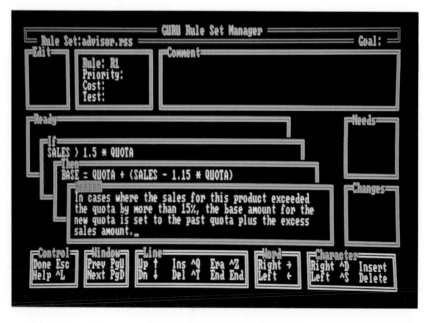

Screen 5. Two Windows into an Advertising
Spreadsheet

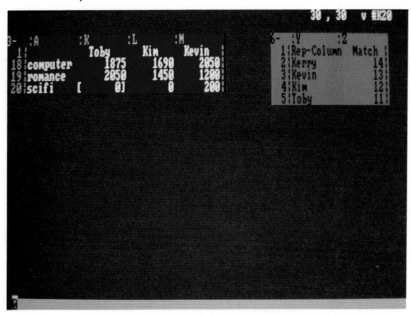

Screen 6. An Example of Inference Engine Plotting

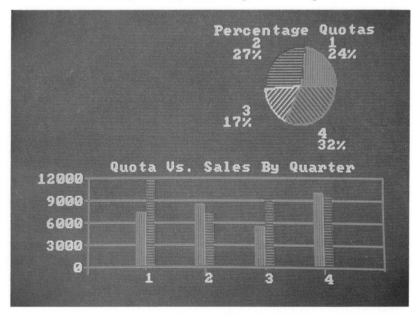

Screen 7. Result of Automatic Menu Construction

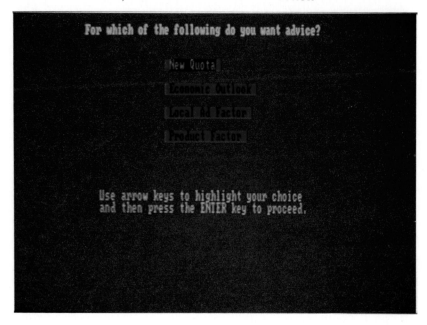

Screen 8. Menu-Guided Definition of the
LOCALADS Variable

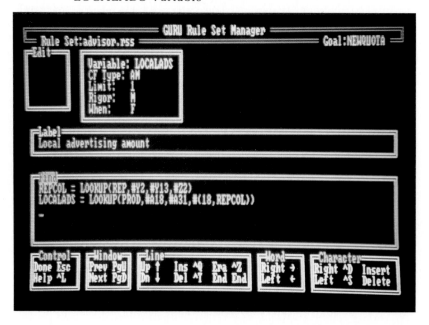

sheet computation, within a procedural model, in the midst of text processing, and so on. These consultation requests can be freely intermixed with other business-computing requests as desired.

AN APPLICATION SCENARIO

The remaining chapters in Part II provide overviews of possibilities available for expressing rules, reasoning with rules, dealing with uncertainty, and invoking an inference engine. These topics are examined in greater detail in Part III. As major points are introduced, examples are provided. All examples are related to the common business problem of establishing sales quotas. The principles and techniques they illustrate can, of course, be applied to any business problem area.

The company of interest here is KC, Inc., a book publisher.* KC has a national sales staff that covers 12 geographic regions. For each region there is a sales manager who is responsible for the sales representatives working within that region. Each sales rep services a prescribed territory within the region. This service includes visiting each retail bookstore in the region on a regular basis to promote existing books, introduce new books, take orders, and inquire about bookstore needs that KC may be able to fulfill. A sales rep is also able to solicit and take book orders via the telephone. In addition to a base salary, each sales representative receives a commission for all books sold to retail bookstores within his or her territory. The company establishes different commission rates for different product lines.

There are presently 14 product lines. One product line consists of general reference books. Another is composed of romance novels. Other lines include science fiction, psychology, photography, and computer books. Toward the end of each year, each regional manager is responsible for deciding on quarterly sales quotas for each of the sales reps in the region. Each sales rep will be assigned a quota for each product line for each quarter of the upcoming year. A sales manager will therefore need to decide on 56 quotas for each sales rep. Because a region has anywhere from 7 to 12 sales reps, a sales manager must set in the neighborhood of 400–700 quotas at the end of each year.

KC's vice president of sales realizes that establishing quotas is not only a big task, but a complicated one as well. Each quota could possibly be influenced by a wide variety of factors including product line characteristics, seasonal trends, territory demographics, past performance of the salesperson, sales training programs, the expected number of new titles in a product line, expenditures for local and national adver-

---

*The company and its employees described here are hypothetical. While its operations and needs are both typical and realistic, KC is unrelated to any actual company.

tising, general economic conditions (e.g., unemployment and growth expectations) in the territory, and much more. The vice president is concerned about the consistency and fairness of quotas assigned to sales reps both within a region and across regions. This is important because various bonuses are paid to sales reps who exceed their quotas. Also, the three sales reps who exceed their total quotas by the greatest amounts receive expense-paid vacations to overseas resort areas.

To help sales managers quickly establish reasonable and fair quotas, the vice president has budgeted funds for developing a computer-based system that can support decisions about quotas. This is actually part of a larger project that will supply each sales manager with a microcomputer to be used for a variety of purposes beyond supporting quota decisions. It will also be used throughout the year to track and analyze the performance of sales reps, for preparing reports and letters, for communicating with the large computer at KC's corporate headquarters, and for various budgeting activities.

The problem of setting quotas requires considerable expertise. Some sales managers seem to have a knack for it, while for others it is a struggle. The vice president has, over the years, been especially impressed with the quota decisions made by a sales manager named Jack Vander, and plans to capture Jack's expertise in an expert system that is able to recommend quota levels. The resultant expert system will then be made available to all sales managers for use on their microcomputers.

POTENTIAL BENEFITS

To the extent that expert systems can be successfully built for business applications, they offer many benefits. These potential benefits are what make the study of expert systems interesting and worthwhile. An overview of the benefits is presented here. It is advisable to keep them in mind as you read the chapters that follow. These chapters will help you to more fully appreciate how the benefits can be achieved.

An expert system is able to provide timely advice when a human expert is unavailable. Unlike its human counterpart, an expert system can operate around the clock, seven days per week, every day of the year. An expert system does not get sick, take holidays, go on vacations, or resign. An expert system is not tied up in meetings, away on business, or otherwise incommunicado. In the case of KC, Jack Vander is simply unavailable as a consultant for other sales managers to contact for help in setting their quotas: Jack has his own sales reps to manage.

Unlike the human experts that it emulates, an expert system can be readily replicated. The same expert system can be used simultaneously in many sites across the country or around the world. Once an expert system has been constructed, it is relatively inexpensive to distribute, particularly if run-time versions of the development tool are available at a low cost. A good expert system functions as a clone of the human expert. Each of the KC sales managers will, in effect, have Jack at his or her side to provide advice if and when it is desired. Notice that this does not threaten to put either Jack or the other sales managers out of work. The expert system is not a substitute for Jack. Instead, it will provide an expert advisory service not previously available, with the intention of improving KC's overall sales effort. The likely impact on Jack will be a bonus, raise, or promotion in recognition of his contribution. Nor is the expert system a substitute for the other sales managers. It simply offers quota advice to them as an aid to managerial effectiveness.

In some cases, a human expert may already be in place providing advice. The introduction of an expert system that can offer comparable advice should have a very positive impact on the human expert. It can reduce the demands on that human expert's time by insulating him or her from many kinds of consultation requests. This allows the human expert to focus on the most challenging problems and to concentrate on new creative activities. Human experts are normally a scarce resource for an organization. To the extent that their productivity can be increased by off-loading consultation activity to expert systems, the organization's human resources can be more effectively utilized. The human expert does not have to spend as much time directly providing advice and those seeking advice do not encounter the usual bottleneck of competing for the human expert's attention.

Another benefit of an expert system is that it provides consistent, uniform advice. It is thorough and methodical. Unlike the human expert, an expert system does not have lapses that cause it to overlook important factors, skip steps, or forget. It is not politically motivated, temperamental, or biased (unless the developer designs it to be so). An expert system functions as a standardized problem solver that can be a substitute, supplement, or verifier for a human expert. Once Jack has built the expert system for providing quota advice, he will probably consult it himself when he sets quotas for his sales reps. Not only might it determine quotas faster than Jack could himself, it will do so in an entirely consistent and error-free manner.

Like a human expert, an expert system is able to explain the line of reasoning it uses for each problem it solves. The flow of reasoning used for one problem may be quite different than that used for a different problem. This explanation ability enables the expert's advice to be critiqued. A user can study the rationale on which the advice is based and is free to accept it or reject it. A sales manager may want to see why a particular quota level is being recommended. The built-in explanation ability sets expert systems quite apart from traditional application systems for record-keeping and decision support. Because those traditional systems were unable to reason, there was never an issue of explaining their lines of reasoning.

Human experts are able to reason with uncertainties. These uncertainties are reflected in the advice that is given. Though all expert systems do not have a comparable capacity, many do. For instance, Jack may want his expert system to take uncertainties about possible states of the local economy into account when it reasons about quotas. As a result, the expert system might indicate that it is 80 percent confident that $20,000 is a proper quota and 60 percent confident that $18,500 is a reasonable quota. This built-in ability to reason about uncertainties and alternative ("fuzzy") values is yet another benefit that differentiates expert systems from traditional application systems.

Expert systems are able to evolve in a straightforward manner. Because the reasoning knowledge is represented as rules in a rule set, new expertise can be added by simply adding new rules or modifying existing rules. This modularity of rules means that there is no issue of programming or reprogramming. The developer of an expert system need not be a programmer, provided a modern development tool is being used. Jack Vander is certainly not a programmer. As examples in the following chapters illustrate, Jack can start out with a simple rule set that is initially useful, yet easily capable of many kinds of elaboration. Over time, the reasoning knowledge embodied in the rule set can be tailored, revised, and expanded, allowing the expert system's expertise to gradually evolve just as human expertise evolves.

A somewhat subtle, yet quite significant, benefit of expert systems is their effect of formalizing an organization's reasoning knowledge. The activity of converting an expert's reasoning knowledge into explicit rules can lead to a better understanding of the nature of an application problem area, as well as clearer insight about how the application's problems are solved. This introspection may well result in better decision making. At the very least, an expert system's formalization of reasoning knowledge provides a way of preserving that knowledge long after its human progenitor has left the scene. It can also provide a valuable basis for training new human experts.

STRATEGIC CONSIDERATIONS

In addition to the foregoing intrinsic benefits of business expert systems, there is also an important strategic role that such systems can play in contributing to an organization's competitive position. The remainder of this chapter is concerned with the strategic benefits and opportunities that business expert systems can offer. Top-level management should be aware of (or be made aware of) the far-reaching implications that business expert systems have for an organization's competitive strategy or outright survival. In what ways can business expert systems give an organization an edge over its competitors? What impacts can business expert systems have on a competitive environment and on the implementation of a competitive strategy?

Competitive Strategy

A company's long-term viability depends on its ability to effectively compete. Recent studies have pointed out that management information systems can be used to achieve competitive advantages [3,5]. For instance, a large airline carrier's reservation system is used not only to book its own flights but also those of its competitors. As a result, the large airline has access to reservation levels of all flights offered by those competitors. This information, which is not fully available to its competitors, enables the large airline to identify competing flights that are performing well and install aggressive competitive countermeasures for those routes [5]. Other examples include interorganizational information systems for order entry and purchasing. These provide electronic pathways between companies, pathways that can not only yield competitive advantages but can also shift the balance of power between buyers and suppliers [3].

These systems are concerned with the storage, maintenance, retrieval, and transmission of information. As discussed in Chapter 2, what we normally think of as information or data is but one kind of knowledge: descriptive knowledge about an organization's environment. Of course, reasoning knowledge is also important to an organization. Just as the computerization of environmental knowledge in the guise of information systems can lead to a competitive edge, so too can the computerization of reasoning knowledge in the guise of business expert systems. Although business expert systems do not have the same long history as management information systems, it is not too early to consider their strategic implications for an organization's competitive stance.

Traditionally, the expertise embodied in an organization's employees has provided an important basis for achieving, improving, and maintaining its competitive position. All else being equal, organizations without comparable expertise are at a disadvantage. With business expert systems, there is an opportunity to amplify the competitive advantage derived from superior know-how. To the extent that the expertise captured in an expert system is unique or not widely known, a sustained advantage results. Unlike information systems, interesting expert systems cannot be readily reproduced without access to the details of their stored expertise. Such an expert system can be used openly, but as long as it has sufficient security provisions to protect the details of its reasoning knowledge from disclosure, the competitive advantage it furnishes endures. In a sense, it is an intellectual property right, similar to a patent without a predetermined expiration date.

Like information systems, expert systems can be used to implement a competitive strategy. Competitive strategies fall into three categories [6]. One strategy is based on the idea of producing goods or services at a lower cost than competitors. Another strategy is based on brand differentiation, which involves offering a unique and attractive mix of product features. A third basic strategy is to concentrate in a special market niche with a product that has little direct competition because of its remarkable features or cost advantages. These basic strategies suggest three ways in which business expert systems can contribute to an organization's competitiveness:

- Enhancing internal productivity.

- Providing enhanced services.

- Providing new services.

On a larger scale, an organization could look to business expert systems as part of a strategy aimed at spawning a completely new industry.

Enhancing Internal Productivity

The purpose of the expert system for setting sales quotas is to enhance sales manager productivity. It does so in two ways. First, it can increase efficiency by reducing the time and effort that a sales manager expends on this activity. The gain can be applied to other activities (e.g., rep training) that have a positive impact on sales within the region. As a result the company is more competitive because its sales managers have an efficiency advantage over their counterparts in competing companies. Second, the expert system can increase effectiveness by utilizing expertise that is otherwise unavailable to many sales managers. The best that the company can offer in this area is replicated in a consistent fashion throughout the organization. A competitor may have persons whose expertise rivals Jack's; however, so long as that expertise is not distributed within the competing organization, it operates at a disadvantage relative to KC. It does not maximize the productivity of its sales managers. All else being equal, KC has a competitive advantage due to a more cost-effective use of its sales management resources.

The sales quota case is but one example of how an organization can use expert system technology to implement a competitive strategy that aims at enhanced internal productivity. It can be applied at all levels of organizational decision making. Anthony has identified three levels in the continuum of decision processes: strategic planning, management control, and operational control [1]. At one end of the decision-making spectrum, strategic planning is concerned with decisions about objectives and policies. Management control is concerned with managing resources to meet objectives and conform to policies. At the other end of the spectrum operational control involves the exercise of precisely specified decision rules to decide what actions to undertake. At one extreme, operational control problems tend to be routine and highly structured. At the other extreme, strategic planning problems tend to be less routine and less structured (i.e., "fuzzy") [7].

In the case of KC, setting sales quotas is an example of a management control problem. An expert system that offers sales quota advice can assist in the effective utilization of a sales manager's resources. A different kind of problem that confronts KC from time to time is whether to take on a new product line or eliminate an existing product line. These are examples of strategic planning problems. They require considerable expertise to solve and could also benefit from expert systems. Many of KC's operational control problems are also appropriate for expert systems. For instance, the shipping department has a few simple rules that clerks use to determine how regular shipments are to be sent. But rush orders are not unusual and they require much greater expertise to handle effectively. The carrier selected for such a shipment depends on factors such as the time of day, day of the week, holiday proximity, destination, and shipment size. An expert system that can offer customized shipping advice for the exceptional cases enhances the productivity of the clerks and their supervisor alike.

At each level of decision making, there are problems amenable to expert system assistance. All of these should be considered as ways for implementing a competitive strategy based on the notion of enhancing internal productivity. Some of these productivity increases may lead to cost advantages, as suggested by Porter. But lower cost is not the only possible manifestation of enhanced productivity. As in the case of the quota expert system, there may also be more effective and efficient decision making. Though this expert system will not significantly impact the cost or price of books, it can still lead to a competitive advantage. It can yield increased sales or market share through the more responsive and motivated sales force that results from fair and consistent quotas, as well as through the removal of a burden to the sales managers.

Providing Enhanced Services

An important business of a certain large chemical company involves the marketing of numerous chemicals to industrial customers. Many of the chemicals have multiple uses and often there may be several chemicals that could, alternatively or in tandem, meet a particular customer need. Sometimes a customer already knows what chemicals it wants and the needed amount of each. However, in many cases a customer does not know what amounts of what chemicals will satisfactorily meet its needs. Management decides to implement a competitive strategy that aims to enhance the services provided to customers. Instead of merely selling chemicals, the company will provide solutions. The company will help a customer to clarify the problem faced, offer expert advice about solving that problem, and justify the advice that is offered.

Sufficient in-house expertise exists for handling the diverse, technical problems that customers face. But the catch to implementing the full solution strategy is the delivery of this expertise. Training technical sales reps to effectively communicate the traits and uses of the company's products is already a costly, lengthy, and ongoing endeavor. Even with extensive training, sales reps often find it difficult to match customer's perceived needs (typically described in very technical terms) with product offerings. Further training that enables a rep to help in clarifying a customer's actual problem, to offer expert advice about solutions, and to convincingly justify that advice may have some value. However, such training cannot be expected to result in a satisfactory implementation of the competitive strategy. There is the prospect that highly trained reps can be lured away by competitors, so that the company serves as a training ground for its competitors. Furthermore, there are limits to what a sales rep can absorb while still actively making sales calls. Even the problem-solving ability of an in-house expert has limits. Individuals who are experts about everything are rare indeed. However, the collective know-how of these experts is formidable.

A possible alternative to implementing the full solution strategy would be to make the in-house experts directly accessible to customers. Together they would form a technical sales support staff. When a rep encounters a problem that he or she cannot handle, it would be referred to an appropriate expert in the support staff. This expert would then help define and solve the problem and explain the solution. There are several difficulties with this implementation approach. The experts typically are not especially skilled in sales techniques. Their expertise is important for postsale customer support and for the research and development of new products. The experts are neither numerous nor inexpensive. As a result, customer referrals would need to be queued. Responses may not be timely and unhealthy contention for expert support may arise among the sales reps.

If it were not for the scarcity and cost of experts, the ideal implementation strategy would be for each sales rep to have an agreeable technical support staff at his or her side as sales calls are made. The rep would be in control of the sales call as it unfolds and would be able to directly draw on the staff's expertise if and when it is needed for clarifying customer problems, offering recommendations, and justifying advice that is given. The company's top management has opted for this approach to implementing its competitive strategy, but with one exception. Rather than the impracticality of a technical support team physically accompanying each sales rep, the team's expertise is captured in one or more expert systems. With a portable microcomputer, each sales rep will be accompanied by an appreciable portion of the support team's expertise. Rather than attempting to train reps to an expert level, the in-house experts train expert systems. The company therefore has a controllable asset that cannot be lured away by the competition.

The competitive advantage that results from enhanced service may or may not be reproducible. To the extent that a competitor has equivalent (or superior) in-house expertise and can harness it in a comparable way, the initial competitive edge may not be fully sustainable. Nevertheless, the first entrant into the marketplace with this enhanced service may have created some entry barriers for competitors that consider following its lead. For instance, it may establish itself in customers' eyes as the leader in providing this service. This positive image can be difficult to overcome. As customers become accustomed to the leader's expert systems, they may find it inconvenient or uninteresting to bother with others. Furthermore, the leader has a learning curve edge in applying the technology to achieve a competitive advantage. Followers are likely to be a step behind as the sales support expert systems continue to evolve.

Providing New Services

Related to the idea of enhanced services is the notion of new services. As in the case of the chemical company, an enhanced service is concerned with improved features, greater timeliness, greater thoroughness, and so on. A competitive strategy could also be aimed at furnishing a new service that draws customers to a company. For instance, top management of a retail bank has decided to introduce a new service that has not been offered by other banks of its type and size. In considering consumer loans, these banks presently use rigid scoring protocols that lead to either the acceptance or rejection of a loan request. This retail bank intends to increase its customer base by offering an investment banker's services to its customers.

In traditional investment banking, an expert works out a customized financing arrangement suitable to a client company's needs. Thus, the retail bank's competitive strategy is based on providing a new service in which loan instruments are tailored to individual consumer situations. In considering how to implement this strategy, it is clear that substantial expertise would be required to effectively handle the creation of customized consumer loans. However, the bank would not be financially justified in hiring sufficient investment bankers to handle the relatively large number of relatively small (dollar-wise) applicants. But an expert system that embodies the sophisticated reasoning behavior that an investment banker would display for consumers could be financially attractive, especially if it were shared by a consortium of banks. As in the case of enhanced services, reproducibility and entry barriers are important issues when considering new services implemented via expert systems.

Spawning New Industries

Some businesses may choose to participate in new industries that are made possible by the advent of powerful and flexible tools for expert system development. This participation can produce a diversification that helps the company compete more effectively. An example is a new industry concerned with the publication and use of expertise.

There are two traditional ways of delivering advice. One is by means of books, articles, and lectures. This often requires considerable effort to ferret out the pertinent recommendation. Sometimes the advice is not explicit, but must be inferred by using reasoning expertise that is presented in books, articles, and lectures. The second major delivery method involves consulting firms and professional service companies such as lawyers, accountants, and physicians. Here, the generation of advice is more specialized to individual client needs. It requires less effort by the client than reading books or attending lectures. However, the availability of this delivery method is relatively limited and costly.

Expert system technology offers a striking alternative, supplement, and complement to traditional ways of delivering advice. It would not be surprising to see the emergence of a new industry concerned with the publication of computerized expertise. For instance, there will likely be new businesses concerned with producing and distributing chunks of reasoning knowledge, each addressing one of a wide variety of problem areas from vehicle maintenance to financial management. Each chunk will be capable of being "plugged in" to a standard, generalized inference engine. We may even see "expert-of-the-month" offerings akin to the idea of book-of-the-month selections. There will be subscription services for providing new and updated expertise. The net effect will be widespread distribution of expertise which, when plugged in to an inference engine, results in responsive consultations at relatively low prices.

As another example, there is a need to distribute expertise on the uses and applications of the masses of knowledge that will soon be commonplace on optical compact disks (which can contain 500 million characters on a single small compact disk). Any of the various kinds of knowledge identified in the prior chapter could reside on a compact disk (CD). Effective usage of such knowledge storehouses will be a paramount issue. The availability of expert systems that can help users dig out and apply the immediately relevant subset of knowledge is akin to having the assistance of a combination librarian/teacher. We expect that an entire industry can develop around the automated, intelligent delivery and application of all types of knowledge. Interestingly, this industry could have a significant impact on third-world countries, by greatly expediting the transfer of knowledge to them in a cost-effective manner. The resultant computer-based "peace corps" could be a valuable complement to its human counterpart.

A third example of a new industry made possible by advances in expert system technology is an industry concerned with constructing artificially intelligent application systems for record-keeping and decision support. Some may prefer to characterize this as a redefinition of an existing industry. In any case, the implications are far reaching. Rather than their traditional passive nature, the management information systems and decision support systems built by this new industry will display an active, inquisitive, insightful behavior. As discussed in Chapter 7, artificially intelligent application systems are a natural result of the integral treatment of expert system and familiar business-computing capabilities. Chapter 13 speculates about how this idea can be carried even farther in the realization of future knowledge-based organizations.

Challenges

The strategic implications of expert systems for business present a challenge and opportunity for top-level management. Management that pays attention to these implications and is alert to the possibilities can find itself with a competitive edge, rather than being out on a competitive ledge. In addition to a managerial challenge, there are also technical challenges to be faced in building business expert systems. These include the selection and use of an appropriate development tool (a programming language, shell, or integrated AI environment). Chapters 4 through 12 concentrate on the many technical aspects of business expert systems. Technical issues have significant impacts on the cost, time, and training requirements of business expert system development. Understanding at least the basics of these issues is crucial for successfully meeting the managerial challenge that exists today.

CONCLUSION

This chapter has laid a foundation for the four chapters that remain in Part II by identifying four major expert system topics: expressing reasoning knowledge as rules, reasoning with those rules, dealing with uncertainty, and invoking the inference engine. These will be illustrated with examples based on a typical business application. The potential benefits of expert systems for business can today be turned into reality. The key to accomplishing this in a timely, cost-effective way is the existence of development tools specially designed for building business expert systems. As the following chapters show, you do not need a graduate degree in artificial intelligence in order to use such a tool for building your own business expert systems or for understanding enough about this technology to assess its implications for a particular organization's competitive strategy.

EXERCISES

1. Identify three kinds of problem areas where expert systems could help a salesperson.
2. Give an example of a business problem that is not particularly well suited to expert system development.
3. What are the three aspects of an expert system?
4. How does a conventional expert system differ from a conventional decision support system?
5. What are the two software components of an expert system development tool? What role does each play in the development process?
6. How do business expert systems differ from conventional expert systems?
7. What are some of the important ways in which inference engines can differ from one another?
8. Describe some of the major potential benefits of business expert systems.
9. Explain why a business expert system should not be regarded as a threat to the human expert who furnishes its rules.
10. Explain why a business expert system should not be regarded as a threat to nonexperts.
11. Discuss the importance of inexpensive expert systems to small businesses and third-world countries.
12. What properties must a system have in order to qualify as an expert system?
13. Identify three classic types of competitive strategy.
14. In what ways can expert system technology be instrumental in implementing a competitive strategy?
15. Discuss the difference between using an expert system in strategic planning and using an expert system in the implementation of a strategic plan.
16. Give examples of how expert systems can be applied at each level of decision making.
17. Explain how a competitive strategy implemented with expert systems can lead to a sustainable competitive advantage.

References

1 Anthony, R. N. *Planning and Control Systems.* Boston: Harvard Business School, 1965.

2 Bonczek, R. H.; C. W. Holsapple; and A. B. Whinston. *Foundations of Decision Support Systems.* New York: Academic Press, 1981.

3 Cash, J. I. Jr., and B. R. Konsynski. "IS Redraws Competitive Boundaries." *Harvard Business Review,* March–April 1985.

4 Findler, N. V., ed. *Associative Networks: Representation and Use of Knowledge by Computers.* New York: Academic Press, 1979.

5 McFarlan, E. W. "Information Technology Changes the Way You Compute." *Harvard Business Review,* May–June 1984.

6 Porter, M. E. "How Competitive Forces Shape Strategy." *Harvard Business Review,* March–April 1979.

7 Simon, H. A. *The New Science of Management Decision.* New York: Harper & Row, 1960.

8 Stefik, M. J. "An Examination of a Frame-Structured Representation" in *Proceedings of International Joint Conference on Artificial Intelligences.* Los Altos, Calif.: Kaufmann, 1979.

Here we see the most important rule of all: <u>If</u> expertise captured in rules increases, <u>then</u> human productivity rises.

Chapter Four

Rules for Reasoning

A rule tells the inference engine what to do if a certain situation exists. A rule, therefore, has a premise and a conclusion. If the inference engine can determine that the rule's premise is true, then the rule's conclusion is known to be valid. A premise consists of one or more conditions. A conclusion consists of one or more actions. If the inference engine discovers that a rule's conditions are satisfied, then the engine will carry out whatever actions are contained in the rule's conclusion.

This chapter describes how a developer can express reasoning knowledge in the form of rules. It shows that both premises and conclusions can be easily specified. With Guru, rules can be specified in a free-form manner. The indentation conventions used for the rule examples shown here are strictly for reading convenience. You are free to use other conventions if you like. After examining the basics of stating rules, the text processing and menu-driven approaches to rule set management are described. The topic of rule induction is also discussed.

EXPRESSING RULES

When Jack Vander thinks about setting a new quarterly quota for a product, his overall strategy is to come up with some reasonable base amount and adjust that amount based on a variety of factors. He likes to set the base to reflect the sales rep's past performance. If the sales rep's sales exceeded quota by more than 15 percent, then the excess is combined with that quota to determine the base amount. This is easily expressed as a rule in a rule set.

```
RULE: R1
  IF: SALES > 1.15*QUOTA
  THEN: BASE = QUOTA + (SALES - 1.15*QUOTA)
```

In this way, Jack has formally expressed a fragment of the reasoning knowledge he uses in setting quotas. Another similar piece of knowledge is that he uses the present quota as the base amount if the sales did not exceed the quota by at least 15 percent.

```
RULE: R2
  IF: SALES <= 1.15*QUOTA
  THEN: BASE = QUOTA
```

Each of these rules has a single condition for its premise and a single action in its conclusion.

One of the factors Jack uses to adjust a base amount is related to local advertising expenditures for the product line. He believes that if the local economy is good and the advertising expenditure exceeds $2,000, then the local advertising factor should be 1 percent for every $1,000 spent. To incorporate this rule into the rule set, the rule set management software would be used to enter the new rule:

```
RULE: R10
  IF: ECONOMY = "good" AND LOCALADS > 2000
  THEN: LAFACTOR = LOCALADS/100000
```

Notice that this premise has two conditions that must be met before the conclusion is valid.

Similarly, it is permissible to have a rule with multiple actions in its conclusion. For example, Jack expects that if the economy is fair, then the local advertising factor should be 1 percent for every $1,200 spent and the economic factor should be one third of the anticipated economic growth rate. He realizes that values must be known for both the LOCAL-ADS and GROWTH variables before LAFACTOR and EFACTOR can be calculated. All of this is concisely expressed as follows:

```
RULE: R4
  IF: ECONOMY = "fair" AND KNOWN("LOCALADS") AND KNOWN("GROWTH")
  THEN: EFACTOR = GROWTH/3
        LAFACTOR = LOCALADS/120000
```

Rule R4 has three conditions in its premise and two actions in its conclusion.

Notice that the KNOWN functions were not used in the premises of rule R1, R2, or R10 because each of those premises already contained references to all of the variables needed in order to carry out their respective actions. Therefore, it is guaranteed that values of these variables will be known before the rules' actions are taken. In the case of R4, the KNOWN functions ensure that values are known for LOCALADS and GROWTH before the actions in R4's conclusion are taken. In general, if a variable on the right side of an assignment statement in a rule action does not appear in the rule's premise, then it is advisable to put it in the premise with a KNOWN function.

A good expert system development tool should be able to support any number of conditions in the premise of a rule and any number of actions in its conclusion. Not only should it allow conjunctions in a rule premise, but disjunctions should be allowed as well. For instance, Jack needs to represent the fact that he considers the economy outlook to be poor if growth projections fall below 2 percent or it appears that the unemployment rate will exceed 8.2 percent:

```
RULE: R9
  IF: GROWTH < .02 OR UNEMPLOYMENT >= .082
  THEN: ECONOMY = "poor"
```

This rule's premise is an example of a disjunction. It says that if either condition is satisfied, then the conclusion is valid.

The AND (conjunction) and OR (disjunction) in rules R10 and R9 are called Boolean operators. They are a natural part of everyday reasoning processes. Two other valuable Boolean operators are XOR (exclusive OR) and NOT (negation). The exclusive OR is like the common OR shown above, except that if both conditions are true, then the overall premise is considered to be false. In other words:

```
GROWTH < .02 XOR UNEMPLOYMENT >= .082
```

would be true only if one, but not both, of the conditions is satisfied. Negation is also an important ingredient of problem-solving rules. For instance, Jack decides that once a base and factors for the economy, product, and local advertising are known, then they can be combined in a certain way to determine the new quota for the product. However, he believes that this formula is only valid if the product is neither a strong nor weak product. Thus, his rule might be stated:

```
RULE: R17
  IF: NOT(WEAK OR STRONG) AND KNOWN("BASE") AND KNOWN("EFACTOR")
      AND KNOWN("PFACTOR") AND KNOWN("LAFACTOR")
  THEN: NEWQUOTA = BASE*(1+EFACTOR+LAFACTOR+PFACTOR)
```

Here again the KNOWN function is used to ensure that the values of certain variables are known before an attempt is made to use them in a calculation. Observe that there is no need to number the rules in any particular order. In fact, a rule's name does not need to contain any numbers at all. For instance, Jack could have named this rule MEDIUM instead of R17.

Notice that some of Jack's rules involved numeric calculations. In some cases these calculations may be needed in the premise of a rule (e.g., rules R1 and R2). In other cases, they may be needed in a rule's conclusion (e.g., rules R1 and R17). Such calculations are indispensable in most business reasoning. A tool for business expert system development should allow rules to involve all the common numeric operations of addition, subtraction, multiplication, division, and exponentiation. It should also provide the person developing rule sets with built-in math functions for automatically calculating square roots, logarithms, and so forth. Of course, all calculations actually carried out when a rule set is consulted should be done with a reasonable degree of numeric accuracy.

All of the foregoing rule examples have had conclusions consisting of one or more assignment actions. An assignment action merely indicates what value to assign to a variable. For instance, in rule R2 the value of QUOTA is assigned to the BASE variable, if the premise is true. Another kind of action that could appear in a rule's conclusion is an input statement, which will prompt the user to type in the value for a variable. For instance, if there is strong interest in a particular product, the base amount is known, and various adjusting factors are known, then Jack wants to prompt the expert system's user for a subjective estimate of the percentage of sales increase due to rising interest in the product line. This percentage is then used in determining the new quota for the product. The corresponding rule is:

```
RULE: R15
  IF: STRONG AND KNOWN("BASE") AND KNOWN("EFACTOR")
      AND KNOWN("PFACTOR") AND KNOWN("LAFACTOR")
  THEN: INPUT RISE NUM WITH\
      "Enter percent increase due to rising interest in "+PROD
      NEWQUOTA=BASE*(1+EFACTOR+LAFACTOR+PFACTOR+RISE/100)
```

If the premise is true, the conclusion's first action is to input the desired percentage into the RISE variable. The NUM in this INPUT command guarantees that the user's entry will be numeric.* The prompt that the user will see consists of the quoted message with the product of interest concatenated to it. If the product line happens to be computers, then the user sees the prompt:

```
Enter percent increase due to rising interest in computers _____
```

---

*A backslash at the end of a line indicates that the command is continued on the next line. Though Guru allows each line to be up to 255 characters, commands shown here are sometimes broken into multiple lines in order to fit within the margins of this book.

The user's response becomes the value of RISE, which is used in the conclusion's second action for determining the new quota.

The rule examples shown here illustrate the basics of specifying rules. Subsequent chapters show more advanced kinds of rules having more elaborate actions and allowing varying degrees of uncertainty to be expressed. You will also see that there can be more to a rule than just its premise and conclusion. Furthermore, a rule set can contain much more than just rules.

MANAGING RULES

An expert system development tool must provide some way of managing a rule set's rules—creating, revising, and deleting them as desired. The software for accomplishing this is called a rule set manager. Various kinds of rule set managers are possible. At one extreme, a text processor can serve as a rule set manager. At the other extreme is software that allows rules to be managed by responses to menu options. Guru supports both approaches to managing rules [2]. Each one is examined here.

Rule Set Management with a Text Processor

Jack can use Guru's integral text processor to build and maintain a rule set's rules in a text file. As described in later chapters, this general-purpose text-processing component can also be used for preparing memos, reports, programs, and so forth. To create a file containing the quota advisor rule set, Jack would type:

```
TEXT "ADVISOR.RSS"
```

where ADVISOR is the name Jack wants to use when referring to this rule set. The console screen takes on the appearance shown in Screen 1 in the color insert and Jack can begin entering rules in the space provided. He simply types in the desired rules using the syntax shown earlier in this chapter. For instance, after entering rules R1 and R2, the screen would have the appearance shown in Screen 2 in the color insert. Notice that for each rule, Jack has specified a reason. As described later in Chapter 7, a rule's reason message is used by the inference engine when explaining its line of reasoning to a user.

As Jack enters the ADVISOR rules, there are many control keys available for controlling cursor movement. These include character-at-a-time movement in any of four directions, moving a word at a time, jumping to the start or end of a line, and automatic vertical and horizontal scrolling. Other control keys are available to insert and delete characters, to toggle between character insertion and replacement pro-

cessing, to insert and delete lines, to split and join lines, to restore a previously deleted line, and to bring help information about control key
usage into view. In addition to control keys, Jack can also use any of
two dozen commands for manipulating the text. These include commands for working with blocks of text (e.g., moving or copying them),
combining text from other files, turning the display of text line numbers
on and off, saving the present version of text on a disk file, searching for
desired character patterns in the text, and replacing one character pattern with another. The automatic search and replacement commands
are especially powerful, supporting wildcard pattern matching, anchor-
ing, and selective scopes of operation.

When Jack has finished entering the rule set's rules, he can save
them by typing on the text-processing command line:

```
WRITE
```

All of the rules are now saved in the ADVISOR.RSS disk file. The RSS
file extension indicates that this file contains the source version of a rule
set. Jack is free to later use the TEXT command to make changes to the
rules held in a rule set's source file. When Jack is satisfied with a rule set,
he then compiles it in order to generate a version of the rule set that can
be efficiently processed by the inference engine. This is accomplished by
typing the command:

```
COMPILE ADVISOR
```

This command results in a file named ADVISOR.RSC. The RSC file extension indicates that this file contains the compiled version of the
ADVISOR rule set.

During this compilation process, Guru analyzes the rules that Jack
has constructed. The compilation analysis looks for possible oversights, inconsistencies, syntactic mistakes, and logical errors in the rule
set. If any potential problems are detected, Guru would issue pertinent
warning messages to Jack. If warning messages do appear, Jack can immediately use the TEXT command to correct the source version of the
rule set. It is then recompiled.

Rule Set Management via Menus

A different approach to rule set management presents the developer
with a menu interface. This provides an alternative way for creating
and revising the source version of a rule set. For instance, rather than
using Guru's TEXT command, Jack could have typed:

```
BUILD ADVISOR
```

This command produces the menu of options shown in Screen 3 in the color insert. Each of the first five options allows Jack to work on a different aspect of the ADVISOR rule set. The only one of these that is of interest for the present is the Rules option. As mentioned earlier, Guru allows a rule set to consist of more than just a list of rules. These other aspects of a rule set are introduced in Chapter 5. The last two options in the main menu are for printing a rule set and for exiting from the rule set manager.

In order to work on the rules for the ADVISOR rule set, Jack would select the Rules option from the main menu. This causes another menu to pop down on top of the main menu. The options in this Rules menu allow Jack to work on the rules in various ways. These include browsing through selected rules and possibly editing them as the browsing proceeds, looking up a specific rule, creating a new rule, renaming a rule, and deleting a rule. In building the ADVISOR rule set from scratch, Jack would choose the Create option. He is then prompted to enter the new rule's name. Once the name has been provided, he can proceed to type in the rule's premise, conclusion, and reason. Screen 4 in the color insert shows what Jack would see after creating rule R1. Notice that other optional characteristics of a rule could also be entered. Jack ignores them for the present. These advanced options will be discussed in Part III. The remaining ADVISOR rules can be created in the same way.

When Jack chooses the main menu's Exit option, he will be presented with an exit menu that gives him a chance to save the source version of the rule set and to produce a compiled version of the rule set. Upon exiting from the BUILD command, Jack is immediately able to execute any other Guru command. The source rule set file produced by the BUILD command can later be modified by using either the BUILD or TEXT command. The BUILD command is probably more appropriate for beginning and infrequent rule set developers than is the TEXT command. Experienced rule set developers are likely to prefer the TEXT approach to rule set management.

The facilities that a tool provides for rule set management are important for developer productivity. They should, of course, be carefully considered when selecting an expert system development tool. Some general guidelines about what features a developer should expect in rule management software are provided in Part IV.

Rule Induction

For some small-scale applications, rule induction may be a workable alternative to directly specifying and modifying rules with a rule set manager. Rule induction is based on the idea of translating specific examples into one or more general rules. For instance, if Jack had to use rule induction software rather than a rule set manager, he would specify a collection of examples rather than directly stating the desired rules. In each example, Jack would need to supply a value for every variable that could influence the new quota. He would also need to specify what new quota should correspond to those values. For instance, Jack would need to indicate that for SALES of $8,729, QUOTA of $9,205, GROWTH of .024, UNEMPLOYMENT of .055, LOCALADS of $875, and so on, the NEWQUOTA should be $9,472. It would be up to Jack to invent and type in enough of these examples to allow the rule induction software to produce the necessary rules for solving quota problems. Even for the modest quota application, this would be quite a challenge.

In general, rule induction can in no way be regarded as an adequate substitute for a good rule set manager. Its most obvious drawbacks are inconvenience and the likelihood of oversights. Contriving and entering enough examples to clearly cover all possibilities for a particular problem area become extremely cumbersome for nontrivial problems. How can the developer be sure all possibilities are covered and that the induction software will produce the desired rule? In contrast, the direct specification of a rule immediately captures a more general pattern of reasoning without the need to make up sufficient examples to convey the same module of reasoning knowledge. There are other drawbacks that are not quite as glaring, yet just as vital. They center around the lack of power and flexibility that examples furnish for adequately representing reasoning knowledge. Many of the expert system capabilities described in the following chapters are not practical if rule induction is all that is available to a developer. On the other hand, a supplemental rule induction capability may be useful for certain limited classes of problems, such as those that are restricted to categorization.

CONCLUSION

As the rule examples in this chapter suggest, rules provide a modular way of representing reasoning knowledge. This is a very different concept than trying to use a programming language to embed such knowledge in a program. Instead of sequencing program statements within traditional control structures, a modular collection of fragments of reasoning knowledge is put together. This is accomplished with a development tool's rule management software, which may be a text processor or a menu-driven facility. It is then the inference engine that determines how to make use of these pieces of reasoning knowledge in response to a particular problem posed by a user. As described in Chapter 8, knowledge integration permits much more powerful and flexible rule specification than the examples shown here. This integration permits rule-oriented reasoning knowledge to play the role of metaknowledge in artificially intelligent decision support systems for business [1].

EXERCISES

1. Explain the relationship between conditions and a rule's premise.
2. Describe the structure of a condition.
3. Give an example of a condition involving a relational operator.
4. Give an example of a condition involving no relational operators.
5. What possible values can the condition SALES< = 1.15*QUOTA have? Describe situations that lead to these values.
6. Explain the relationship between actions and a rule's conclusion.
7. What are the two kinds of actions introduced in this chapter?
8. What other kinds of actions might be useful in the conclusions of rules existing in a business expert system?
9. Why are the two KNOWN conditions necessary for rule R4?
10. Why is a KNOWN condition unnecessary in rule R10?
11. Explain the relationship between a rule's premise and conclusion.
12. What are the advantages of having extensive freedom and flexibility in the specification of a rule?
13. Suppose your inference engine permits only one action per conclusion. How would you capture the reasoning knowledge represented in rule R4?
14. Suppose your inference engine does not permit conditions to be connected by OR in a premise. How would you capture the reasoning knowledge inherent in rule R9?
15. Suppose your inference engine is unable to comprehend the XOR Boolean connector. If you need a premise of GROWTH< .02 XOR UNEMPLOYMENT> = .082, what would you do?
16. Instead of determining the BASE with respect to a fixed 15 percent criterion, Jack wants the percentage to be the ratio of the square root of twice the quota relative to half the quota. Assume that the inference engine is able to recognize and process a square root function named SQRT. Restate rules R1 and R2 accordingly.
17. How would the prior situation be handled if the inference engine is unable to compute square roots with a built-in function?
18. What is the purpose of rule management software?
19. Contrast the text-processing and menu-oriented approaches to rule set management.
20. What are some of the advantages of rule set compilation?
21. Explain the difference between inference performed by an expert system and rule induction performed by a rule set manager.

22. Contrast the activity of developing a rule set with the activity of writing a program.

23. Discuss the limitations of rule induction.

References

1   Bonczek, R. H.; C. W. Holsapple; and A. B. Whinston. *Foundations of Decision Support Systems.* New York: Academic Press, 1981.

2   *Guru Reference Manual*, vols. 1–2. Lafayette, Ind.: MDBS, Inc. 1985.

Chapter Five

Reasoning with Rules

Once a rule set has been built, the reasoning knowledge it contains can be used by an inference engine. Remember that each rule is a module of knowledge that tells the inference engine what actions to take, provided the conditions stated in its premise are satisfied. When confronted with a problem, the inference engine reasons with the rules in an effort to derive a solution to the problem. This reasoning involves the ability to select those rules that are pertinent to the specific problem, determine whether a rule's premise is satisfied, carry out the actions specified in a rule's conclusion, and acquire additional knowledge (e.g., from the user) if an impasse is reached. Each of these abilities is explored in this chapter.

THE ADVISOR RULE SET

Suppose that Jack Vander has developed the ADVISOR rule set having the 18 rules shown in Figure 5–1. Notice that in addition to its premise and conclusion, each of the rules has a reason. This is simply a text description of the rule. If a rule was involved in solving a problem, then its reason can be displayed to the user when the inference engine is asked to explain the line of reasoning used to reach a solution. The developer of a rule set is free to make a rule's reason as specific (e.g., rule R1) or general (e.g., rule R8) as warranted by the application. It may be desirable to avoid overly specific reasons, especially if the rule is too technical or complex for a user to understand in detail or if the rule's reasoning knowledge cannot be disclosed to users for security reasons. A rule's reason can be omitted from the rule set if desired.

A sales manager may now want to consult the ADVISOR rule set to get advice about what quarterly quota to set for a particular sales rep on a particular product line. This could be accomplished with a command such as:

CONSULT ADVISOR TO SEEK NEWQUOTA

FIGURE 5-1   Sample rules in the ADVISOR rule set

RULE: R1
    IF: SALES > 1.15 * QUOTA
    THEN: BASE = QUOTA + (SALES − 1.15 * QUOTA)
    REASON: In cases where the sales for this product exceeded the quota by more
           than 15%, the base amount for the new quota is set to the past quota
           plus the excess sales amount.

RULE: R2
    IF: SALES < = 1.15 * QUOTA
    THEN: BASE = QUOTA
    REASON: The base amount for the new quota is the same as the past quota
           because this product's sales did not exceed the past quota by more than
           15%.

RULE: R3
    IF: ECONOMY = "good" AND KNOWN ("GROWTH")
    THEN: EFACTOR = GROWTH
    REASON: When the local economic outlook is good, the economic factor is equal
           to the economy's anticipated growth rate.

RULE: R4
    IF: ECONOMY = "fair" AND KNOWN ("LOCALADS")
        AND KNOWN ("GROWTH")
    THEN: EFACTOR = GROWTH/3; LAFACTOR = LOCALADS/120000
    REASON: When the local economic outlook is fair, the economic factor is one
           third of the growth rate and the local advertising factor is 1/120,000th
           of the amount budgeted for local advertising.

RULE: R5
    IF: ECONOMY = "poor" AND KNOWN ("GROWTH")
        AND KNOWN ("UNEMPLOYMENT")
    THEN: EFACTOR = MIN (GROWTH, .085 − UNEMPLOYMENT)
    REASON: If the local economic outlook is poor, then the economic factor should
           be the lesser of the growth rate and the result of subtracting the
           unemployment rate from 8.5%.

RULE: R6
    IF: GROWTH > = .04 AND UNEMPLOYMENT < .076
    THEN: ECONOMY = "good"
    REASON: The economic outlook is good because the projected unemployment
           rate is below 7.6% and the anticipated growth rate is at least 4%.

RULE: R7
    IF: GROWTH > = .02 AND GROWTH < .04
        AND UNEMPLOYMENT < .055
    THEN: ECONOMY = "good"
    REASON: The economic outlook is good because projected unemployment is less
           than 5.5% and the anticipated growth rate is between 2% and 4%.

RULE: R8
    IF: GROWTH > = .02 AND GROWTH < .04
        AND UNEMPLOYMENT > = .055 AND UNEMPLOYMENT < .082
    THEN: ECONOMY = "fair"
    REASON: The economic outlook is fair because of moderate growth and
           unemployment expectations.

FIGURE 5-1   *(continued)*

RULE: R9
    IF: GROWTH < .02 OR UNEMPLOYMENT > = .082
    THEN: ECONOMY = "poor"
    REASON: The economic outlook is poor because either the anticipated growth
        rate is very low or projected unemployment is high or both.

RULE: R10
    IF: ECONOMY = "good" AND LOCALADS > 2000
    THEN: LAFACTOR = LOCALADS/100000
    REASON: When the economy is good and local advertising exceeds $2,000, the
        local advertising factor is 1% for every thousand dollar expenditure.

RULE: R11
    IF: ECONOMY = "poor" AND LOCALADS < 1500
    THEN: LAFACTOR = − .015
    REASON: When the economic outlook is poor and local advertising expenditures
        for the product are modest, then the local advertising factor is
        negative.

RULE: R12
    IF: (ECONOMY = "poor" AND LOCALADS > = 1500)
        OR (ECONOMY = "good" AND LOCALADS < = 2000)
    THEN: LAFACTOR = 0
    REASON: The local advertising factor is negligible because of low advertising in a
        good economy or a poor economy coupled with substantial local
        advertising for the product line.

RULE: R13
    IF: PROD IN ["computer", "romance", "scifi"]
    THEN: PFACTOR = (NEWTITLES + OLDTITLES)/OLDTITLES − 1
        STRONG = TRUE
        WEAK = FALSE
    REASON: This is a strong product line. The product factor is based on the growth
        in the number of titles in this line.

RULE: R14
    IF: PROD IN ["reference", "biography", "psychology", "sports"]
    THEN: PFACTOR = .75*((NEWTITLES + OLDTITLES)/OLDTITLES − 1)
        STRONG = FALSE
        WEAK = FALSE
    REASON: This is neither a strong nor weak product line. The product factor is
        proportional to three fourths of the growth in the number of titles in
        this line.

RULE: R15
    IF: STRONG AND KNOWN ("BASE") AND KNOWN ("EFACTOR") AND
        KNOWN ("PFACTOR") AND KNOWN ("LAFACTOR")
    THEN: INPUT RISE NUM \
        WITH "Enter estimate of percentage sales increase " \
        + "due to rising interest in " + PROD
        NEWQUOTA = BASE * (1 + EFACTOR + LAFACTOR + \
            PFACTOR + RISE/100)
    REASON: This is a strong product line. The base amount, economic factor,
        product factor, and local advertising factor for calculating the new
        quota are all known. A subjective assessment of the expected sales
        increase due to general rising interest in the product is requested. The
        new quota is then calculated.

FIGURE 5-1   *(concluded)*

RULE: R16
        IF: WEAK AND KNOWN ("BASE") AND KNOWN ("EFACTOR") AND
            KNOWN ("PFACTOR") AND KNOWN ("LAFACTOR")
        THEN: INPUT FALL NUM \
                WITH "Enter estimate of percentage sales decrease " \
                + "due to falling interest in " + PROD
                NEWQUOTA = BASE * (1 + EFACTOR + LAFACTOR + \
                        PFACTOR − FALL/100)
        REASON: This is a weak product line. A subjective assessment of the expected
                sales decrease due to general declining interest in this product line is
                requested. The new quota can then be calculated.

RULE: R17
        IF: NOT (WEAK OR STRONG) AND KNOWN ("BASE")
            AND KNOWN ("EFACTOR") AND KNOWN ("PFACTOR")
            AND KNOWN ("LAFACTOR")
        THEN: NEWQUOTA = BASE*(1 + EFACTOR + LAFACTOR + PFACTOR)
        REASON: This is neither an especially strong nor weak product line. Its new
                quota is calculated from the base amount and factors for the economy,
                local advertising, and product line expansion.

RULE: R18
        IF: NOT (PROD IN ["computer", "romance", "scifi", "reference", "biography",
            "psychology", "sports"])
        THEN: WEAK = TRUE; STRONG = FALSE
                PFACTOR = .45*((NEWTITLES+OLDTITLES)/OLDTITLES−1)
        REASON: This is a weak product line. The product factor is proportional to less
                than half of its growth in titles.

Imagine for a moment that you are the inference engine. You have access to all 18 rules. How will you reason with these rules that Jack built, in order to find a new quota? How will you select which rule to consider next as your reasoning proceeds? How will you determine whether that rule's premise is satisfied? How will you carry out the actions in its conclusion if the premise is satisfied? These are the issues confronting the inference engine each time a consultation is requested.

CHALLENGE OF THE UNKNOWN VARIABLES

It is clear that the user wants you (the inference engine) to reason with the expertise embodied in the ADVISOR rule set in order to determine a value for the NEWQUOTA variable. If you pause to examine the rules in Figure 5-1, you will notice that values of the variables in the rules are unknown. In rule R1 for instance, you do not presently know the value of SALES or the value of QUOTA. Therefore you have no way of determining whether the premise of R1 is true or false. Because the premise is unknown, you do not know whether it is permissible to fire the rule (i.e., to take the action specified in its conclusion).

Look at rule R16. Even if you knew the value of WEAK (true or false), the rule could not be fired because the base amount and various factors indicated in the premise are unknown. The KNOWN function has an unknown value if the indicated variable's value is unknown but could perhaps become known in the reasoning process. If the inference engine has discovered that the variable's value cannot become known during the reasoning process, then the KNOWN function has a false value. Initially, the KNOWN functions in R16 are unknown (not false) because their variable's values could possibly become known during the reasoning process. As a result, R16 cannot presently be fired. In fact, you are currently unable to fire any rule in the ADVISOR rule set because the premise of each rule is presently unknown.

Three Approaches to Knowing

So, how does an inference engine overcome this apparent impasse? The conventional solution is that it can ask the user to supply the values of unknown variables. Of course, the inference engine needs to know precisely what question to ask for each variable that could be unknown. This information can be incorporated into the rule set in any of several ways: as a rule's conclusion, as a variable description, or in an inference initialization sequence. The first approach is most common with conventional expert system development tools. All three approaches are supported by Guru and an example of each is provided here.

Rule conclusion. In looking at R13, for instance, Jack notices that a value must be established for PROD before the premise can be determined to be either true or false. Because none of the other rules has a conclusion that could change the value of PROD, Jack decides that the user of the ADVISOR system should be prompted to indicate which product is of interest for a particular consultation. This can be accomplished by adding the following rule to the ADVISOR rule set.

```
RULE: VARPROD
  IF: NOT KNOWN("PROD")
  THEN: INPUT PROD STR WITH "Enter product line:"
  REASON: You must tell me what the product line is before
          I can determine what its new quota should be.
```

The inference engine now has a way of getting a string value for PROD when the product line is not known during a consultation. Jack could devise similar rules for acquiring values of other variables that could be unknown during a consultation.

Variable description. A drawback of inventing rules such as VARPROD is that many of them may be necessary in a rule set that has many variables. In general, increasing the number of rules in a rule set slows the expert system's response time. All else being equal, an inference engine can normally reason with a small number of rules faster than it can reason with a significantly larger number of rules. A more important drawback for advanced expert system developers is that a rule such as VARPROD gives no way of characterizing the nature of the variable itself. Such characterizations are of no concern for the moment, but will be examined later.

Rather than the VARPROD rule, Jack could incorporate the following variable description into the ADVISOR rule set:

```
VARIABLE: PROD
  FIND: INPUT PROD STR WITH "Enter product line:"
```

This yields the same prompting effect as the VARPROD rule, but without the cost of processing a rule. The FIND portion of a variable description simply tells the inference engine how to find a value for the variable whenever the value is needed but unknown during a reasoning process.

Inference initialization. In addition to rules and variable descriptions, an advanced development tool like Guru allows a rule set to contain an inference initialization sequence. This is simply a series of actions that the inference engine will automatically carry out as soon as a user consults the rule set. These actions are taken before the inference engine even begins to consider how the rules will be used in reasoning about the specific problem that has been posed. This is an ideal spot to include a sequence of INPUT actions for:

1. All of the rule set variables that are needed for every consultation, regardless of the specific problem posed by the user.

2. All of the rule set variables whose values are known to the user at the very start of every consultation.

For instance, Jack might build the following initialization sequence into the ADVISOR rule set.

```
INITIAL:
  LET E.LSTR = 50
  INPUT REP STR WITH "What is the sales rep's name?"
  INPUT PROD STR WITH "Enter product line:"
  INPUT SALES NUM WITH "How much " +\
    TRIM(PROD) + " did " + TRIM(REP) + " sell?"
  INPUT QUOTA NUM WITH "What was the " + TRIM(PROD)\
    + "quota for " + TRIM(REP) + "?"
```

FIGURE 5-2 A sample of inference initialization

Guru> *CONSULT ADVISOR TO SEEK NEWQUOTA*
What is the sales rep's name? *Toby*
Enter product line: *romance*
How much romance did Toby sell? *13750*
What was the romance quota for Toby? *12560*

Whenever the ADVISOR rule set is consulted, the inference engine would carry out the four INPUT actions before considering any of the rule set's rules. It would first ask the user which sales rep is of interest and then ask which product line is of interest. The user's responses become the new values of the REP and PROD variables, respectively. Furthermore, these responses automatically become part of the subsequent sales and quota questions. TRIM is an example of a built-in Guru function. It automatically trims off any blanks from the end of a string variable's value. A sample of the user interaction for this initialization sequence is shown in Figure 5-2, with the user's responses to prompts being shown in italics. Notice that an initialization sequence allows Jack to easily control the order in which questions are posed to the expert system user. Of course, many more INPUT actions could have been included in the initialization sequence (e.g., for GROWTH and UNEMPLOYMENT). This particular initialization sequence began with an assignment command that tells the inference engine to let the length of prompt strings be up to 50 characters. The E.LSTR variable is one of more than 100 environment variables (each beginning with E.) built into Guru. By setting these variables as desired, Jack can customize the AI environment provided by Guru. Further examples of environment variables are sprinkled throughout the remainder of this book.

Customizing the User Interface

Each of the three approaches made use of one or more INPUT commands. The INPUT examples shown here have been of a very basic nature. There are more elaborate INPUT variations available, allowing the developer to control the screen location where the input will occur and the kinds of characters that can be input. For instance:

```
AT 5,11 INPUT PROD STR USING "LLLLLLLLLLLL"\
 WITH "Enter product line:"
```

would cause the "Enter product line:" prompt to appear in the fifth row of the console screen, beginning 11 character positions from the left edge of the screen. The USING "lllllllllllll" means that the user's response can consist of up to 12 characters. If any of those characters is typed in upper case, then it is automatically converted to lower case. In contrast, "uuuuuuuu" would indicate that the user could type in up to eight characters, all of which are automatically converted to upper case.* Generally speaking, the character pattern enclosed in quotes following USING is called a picture. The various kinds of pictures supported by Guru are too numerous to describe here.

The facilities that a tool gives to a developer for customizing an expert system's user interface are very important. An ability comparable to the Guru INPUT command is a minimal necessity, but conventional tools' abilities to acquire input from users rarely go any further. However, much more powerful and flexible facilities for constructing sophisticated user interfaces are available in Guru [1]. Any of these can be employed in a rule conclusion, in a variable description's find action, or in the rule set's initialization sequence.

There is a built-in function for automatically building a menu of options, presenting it to the expert system's user, and capturing the user's selection as the value of a variable that can be used for subsequent reasoning. Option positioning and colors are easily controlled. This is described later in Chapter 7. For advanced developers, there is another built-in function that tracks the way in which the user manipulates a mouse device, furnishing an alternative to keystroke input. Also available is a command that causes the meaning of keyboard function keys to be redefined as needed during a consultation. This allows a user to respond to the inference engine by pressing a desired function key.

Perhaps the most interesting and valuable facility for developing customized user interfaces for expert systems is Guru's forms management component. It allows the developer to build a collection of forms that the inference engine can use for interacting with a user. The developer can design or modify each form by "painting" its layout, colors, contents, and special effects (e.g., blinking or reverse video) directly on the console screen. There is a group of commands available for processing an entire form at a time. This includes displaying a form to the user at a desired screen location, assigning values that the user types into the form to proper variables, resetting the form's contents, and clearing a form from the screen. For instance, an entire series of INPUT commands could be replaced by a single form command. Many forms can be "windowed" on a screen simultaneously and can overlap as desired. Although the user interface examples shown in this book deal primarily

---

*As a shorthand notation, it is permissible to use "%8u" in place of "uuuuuuuu"" or "%12l" in place of "lllllllllllll."

with the line-oriented INPUT and OUTPUT commands, expert system developers should remember that high-level forms management commands are available as a sophisticated alternative.

BEYOND USER INTERACTION—THE POWER OF INTEGRATION

The rules of an interesting rule set will inevitably refer to some variables whose values are unknown at the outset of a consultation. In order to fully grasp the nature of a problem posed by an end user, the inference engine needs to somehow establish the values for at least some of these unknown variables. A human expert can draw on expertise about a problem area in order to know what questions to ask of a client and when to ask them. Similarly, an expert system's inference engine is able to draw on a rule set to determine what questions to ask of a user and when to ask them. As briefly described above, the interface styles (line-oriented, menu-oriented, mouse-oriented, forms-oriented) for getting values from the user can also be designed into a rule set.

A human expert is not limited to asking the client questions whenever the reasoning process pauses because of insufficient knowledge. The client may not know all the answers anyway. Thus, instead of always asking the client, the expert gets the knowledge needed to continue the reasoning process from other sources. This could involve reading a textual passage, making a calculation, conducting an analysis with some procedural model (e.g., regression analysis), selectively computing a desired statistical measure (e.g., standard deviation), looking up values that exist in a data base, telephoning an external source to ask for needed knowledge, consulting other experts, and so forth. Any or all of these could happen as the expert ponders a particular problem. Because there are no barriers in the human mind, these kinds of activities can be blended together as desired in the course of reasoning about a problem. This synergy is an important factor in effective human problem solving. It is just as important for expert system problem solving.

If an expert system is to be able to truly emulate the human expert, it must not be limited to merely asking the user for a variable's value whenever there is insufficient knowledge to continue reasoning about a problem. A tool that imposes this restriction on developers leads to expert system behavior that could well be regarded as mentally handicapped if it were observed in a human. Resultant expert systems may not resemble outstanding human experts as closely as we might like. A few conventional expert system development tools have made a small start at addressing this restriction.

Such tools support "hooks" to outside data files or programs. This means that a rule set is able to access data in files that have been produced as a result of executing external programs or request the execution of an external program. The exact details of these hooks vary widely from one tool to another, but all fall far short of the effects that can be achieved with true integration. Hooking therefore receives little consideration here. The emphasis is on the much more powerful and convenient integral facilities that are today available for acquiring knowledge.

Recall that there are three distinct approaches to incorporating desired prompting behavior into a rule set: as the conclusion of a rule, in the find action of a variable description, or in the rule set's initialization sequence. In each case, it was shown how an INPUT command could be used to give the inference engine a way of asking the user for a variable's value. In each case, it is possible to replace or supplement INPUT commands with other kinds of commands. An INPUT command is not used in situations where the developer believes that it makes more sense to acquire an unknown variable's value without asking the user. In other situations, the developer may want the inference engine to do some preliminary work and present the results (e.g., a graph or report) to the user before asking for user input. The following examples illustrate some of the possibilities.

Data Base Management within a Rule Set

Because Guru has a full-scale relational data base management component [1], KC's vice president of sales has decided that each sales manager will use Guru to track quarterly sales and quotas of all their sales reps for each product. KC's MIS department has designed the data table structure shown in Figure 5-3 for this purpose. The table's name is THISYR and it identifies five categories of data that are of interest: sales rep name, product line name, quarter number, quota, and sales. Each category is called a field and has its own unique name (REPNAME, PRODNAME, QTRNUM, QUOTA, SALES). Figure 5-4 shows some of the actual data content of this table for one of the sales managers. Each row in the table is called a record. It records the quota and sales of a particular product in a particular quarter by a particular sales rep. For instance, in this year's second quarter Toby's romance sales were $13,750 against a quota of $12,560. Each sales manager maintains his or her own reps' data in a THISYR table. The manager can use Guru's SQL query, statistical analysis, graphics generation, and other capabilities to monitor and evaluate sales rep performance during the course of the present year.

FIGURE 5–3   Structure of the THISYR table

THISYR

REPNAME	PRODNAME	QTRNUM	QUOTA	SALES

FIGURE 5–4   Sample records in the THISYR table

THISYR

REPNAME	PRODNAME	QTRNUM	QUOTA	SALES
Toby	computer	1	14051	11010
Toby	romance	1	16820	17520
Toby	computer	2	18000	16958
Toby	romance	2	12560	13750
Kim	scifi	1	6750	7120
Kim	computer	1	14444	12982
Kim	romance	1	12820	12147
Toby	scifi	1	7980	8796
Kim	computer	2	15582	16125
.	.	.	.	.
.	.	.	.	.
.	.	.	.	.

Jack realizes that a sales manager's THSYR table contains data that are pertinent to the expert system he is developing. For instance, why should his expert system force a user to look up and then type in sales and quota figures when they are already available in the THISYR table? Not only does this take more time and place a burden on the user, it also increases the chance of errors due to undetected typing mistakes. As a convenience to the user, Jack might build the following initialization sequence into the ADVISOR rule set:

```
INITIAL:
  LET E.LSTR = 50; LET E.SUPD = TRUE
  INPUT REP STR WITH "What is the sales rep's name?"
  INPUT PROD STR WITH "Enter product line:"
  INPUT QTR STR USING "n" WITH "Enter quarter:"
  IF NOT INUSE("THISYR") THEN USE THISYR; ENDIF
  OBTAIN RECORD FROM THISYR FOR\
   REPNAME=REP & PRODNAME=PROD & QTRNUM=QTR
```

This initialization sequence begins in much the same way as the one presented earlier. By letting the E.SUPD environment variable be TRUE, Jack causes Guru to suppress the on-screen display of data subsequently obtained from data tables. Here, the user is prompted for the quarter number in addition to the rep name and product line. The "n" picture means that Guru will accept only a single numeric character in response to the "Enter quarter:" prompt. If the THISYR table is not already in use, then the USE command tells the inference engine the THISYR is going to be used (the data base could consist of many tables, not all of which need to be used by the expert system). The OBTAIN command obtains the THISYR record whose rep name, product, and quarter match those specified by the user. In general, & symbol is interchangeable with the Boolean AND operator.

After the inference engine carries out this initialization sequence, both the SALES and QUOTA variables will have the correct values.* The inference engine simply obtains them from the table, rather than forcing a user to look them up and enter them in response to prompts. In general, there is no limit on the number of tables that an expert system can use simultaneously. Multikey indexed access to data tables is fully supported, as is the retrieval of related data from multiple tables via a single command. Guru's table capacities are generous: unlimited tables/data base, 255 fields/table, over 2 billion records/table, 65,535 characters/field value, and so on. To do justice to the Guru data base management capabilities would require an entire book in and of itself. Here, we can only touch on a few of the basic capabilities of this Guru component. Suffice it to say that novices can do productive data management right away, while professional developers will discover features that are at least on a par with the most extensive stand-alone data management systems. Furthermore, professionals should not overlook the more sophisticated postrelational data base management capabilities that are optionally available for integral use in this environment [1].

---

*In the initial release of Guru, every rule set reference to a field name must be qualified by its table name. For instance, each mention of the SALES field in the initialization sequence and in rules should appear as: THISYR.SALES

Spreadsheets within a Rule Set

Just as it is commonplace to have data values stored in a data base, it also frequently happens that a spreadsheet may contain values that could be pertinent to expert system processing. Because spreadsheet processing is an integral component of Guru [1], the inference engine always has immediate access to the value of any cell of the presently loaded spreadsheet. The spreadsheet need not be showing on the screen in order to access its contents. Thus there is no need to prompt a user to reenter any value that already exists in a spreadsheet.

KC's sales managers use Guru's spreadsheet for preparing advertising budgets. Each quarter, the manager receives a discretionary amount to spend on local advertising. Sales managers use their own formulas for allocating advertising funds to product lines and sales reps. Screen 5 in the color insert shows a console screen having two window views into different parts of an advertising spreadsheet. Four rows (1, 18, 19, 20) and four columns (A, K, L, M) are visible in window 3. In general, a sales manager's spreadsheet will contain many local advertising amounts like the nine shown here, but only one is pertinent to a particular consultation.

Jack wants the inference engine to look up the proper value for the LOCALADS variable in the sales manager's spreadsheet. He has reached an agreement with the sales managers that rows 18 through 31 of their spreadsheets will always contain budgeted advertising amounts by product line. The product lines are in alphabetical order (e.g., scifi cannot precede romance in any spreadsheet). He has also reached an agreement that the 2nd through 13th rows of columns Y and Z will show which column of advertising amounts belongs to which sales representative. This is partially shown in window 6 of Screen 5 in the color insert. Beyond those conventions, the managers can arrange their spreadsheet contents as desired.

To let the inference engine know how to find a value for the LOCALADS variable, Jack could build the following variable description into the ADVISOR rule set:

```
VARIABLE: LOCALADS
   FIND: REPCOL = LOOKUP(REP,#Y2,#Y13,#Z2)
         LOCALADS = LOOKUP(PROD,#A18,#A31,#(18,REPCOL))
```

There are two ways to refer to a spreadsheet cell. One is to use a crosshatch symbol in front of the cell's column and row (e.g., #Y2). The other is to use the crosshatch followed by the parenthesized row number and column number. For instance, #Y2 is equivalent to #(2,25).

Here, Guru's spreadsheet LOOKUP function is used twice. The first time, it looks up the sales rep (between #Y2 and #Y13) and finds the associated column number (beginning at #Z2) for that rep. The second time, it looks up the product (between #A18 and #A31) and finds the associated advertising amount in the proper sales rep's column. Thus, when the inference engine needs to find a value for LOCALADS during a consultation, it simply looks up the proper value in the sales manager's own advertising spreadsheet. Remember, there is no switching among separate programs and no intermediate file construction. The manager can use Guru to work on the advertising budget and, in the very next command, consult the ADVISOR rule set. As soon as the consultation is completed, the manager may decide to adjust some of the spreadsheet assumptions and then immediately reconsult ADVISOR to see the effect on the recommended new quota amount.

Procedural Modeling within a Rule Set

In order to carry out its reasoning about quotas, the inference engine will need to know about the growth and unemployment outlooks for the local economy. The sales managers themselves are unable to make such projections. In the past, Jack has relied on KC's economic forecasting staff for producing reliable growth and unemployment estimates for the various territories in his own region. In building the ADVISOR expert system, he would like the inference engine to similarly rely on the economic forecasting staff. These economists have invented an economic model for making growth and unemployment projections. Because Guru provides a complete structured programming language [1], it is straightforward to represent the model as a Guru program. As a result, the inference engine can itself invoke this program in the course of a consultation to perform an economic analysis that determines the growth and unemployment rates.

The program is named ECON, so Jack adds the following action to ADVISOR's initialization sequence:

```
PERFORM ECON
```

This command performs the desired economic analysis. Within this program there are instructions that set the values of the GROWTH and UNEMPLOYMENT variables, based on the model's analysis. While it is being performed by the inference engine, the ECON program may draw on Guru data bases and spreadsheets, prompt the user for various inputs, make use of the values of any variables that have been previously set by the inference engine, get needed inputs from the mainframe computer at KC's headquarters, and so forth. A program can itself use all knowledge that is available to the inference engine and can create new knowledge that is directly available to the inference engine as soon as the program's execution terminates. There is no barrier between procedural modeling and expert system reasoning.

Consultation within a Rule Set

Suppose that KC's economists had implemented their forecasting knowledge as an expert system rather than a procedural model. Then the PERFORM command shown above would be replaced by:

```
CONSULT ECON
```

This command allows the ADVISOR expert system to consult an ECON expert system. The ECON rule set would contain the expertise needed to establish values for the GROWTH and UNEMPLOYMENT variables. As soon as the inference engine finishes consulting ECON, it continues the ADVISOR consultation—with all of the ECON results available to it.

Graphics within a Rule Set

In reviewing the ADVISOR rules, Jack decides that rule R2 should give the user some discretion in determining the base amount for the new quota. So he uses the rule set manager to alter R2.

```
RULE: R2
  IF: SALES <= 1.15 * QUOTA AND KNOWN("SUBJ")
  THEN: BASE = QUOTA * (1 + SUBJ/100)
  REASON: If the sales-to-quota ratio is not exceptional,
          then the base amount will be based on your
          subjective assessment of how reasonable last year's
          quota was. The subjective assessment indicates the
          percentage by which the base should differ from
          last year's quota.
```

Here, Jack has introduced a new variable, SUBJ. He wants the inference engine to ask the manager for the value of SUBJ in the event that R2 is considered during a consultation. But he wants the inference engine to put the past sales and quota levels in perspective before prompting the user.

Specifically, Jack wants the inference engine to produce a bar graph comparing the rep's quotas to sales for the product line over the last four quarters. He also wants the inference engine to generate a pie graph portraying the relative percentage breakdown of quota amounts by quarter. For convenient viewing, both graphs should appear on the console screen at the same time. When the manager has finished viewing the graphs, the inference engine should prompt for a subjective opinion based on the graphical content. All of this is incorporated into the ADVISOR rule set via the following variable description:

```
VARIABLE: SUBJ
   FIND: OUTPUT "You will be shown two graphs."
         OUTPUT "Please examine them carefully."
         OUTPUT "You will be asked for the percentage "\
          + "by which last year's quota was too high or low."
         LET PRESENT = CURREC(THISYR)
         OUTPUT "Press the space bar when finished viewing."
         DIM DS(4,3)
         CONVERT QTRNUM, QUOTA, SALES FROM THISYR\
          FOR REPNAME=REP & PRODNAME=PROD TO ARRAY DS(1,1)
         LET #TITLE = "Quota vs. Sales By Quarter"
         RANGE UP FROM 0
         E.DECI=0
         PLOT BAR FROM DS(1,1) TO DS(4,3) AT BOTTOM
         LET #TITLE = "Percentage Quotas"; E.DECI=1
         PLOT ONTOP LABELED % PIE FROM\
          DS(1,1) TO DS(4,2) AT TOP RIGHT
         INPUT SUBJ NUM WITH\
          "By what percentage should the quota be adjusted?"
         OBTAIN PRESENT RECORD FROM THISYR
```

Instead of simply having the inference engine use a solitary INPUT command to get a value for SUBJ, Jack has the inference engine carry out other common business computing actions as a prelude to the INPUT command. These have been devised to help the user make a reasonable response to the INPUT prompt. If the inference engine needs to find a value for SUBJ during a consultation, it will carry out the sequence of find actions in the variable description for SUBJ.

These actions begin with OUTPUT commands that alert the user to what is about to happen. Because the commands that follow are going to rummage about in the THISYR table's records, Jack has the inference engine remember which record is presently the current record (obtained during the initialization sequence). It can then be quickly obtained again after the user has provided a value for SUBJ. The DIM command dimensions a data source for the graphs that are to be generated. This data source happens to be called DS and it consists of four rows (one for each quarter) and three columns (for quarter, quota, and sales). The CONVERT command sets the 12 values in this data source by taking the quarter number, quota, and sales values of each record in the THISYR table for the indicated sales rep and product line. Each such record results in a row in the DS data source.

This data source can then be used to generate various graphs. Before each graph is generated, there is an assignment command that indicates what its title should be. The E.DECI environment variable controls how many decimal digits will be displayed by a graph. The inference engine uses all of the data in the data source to plot a bar graph on the bottom half of the console screen. Because there are four rows in the data source, there will be four clusters of bars in the graph—one for each quarter. The first value of each row is a quarter number that will serve as the X-axis label for that cluster. The other two values in the row indicate the heights of the quota and sales bars that will appear in the cluster.

The desired pie graph is then plotted on the same graphics screen, in the top right corner. Because it is a graph of quotas, only the first two columns of the data source are used. The quarter numbers become labels for the four pie slices. The size of each slice depends on the corresponding quota. Screen 6 in the color insert shows an example of what the user would see on the console screen after the inference engine has plotted the two graphs. By pressing the space bar, the user clears the graphs from the screen and is then prompted for the value of SUBJ. With the final OBTAIN command, the inference engine once again obtains the particular THISYR record that was initially accessed at the start of the consultation.

This example only touches on the graphics capabilities that are available in Guru [1]. Like the data base management, spreadsheet, programming, and other business-computing components, it would take an entire book to describe them in detail. All that can be done here is to provide a taste of the possibilities within an expert system context. The principle of having the inference engine automatically present a user with preliminary or stimulatory information before prompting is not restricted to graphics generation. It can involve any Guru component—from customized report generation to program execution [1].

Integrated Knowledge Acquisition

All of these examples serve to illustrate one central point: There is no need for a modern expert system to blindly prompt the user every time it has insufficient knowledge to continue its reasoning about a problem. When an inference engine is effectively integrated with all the familiar knowledge management capabilities, it can use any of them to acquire the knowledge needed to continue its reasoning. This results in expert systems that much more closely resemble human experts' problem-solving abilities. Sometimes it is best to prompt a user for the value of an unknown variable. Other times it places an unnecessary burden on the user, decreasing the efficiency of both the user and the inference engine. It increases the likelihood of erroneous consultation responses due to undetected mistakes in user responses. In yet other cases, the user may not possess a meaningful answer. All of these issues are resolved by an inference engine that encompasses the knowledge management facilities that are so well known in the business-computing world (see Figure 3–1, Chapter 3).

RULE–BASED REASONING

With this background, it is time to take a look at how an inference engine actually reasons with the rules in a rule set as it attempts to solve a problem. The following discussion assumes that Jack has augmented the ADVISOR rules shown in Figure 5–1 with the initialization sequence and variable description appearing in Figures 5–5 and 5–6 respectively. Notice that the initialization sequence explicitly gives an unknown value to variables whose values are not set by the preceding actions in the sequence. This initialization is important because Guru remembers the values of variables even after a consultation terminates. If a user were to request two consecutive consultations, the second should not normally begin with variable values determined by the first consultation. They should be reinitialized. Figure 5–5 also shows that the default goal of the rule set is NEWQUOTA. If a consultation request does not explicitly identify a goal for the consultation, the rule set's default goal is assumed.

When a user makes a consultation request, the inference engine first carries out all actions specifed in the rule set's initialization sequence. What happens next depends on the kind of reasoning that has been requested. As explained in Chapter 1, there are two basic kinds of reasoning: forward and reverse. Variations of these two are possible, but the focus here is first on forward reasoning and then on backward reason-

FIGURE 5–5   Initialization sequence for the ADVISOR rule set

```
INITIAL:
      LET E.LSTR = 50; LET E.SUPD = TRUE
      INPUT REP STR WITH "What is the sales rep's name?"
      INPUT PROD STR WITH "Enter product line:"
      INPUT QTR STR USING "n" WITH "Enter quarter."
      INPUT OLDTITLE NUM WITH "How many oldtitles for " + \
         TRIM(PROD) + "?"
      INPUT NEWTITLE NUM WITH "How many new titles?"
      IF NOT INUSE ("THISYR") THEN USE THISYR; ENDIF
      OBTAIN RECORD FROM THISYR FOR REPNAME = REP & \
         PRODNAME = PROD & QTRNUM = QTR
      PERFORM ECON
      ECONOMY = UNKNOWN; EFACTOR = UNKNOWN
      LOCALADS = UNKNOWN; LAFACTOR = UNKNOWN
      PFACTOR = UNKNOWN
      BASE = UNKNOWN; STRONG = UNKNOWN; WEAK = UNKNOWN
      NEWQUOTA = UNKNOWN
GOAL:
      NEWQUOTA
```

FIGURE 5–6   A variable description for the ADVISOR rule set

```
VARIABLE: LOCALADS
      FIND: REPCOL = LOOKUP(REP, #Y2, #Y13, #Z2)
            LOCALADS = LOOKUP(PROD, #A18, #A31, #(18, REPCOL))
```

ing. In both explanations, it is instructive to imagine that you are the inference engine. You have carried out the initialization actions and are now ready to begin reasoning with the ADVISOR rules.

REASONING WITH RULES— FORWARD REASONING

Forward reasoning, sometimes called "forward chaining," is based on the idea of examining each rule in a forward direction, looking first at its premise. The conclusion is ignored until the premise is determined to be true. When a rule's premise is found to be true, the rule is fired. The actions in its conclusion are taken. If the rule's premise is false, then the rule is not fired and another rule is considered. A rule whose premise is currently false may be reconsidered later. The firing of other rules may change variables in such a way that its premise could become true.

There is one other possibility when considering a rule during forward reasoning. Its premise may be neither true nor false—it could be unknown. This happens if one or more of the variables referenced in the premise is unknown. The values of these variables were not established during the initialization sequence, nor as a result of firing previously considered rules. If the rule set contains variable descriptions for these unknown variables, then the inference engine can find values for them by carrying out the prescribed actions in these variable descriptions. However, if there are some unknown variables that do not have variable descriptions, then the premise is still unknown. In such a case, the rule is not fired and another rule is considered. A rule whose premise is currently unknown may be reconsidered later. The firing of other rules may establish values for the unknown variables, so that the premise can later be evaluated as either true or false.

An Example of Forward Reasoning

To see how forward reasoning works in practice, think of yourself as the inference engine. A user has just asked you for a consultation to test out the effects of applying the ADVISOR expertise:

CONSULT ADVISOR TO TEST

You conduct the initialization actions of Figure 5–5 to establish initial values for the rule set's variables. Suppose that the following variable values result from the prompts, data base retrieval, and model execution:

REP: "Toby"	SALES: 24000
PROD: "romance"	QUOTA: 20000
QTR: "3"	GROWTH: .03
OLDTITLES: 100	UNEMPLOYMENT: .06
NEWTITLES: 10	

As Figure 5–5 shows, other variables are presently unknown. Now, you turn your attention to forward reasoning with the ADVISOR rules.

The first issue that arises is the order in which rules should be selected for consideration. Should you consider the rules in the order in which they appear in the rule set (see Figure 5–1) or should you select them in some other order? An alternative selection order might be to consider the rules with the fewest number of unknown variables in their premises before considering those with more unknowns. Guru's inference engine can use any one of over 50 different selection orders (discussed later in Chapter 9). The setting of the E.SORD environment variable controls which strategy will be used. The default setting of selecting rules based on their rule set order is what you will use here. This is typically the single selection order supported by the conventional inference engines that allow forward reasoning.

From Figure 5–1 you can see that rule R1 is first in the rule set, so you consider it before any of the other rules. When you evaluate the R1 premise, you discover that it is true. Sales of 24,000 do indeed exceed the quota of 20,000 by more than 15 percent. You therefore fire the rule by taking the action specified in R1's conclusion. As a result, the BASE variable is no longer unknown, but now has a value of $20000 + 24000 - 23000 = 21000$. You proceed to the next rule, R2. When you evaluate its premise, you see that it is false and thus go on to consider rule R3. Because the ECONOMY variable is presently unknown and has no variable description in the rule set, it is impossible to determine whether R3's premise is true or false. Hence, you continue to R4. Its premise is similarly unknown and so is the premise of R5.

When you consider the first condition in the premise of R6, you see that it is false (the growth of .03 is not at the .04 level). Thus you know that the overall premise will also be false, regardless of the unemployment rate. Thus you can immediately discard R6 and go on to rule R7. Here you find that the first two conditions in the premise are satisfied. However, the third is not because the unemployment rate of .06 is not less than .055. As a result the R7 premise is false and you move on to consider rule R8. All four conditions in the premise of this rule are true and thus the overall premise is true. You fire rule R8 to give ECONOMY a "fair" value. When you evaluate the next rule's premise, the first condition is false, but you cannot stop there. Because the OR (rather than AND) operator appears you must try the second condition also. In this case, it too is false. Thus R9's premise is false and you proceed to consider the next rule.

The premises of R10, R11, and R12 are successively discovered to be false. When you reach R13, you find that its premise is true. You therefore fire this rule to take the three actions specified in its conclusion. First, you calculate PFACTOR to be $(10 + 100)/100 - 1 = .10$; then you let the STRONG and WEAK variables have values of TRUE and FALSE, respectively. The premises of each of the remaining rules (R14–R18) are either unknown or false. At this point you have considered all 18 rules and you have fired 3 of them: R1, R8, and R13. By taking the actions indicated by these rules, you realize that some previously unknown or false premises may now be true. Therefore, you make another pass through the rule set, to consider the unfired rules.

R1 was already fired. The R2 and R3 premises are false. When you then consider the R4 premise, you see that the first condition is true. However, the second condition is unknown because the LOCALADS variable value is still unknown, though it could possibly become known.

You (the inference engine) notice that there is a variable description for LOCALADS (Figure 5–6), so you can find a value for LOCALADS by taking the two lookup actions specified there. Suppose that this results in a value of 1200. This makes the second condition true, because a value is now known for LOCALADS. The third condition is true, so the premise of R4 is true. When you fire this rule, .01 is assigned to both EFACTOR and LAFACTOR. You proceed to R5. Its premise is false, as are the premises of R6 and R7.

Rule R8 has already been fired. The premises of rules R9–R12 are false. Rule R13 has already been fired and rule R14's premise is false. Because STRONG is true and all of the indicated variables are known, the premise of rule R15 is true. You can now fire that rule. In so doing, you first ask the user to enter a subjective assessment of the percentage increase in romance books due to the general rise of public interest in this kind of book. Suppose the user responds to the input prompt by entering 5. You then take the action of calculating the new quota:

```
NEWQUOTA = BASE*(1+EFACTOR+LAFACTOR+PFACTOR+RISE/100)
         = 21000*(1+.01+.01+.10+5/100)
         = 21000*(1.17)=24570
```

The premise for each of the remaining three rules is false. On this second pass through the ADVISOR rules, you have fired R4 and R15.

If you were to make one more pass through the unfired ADVISOR rules, you would see that none of them can be fired. By firing R4 and R15, you have done nothing to change the falseness of the other rules' premises. You have reached a point where you can reason no further. You have fully tested the effects of applying the ADVISOR expertise to a particular sales rep for a particular product line in a particular quarter. One effect is that you can now offer advice about what the new quota should be. You also now know what the economic prognosis is, what the base amount is, and what the various adjusting factors are. The consultation is done . . . almost. You still need to do something with the results of your reasoning.

PRESENTING THE RESULTS
OF A CONSULTATION

A conventional expert system would report the value of the rule set's goal variable to the user. Conventional expert system development tools typically offer little developer control over the appearance of this report. A human expert, of course, has broad flexibility when it comes to presenting advice. It is important to present it in a manner that is conducive to user understanding. Furthermore, the human expert is not limited to just presenting the reasoning results, but can immediately process this newly derived knowledge in various ways. It can be stored away (i.e., remembered or recorded) for later reference, used as input to analysis with some procedural model, used as a basis for graphics generation, incorporated into a textual description, communicated to persons at distant sites, used as a basis for data recall, incorporated into a spreadsheet, and so forth.

Guru closely resembles real human experts by supporting all of these capabilities—after reasoning has concluded, but before a consultation terminates. This is accomplished by building a completion sequence into a rule set. Like an initialization sequence, this is simply a series of one or more Guru commands. However, the inference engine executes these commands after reasoning with the rules has concluded, rather than before it begins. A very simple completion sequence for the ADVISOR rule set is shown in Figure 5–7. It begins with the CLEAR command, which simply clears the screen. Notice that Guru's OUTPUT command allows Jack to control the console screen position where each output is to appear. The last two actions are examples of how Jack can have Guru's inference engine carry out desired actions if specified conditions are met.

FIGURE 5–7   A completion sequence for the ADVISOR rule set

```
DO:
    CLEAR
    AT 5,1 OUTPUT "Sales Rep:", REP
    AT 6,1 OUTPUT "Product Line:", PROD
    AT 5,20 OUTPUT "Quarter:", QTR
    AT 8,1 OUTPUT "The recommended new quota is:", NEWQUOTA
    AT 12,20 OUTPUT "Basis for the recommendation."
    AT 14,20 OUTPUT "Base Amount:", BASE
    AT 14,40 OUTPUT "Economic Factor:", EFACTOR
    AT 15,40 OUTPUT "Product Factor:", PFACTOR
    AT 16,40 OUTPUT "Local Ads Factor:", LAFACTOR
    IF STRONG THEN AT 17,40 OUTPUT "Rise Factor:", RISE/100; ENDIF
    IF WEAK THEN AT 17,40 OUTPUT "Fall Factor:", FALL/100; ENDIF
```

The nine OUTPUT commands of Figure 5–7 could be replaced with a couple of form management commands if desired. In addition to presenting consultation results, Jack may want the inference engine to preserve the results as a record in a table. Suppose this table is named NEXTYR and has fields named NREP, NPROD, NQTR, and NQUOTA. The following actions would be added to those shown in Figure 5–7:

```
IF NOT INUSE ("NEXTYR") THEN USE NEXTYR; ENDIF
ATTACH 1 to NEXTYR
NEXTYR.NREP = REP; NEXTYR.NPROD = PROD
NEXTYR.NQTR = QTR; NEXTYR.NQUOTA = NEWQUOTA
```

The first command causes the NEXTYR table to be placed in use if it is not already in use. The second command attaches a new blank record to the end of the NEXTYR table. The inference engine then preserves the appropriate variable values as that new record's field values. In general, there is no restriction on what Guru can do after reasoning with the rules finishes and before the consultation ends. Any of the more than 100 kinds of Guru commands can be incorporated into a rule set's completion sequence.

REASONING WITH RULES— REVERSE REASONING

Reverse reasoning is sometimes called "backward chaining" or "goal-directed" reasoning. It is based on the idea of considering rules in a reverse direction—looking first at a rule's conclusion, rather than its premise. At any moment during the reasoning process, the inference engine is focusing its efforts on trying to establish the value of a particular unknown variable. This is called the current goal variable. At the outset of a consultation, the user can specify what goal should be sought by the inference engine. For instance, a user's consultation request might be:

```
CONSULT ADVISOR TO SEEK NEWQUOTA
```

In this case the word SEEK rather than TEST is used to indicate that reverse reasoning rather than forward reasoning is desired. As an alternative to NEWQUOTA, any unknown variable in the ADVISOR rule set could be specified as the overall goal of the consultation. If no goal variable is indicated following the word SEEK, then the rule set's default goal (see Figure 5–5) is assumed.

As you are about to see, reverse reasoning is a much more intricate process than forward reasoning. Forward reasoning is a relatively "blind" or brute force method for using rules to discover the value of an initially unknown variable. It therefore requires a comparatively brief explanation. Reverse reasoning is a much more sophisticated method of reasoning and requires a more lengthy explanation. In the next section of this chapter the general principles of the reverse reasoning technique are discussed. This is followed by an example of reverse reasoning with the ADVISOR rule set. If you find the general description too detailed, you may want to skip ahead to the example for a broad appreciation of what is involved in reverse reasoning. There you can concentrate on the pattern of processing.

General Description of Reverse Reasoning

As reverse reasoning begins, the inference engine focuses on the consultation's overall goal variable. For the moment this is the current goal and its value is presently unknown. By looking at the conclusions of rules in the rule set, the inference engine can detect which of these rules could possibly establish a value for the goal variable. These rules are candidates for further consideration. The inference engine selects one of these rules and examines its premise. If the premise is true, then the rule is fired to establish a value for the goal variable. Because remaining candidate rules may also affect the value of the goal variable, they too may then be considered in the same way. If the premise is false, then the rule is not fired and another of the candidate rules is selected for consideration. The other possibility is that a candidate rule's premise is unknown. When this occurs, the inference engine attempts to make the premise known. It does this by trying to determine values for the unknown variables in the premise.

There are two ways for the inference engine to make an unknown variable known during reverse reasoning. As with forward reasoning, the inference engine can carry out the actions specified in a variable description. If there is no variable description for an unknown variable, then that variable temporarily becomes the current goal. The inference engine works on this goal in exactly the same way as the consultation's original overall goal. It detects which of the rule set's rules could possibly establish a value for this current goal variable. These are treated as candidate rules for the new current goal. The inference engine selects one of these rules and examines its premise. If its premise is true, the rule is fired to establish a value for the current goal. If the premise is false, then the rule is not fired and another of the candidate rules for the current goal is selected for consideration. If the premise is unknown, then its unknown variables in turn can then be subjected to the same reverse reasoning process. If an unknown variable does not have a variable description showing how to find its value, then that variable temporarily becomes the new current goal.

Thus, reverse reasoning works by using rules to break the overall problem into subproblems. Each of these may itself be broken into its own subproblem. In other words, it meets the current goal by giving a value to the unknown variable that is of immediate interest. If there are any candidate rules for that goal that have not yet been considered, then they too may be processed in the same manner. At this point, the inference engine focuses on a different goal (i.e., problem, unknown variable). There are two possibilities. If solving the former goal does not allow the premise that contains it to be evaluated as being either true or false, then another unknown variable in that premise becomes the new current goal. The inference engine uses reverse reasoning to try to solve the problem posed by this goal.

The second possibility is that the just-solved goal allows the premise containing it to be evaluated as either true or false. The last unsolved goal to have previously been the current goal (before it was broken into subproblems) again becomes the current goal. If the premise was true, the rule is fired and this goal variable's value can therefore change. If the premise is false, the rule is not fired and the goal variable's value remains unchanged. In either case, another candidate rule for that goal variable is selected for consideration. If there are no further candidate rules for the current goal, then no further reasoning is possible for that variable. If this is the consultation's overall goal variable, then reverse reasoning is finished and the inference engine carries out the rule set's completion sequence. On the other hand, if this is the goal of some subproblem, the inference engine proceeds to focus on another subproblem that has yet to be solved. Eventually, the overall goal will again become the current goal—when all of its pertinent subproblems have been processed. Depending on which of its candidate rules have been fired, this variable now has a value that has been determined by reasoning with the expertise embodied in the rule set. If the overall goal variable ends up with an unknown value, then the rule set has insufficient expertise to solve the user's problem.

Controlling the Reasoning Flow

This, then, is the basic flow of reverse reasoning. However, there are a number of more subtle issues involved. Some of these deserve brief comments here. First, there is the issue of the selection order that will be used for considering candidate rules that have been identified for a goal. Any of the selection orders that Guru supports for forward reasoning can also be used for controlling the sequence in which candidate rules are selected for consideration. This selection order is governed by the setting of the E.SORD environment variable. In the example that follows, the default of using the rules' relative order in the rule set is observed.

Second, there is the issue of when the inference engine should use a variable description to establish a value for an unknown variable. Should this happen before (i.e., instead of) having the inference engine try reverse reasoning to determine a value for the variable? Or, should it happen only as a last resort—in cases where reverse reasoning is unable to determine a value? Depending on the nature of the application, one of these alternatives may be preferable to another. Guru supports both approaches. This is controlled by the E.WHN environment variable's setting. In the example that follows, the default of giving preference to the variable description is observed.

Third, there is the issue of how rigorous the inference engine should be. The foregoing description suggests that all candidate rules for the current goal may be considered. While it is highly rigorous to exhaustively consider all candidate rules, it may be overkill for some rule sets. For instance, a rule set may have been built in such a way that no more than one candidate rule's premise will ever be true for a given problem. In such a situation, it is probably a waste of time for the inference engine to consider the remaining candidate rules once one candidate rule has been fired. On the other hand, a rule set may be built so that the premises of multiple candidate rules could be true for a given problem. This is commonplace when the current goal variable is fuzzy.* In such situations it may be important for all candidate rules to be considered. Guru supports three degrees of rigor controlled by the E.RIGR environment variable's setting. In the example that follows, the convention of considering all candidate rules is observed.

Fourth, there is the issue of how an inference engine should go about trying to evaluate the premise of a rule. Should it take a strict approach? This means that the inference engine will try to evaluate the premise only after all of its unknown variables become known. If it happens that the inference engine cannot establish a value for one of these variables, then the rule is immediately abandoned. In contrast is the eager approach. Here, the inference engine tries to evaluate the premise as each of its unknown variables becomes known. The rule is fired as soon as its premise is determined to be true, regardless of whether all of its unknown variables have been processed. Then there is the patient approach, in which the inference engine does not try to evaluate the premise as each of its unknown variables is processed. Instead, there is only one attempt to evaluate the premise and this happens after all of its unknown variables have been processed. Unlike the strict approach, the rule is not abandoned if one of the unknown variables remains unknown. Guru's E.TRYP environment variable can be set to control which approach the inference engine will take. In the example that follows, Guru's default approach of strict evaluation is observed.

An Example of Reverse Reasoning

To see how reverse reasoning works in practice, once again imagine that you are the inference engine. The user has asked you to seek the value of the NEWQUOTA variable. You first carry out the commands in ADVISOR's initialization sequence. Suppose that this yields the same variable values that were used in the forward reasoning example.

---

*Fuzzy variables are described in Chapters 6 and 11.

REP: "Toby"   SALES: 24000

PROD: "romance"   QUOTA: 20000

QTR: "3"   GROWTH: .03

OLDTITLES: 100   UNEMPLOYMENT: .06

NEWTITLES: 10

As Figure 5-5 shows, other variables are presently unknown. Now you turn your attention to reverse reasoning with the ADVISOR rules depicted in Figure 5-1. Remember that you will be examining a rule's conclusion before you look at its premise.

You know that NEWQUOTA is the overall goal variable and at this moment it is also your current goal. Its value is presently unknown. You need to identify those rules whose actions could possibly change the value of NEWQUOTA. These will be the candidate rules for NEWQUOTA. By looking at the conclusions of the ADVISOR rules you can easily pick out those that have a potential for affecting the value of NEWQUOTA. When you look at the conclusion of rule R1, you see that even if R1 is fired it could not alter the present value of NEWQUOTA. It can only affect the BASE variable. Similarly, R2 does not qualify as a candidate rule for NEWQUOTA. As you scan the 18 rule conclusions you can see that there are only 3 rules that have a chance of giving a value to NEWQUOTA. These NEWQUOTA candidate rules are R15, R16, and R17.

You select R15 to consider first.* When you look at its premise you see that it is unknown. In fact, you will need to know the values of five presently unknown variables and STRONG will have to be true, before you can fire this rule and produce a value for NEWQUOTA. Finding out the value of STRONG becomes a new subproblem and the STRONG variable becomes your current goal. There is no variable description that tells you actions to take for finding a STRONG value. Therefore, you proceed to identify the candidate rules for STRONG. These are rules R13, R14, and R18.

You consider R13 first. When you examine its premise, you can evaluate it immediately. Because the premise is true, you fire rule R13. Not only does this result in a value of TRUE for STRONG, but two other actions are also taken. The WEAK variable becomes FALSE and a value of .10 is calculated for PFACTOR. Rule R14 is the next candidate rule for STRONG. Because its premise is false, you proceed to the last STRONG candidate rule. The premise of this rule (R18) is also false, so you are done processing the STRONG variable. Because the value you

---

*As Chapter 9 explains, there are many possible strategies for deciding which candidate rule to choose first, second, and so on. For the present, we shall ignore these alternatives.

have inferred for STRONG does not make the premise of R15 false, you proceed to another subproblem for that rule. In particular, you need to establish a value for the BASE variable, before R15 can be fired. Thus, BASE is now your current goal.

There is no variable description for BASE, so you will use reverse reasoning in an effort to establish its value. You see that there are two rules that could possibly change the value of BASE from its present unknown status. These candidate rules are R1 and R2. You consider R1 first. When you evaluate its premise, you discover that the premise is true. You therefore fire R1, which calculates a value of 2100 for BASE. Considering the other candidate rule for BASE, you discover that its premise is false. Thus you are finished processing BASE. Because BASE now has a known value, you continue working with rule R15 by focusing on the next subproblem: establishing a value for EFACTOR.

With EFACTOR as your current goal, you proceed to identify its candidate rules. These are R3, R4, and R5. Because there is no variable description for EFACTOR, you immediately consider R3. When you try to evaluate its premise, you discover that you cannot because ECONOMY is unknown. Thus you now have a subproblem for EFACTOR that involves establishing a value for the ECONOMY variable. ECONOMY temporarily becomes your current goal. It has no variable description that tells how to find its value, so you identify ECONOMY candidate rules. These are R6, R7, R8, and R9. When you examine the premise of R6, you see that it is false. Similarly, the premise of R7 is false. However when you evaluate the premise of R8, you discover that it is true. Thus you fire R8 and a value of "fair" is assigned to ECONOMY. Because the premise of R9 is false, you are finished processing the ECONOMY variable and EFACTOR is once again your current goal.

You can now evaluate the premise of EFACTOR's first candidate rule (R3), and you discover that it is false. Proceeding to R4, you see that LOCALADS needs to become known before this rule can be fired. Using the actions specified in the LOCALADS variable description (see Figure 5–6), you find its value by doing a couple of spreadsheet lookups. The resultant value for LOCALADS is 1200. The premise of R4 is now true, so you fire it. This establishes a value of .01 for both EFACTOR and LAFACTOR. The last candidate rule for EFACTOR is R5. Because its premise is false, you are now done processing the EFACTOR variable and continue working with rule R15. All variables in R15's premise are now known and you discover that the premise is true when you evaluate it. You now fire R15. Assuming that the user responds with 5 to the RISE prompt, a value of 24570 is calculated for the NEWQUOTA goal.

You proceed to consider the other two candidate rules for NEWQUOTA (R16 and R17), but quickly see that each has a false premise. As a result, your reasoning for this consultation is finished and you complete the consultation by taking the actions specified in the

ADVISOR's completion sequence (see Figure 5–7). In the course of your reverse reasoning you fired five rules in the order: R13, R1, R8, R4, R15. Notice that these are the same five rules that were fired in the forward reasoning example, though the firing order differs (R1, R8, R13, R4, R15 in the forward case).

CONCLUSION

In this chapter you have had an inside look at how an inference engine runs during a consultation. The mechanics of both forward and reverse reasoning have been explored. With forward reasoning, an inference engine takes the attitude of carrying out every action that is logically valid. The user can then study the results. Reverse reasoning is much more focused. The inference engine limits itself to taking only those actions that might help to meet some specified goal. Due to its focused approach, reverse reasoning oftentimes is preferable because it may be able to determine a variable's value much more rapidly than forward reasoning. Forward reasoning is of interest in situations where you do not have a specific goal, where you know that all (or most) rules are to be considered, or where there are relatively few rules in a rule set.

Here, you have also seen various ways that an inference engine can acquire knowledge needed in its reasoning process: from the user (or other external sources) or from its own integral knowledge system, which holds data bases, spreadsheets, procedural models, other rule sets, and so forth. The possibilities that this integration offers to developers are vast. A developer can also make valuable use of such integral facilities in designing a rule set's completion actions.

EXERCISES

1. Beyond its premise and conclusion, what else might be involved in a rule specification?
2. Beyond its rules, what else might a rule set contain?
3. Identify three ways of incorporating prompts for further information into a rule set.
4. Discuss the role of a rule set's initialization sequence.
5. Why is it important to have a variety of ways available for customizing an expert system's user interface?
6. Beyond line-oriented input/output, what other kinds of interface facilities could be of value to a developer?
7. During a consultation, the inference engine may encounter many unknown variables whose values may need to become known if a

solution is to be derived. Suppose the user does not know the value for such a variable. How can the inference engine establish a value for it?

8. Explain why "hooks" to external software are no substitute for true integration.

9. Compare the conditional clauses allowed in SQL inquiries with the premises allowed in Guru rules.

10. Describe several alternative strategies that you would like an inference engine to support for the selection order used when considering a group of candidate rules.

11. What is meant by inference engine rigor?

12. Step through the inference engine's reasoning with the ADVISOR rule set where the initial variable values are as follows:

REP: "Kevin"   SALES: 10000

PROD: "scifi"   QUOTA: 9000

QTR: "3"   GROWTH: .04

OLDTITLES: 50   UNEMPLOYMENT: .06

NEWTITLES: 10

Use reverse reasoning first; then solve the same problem with forward reasoning.

Reference

1   *Guru Reference Manual*, vols. 1–2. Lafayette, Ind.: MDBS, Inc. 1985.

I think we have entered the uncertainty zone.

Chapter Six

Dealing with Uncertainty

Human experts sometimes need to reason about uncertain situations. The person asking for advice may not be 100 percent sure about all of the inputs he or she provides to the expert during a consultation. The expert might not have complete confidence in all of the knowledge acquired from external sources during a consultation. Even if the expert is completely certain about all aspects of the problem being faced, there could be some uncertainty about the validity or applicability of some of the expertise that will be used in reasoning about the problem. All of these uncertainties are factored into the human reasoning process. As a result, the advice that the expert gives may be qualified by some degree of certainty. Jack might say, "I'm 80 percent certain that this is a fair quota."

Similarly, AI techniques exist for factoring varying levels of certainty into the reasoning performed by an expert system. This is accomplished by means of what are called certainty factors [2], [3]. Many conventional expert system development tools do not have built-in mechanisms for dealing with uncertainty. Others are able to deal with certainty factors. The method that one tool uses for handling certainty factors may be different than the method used by another tool. Ideally, a tool should take its cue from human experts who are able to deal with uncertainties in different ways, depending on the nature of the problem. Guru's built-in methods for automatically processing certainty factors are too numerous to enumerate in this introductory chapter [1]. However, several ways in which they can be used are touched on here. More detailed discussion of the possibilities appears in Chapters 10 and 11.

CERTAINTY FACTORS

A certainty factor is a number in the 0 to 100 range* that can be assigned to the value of a variable. It is a measure of how certain or confident the

---

*Though 0 to 100 is a convenient and commonly used range, there are inference engines that use other ranges such as 0 to 10 or −1 to 1.

inference engine is about the value for the variable. A certainty factor of 0 is the lowest possible certainty. A 100 certainty factor represents the highest possible certainty. In the ADVISOR rule set, no certainty factors were explicitly assigned to any of the variable's values. When no certainty factor is mentioned for a variable's value, a certainty factor of 100 is assumed.

Jack realizes that the growth and unemployment projections made by the ECON model are not guaranteed to be completely accurate. In conferring with the economics staff, he finds that they can revise the ECON model slightly so that it will set two additional variables: CGROW and CUNEMP. The values of these variables will indicate the model's level of confidence in the GROWTH and UNEMPLOYMENT values that it produces. Jack decides to incorporate the uncertainty about growth and unemployment into the rule set. This is accomplished by including two additional commands following PERFORM ECON in ADVISOR's initialization sequence.

```
PERFORM ECON
LET GROWTH = GROWTH CF CGROW
LET UNEMPLOYMENT = UNEMPLOYMENT CF CUNEMP
```

When the initialization sequence is carried out at the start of a consultation, the CGROW and CUNEMP confidence levels calculated by ECON become the certainty factors for GROWTH and UNEMPLOYMENT.

THE CERTAINTY OF A PREMISE

Suppose ECON projects a growth rate of .05 with 80 percent confidence and an unemployment rate of .075 with 90 percent confidence. After the initialization, GROWTH has a value of .05 with a certainty factor of 80; the UNEMPLOYMENT variable has a value of .075 with a certainty factor of 90. When the inference engine evaluates the premise of R6, it discovers that the premise is true. (See Figure 5–1, Chapter 5, for rule R6 and other rules mentioned in this chapter.) But how true is it? The .05 value of GROWTH exceeds .04 in the first condition, so that condition is true with a certainty of 80. Similarly, the second condition is true with a certainty of 90. How should the inference engine combine these two certainty factors to determine an overall certainty factor for the premise?

Joint Certainty for a Premise

Keeping in mind that both conditions must be true in order for the premise to be true, it is reasonable that the overall certainty of the premise should not exceed that of the least certain condition. If you are only

80 percent sure about the growth rate, then your joint certainty about both unemployment and growth cannot reasonably exceed 80. Intuitively, this is equivalent to the old argument that a chain is no stronger than its weakest link. Others might reasonably push this argument further, claiming that the joint certainty should actually be calculated by taking the product of the two individual certainties. If one of the certainty factors is 100, then this yields the same result as the approach of taking the minimum certainty factor. However, if both are less than completely certain, then the product method yields a lower certainty than the minimum method. In this case, a joint certainty of 72 would result from the product method (90*80/100) versus a joint certainty of 80 for the minimum method (minimum of 80 and 90).

Regardless of the calculation method, the important point is that all joint certainty factors are automatically calculated by the inference engine during a consultation. It is very important for a development tool to give a choice about the method to be used for calculating a joint certainty factor. A joint certainty calculation method that may be well suited for one application may be poorly suited for some other application area. An inference engine that supports only one way of dealing with certainties can be very restrictive. In contrast, Guru's inference engine supports several built-in methods for calculating joint certainty factors. These include both the minimum and product methods. Others are introduced in Chapter 10. The E.CFJO environment variable controls which of the joint certainty factor methods will be used by the inference engine in a particular consultation. Guru's default is the minimum method.

Confirmative Certainty for a Premise

Suppose that PERFORM ECON yields a growth rate of .01 with a confidence of 70 and an unemployment rate of .085 with a confidence of 50. When the inference engine evaluates the premise of rule R9, the first condition is true (.01 < .02) with a certainty factor of 70. The second condition is true (.085 > = .082) with a certainty factor of 50. This rule has a major difference from R6. Here the two conditions are connected by the OR rather than AND operator. Keeping in mind that only one condition needs to be true in order for the premise to be true, it is reasonable that the overall certainty of the premise should be at least as large as the most certain of the two true conditions. Intuitively, the rationale is that when two "chains" are offered, the strongest will be chosen. Others might reasonably push this argument further, claiming that both can be chosen with one reinforcing the other. In any event, one certainty factor acts to confirm the other.

One approach to calculating the confirmative certainty is to take the maximum of the two certainty factors. Another approach, which always yields a higher confirmative certainty, is commonly called the probability sum. It causes the product of the two certainty factors to be subtracted from their sum. In this case a confirmative certainty of 70 would result from the maximum method (maximum of 70 and 50) versus a confirmative certainty of 85 for the probability sum method (70 + 50 − 70*50/100).

As in the case of joint certainty factors, all confirmative certainty factors are automatically calculated by the inference engine during a consultation. Here too, conventional inference engines usually offer no more than one method for calculating a confirmative certainty factor. Guru's inference engine supports several built-in methods for determining confirmative certainty factors. These include the maximum and probability sum methods. Others are introduced in Chapter 10. The E.CFCO environment variable controls which of the confirmative certainty factor methods will be used by the inference engine in a particular consultation. Guru's default for this environment variable is the maximum method.

THE CERTAINTY OF A VARIABLE'S VALUE

You now see how an inference engine can reason with uncertainty when evaluating a premise. Suppose the inference engine has established that the R6 premise is true with a certainty of 72. How is this certainty reflected for the ECONOMY variable's value of "good" when the rule is fired? Very simply. If the inference engine is 72 percent certain that the premise is true, then it is also 72 percent sure that the ECONOMY value of "good" is correct. This is carried even further when rule R3 is later considered, but the reasoning is a bit more involved for this rule.

As in the case of R6, the R3 premise is true with a certainty of 72. But unlike R6, the R3 action does not consist of assigning a constant to a variable. Instead, it assigns the GROWTH variable's value to EFACTOR. Thus, there are two sources of uncertainty that jointly contribute to the certainty factor that will result for EFACTOR. There is the certainty factor of the premise (72) and the certainty factor of GROWTH (80). How should these be combined to arrive at a certainty factor for the EFACTOR variable? The setting of Guru's E.CFVA environment variable controls which of the joint certainty methods is employed for computing a variable's certainty. As with E.CFJO, the minimum, product, and other methods are supported. Do not confuse E.CFJO with E.CFVA. The former controls joint certainty computations for expressions such as the premise of a rule and arithmetic formulas in a rule's conclusion. The latter controls the joint certainty computation for a variable. The flexibility that results from differentiating between these two distinct uses of joint certainty computation is important for expert system developers.

Suppose that E.CFVA is set to have the inference engine use the minimum method for computing a variable's certainty factor when a rule fires. This would result in a certainty factor of 72 (the minimum of 72 and 80) for EFACTOR's value when rule R3 is fired. The product method would have yielded a certainty factor of 58 (72*80/100, rounded). In either case, a value of .05 is assigned to EFACTOR. If the inference engine later fires rule R15, then the EFACTOR of .05 is used in computing the NEWQUOTA value. The certainty factor of this NEWQUOTA value is influenced by the certainty factor that exists for EFACTOR. Suppose this certainty factor is 72. Assuming that BASE, STRONG, LAFACTOR, PFACTOR, and RISE all have certainties of 100, the certainty factor for NEWQUOTA is then 72.

Reporting the Certainty Factor of a Variable's Value

The certainty factor for NEWQUOTA's value can then be communicated to the user via the rule set's completion sequence shown in Figure 5–7, provided the command:

```
AT 8,1 OUTPUT "The recommended new quota is:", NEWQUOTA
```

is replaced by the following command:

```
AT 8,1 OUTPUT "The recommended new quota is: ",\
  NEWQUOTA USING "nnnnn", " with a certainty of ",\
  HICF(NEWQUOTA) USING "nnn", " out of 100."
```

HICF is a built-in Guru function whose value is the highest certainty factor of the indicated variable (NEWQUOTA, in this case). Suppose that the new quota has been calculated to be 28200. When the inference engine executes this completion action, the following will appear on the eighth line of the console screen:

```
The recommended new quota is: 28200 with a certainty of 72 out of 100.
```

Of course, much more elaborate ways of presenting these consultation results are possible (e.g., with Guru's forms management capabilities).

Capturing a User's Uncertainty

The certainty factors for GROWTH and UNEMPLOYMENT were acquired from the execution of a procedural model. Certainty factors can alternatively be taken from other integral sources—a spreadsheet, a data table, statistical calculations, and so forth. Guru's inference engine can also acquire the certainty factor for a variable's value from sources external to the Guru software environment. These sources include external programs, external files, and the expert system's user. For example, when rule R15 is fired, the inference engine asks the user to provide a value for the RISE variable. It would not be unusual for a user to feel somewhat uncertain about his or her response. Jack can easily have the inference engine capture this uncertainty by inserting the actions:

```
INPUT CRISE USING "nnn" WITH\
 "On a scale of 0 to 100, how sure are you?"
LET RISE = RISE CF CRISE
```

immediately after the input action that already exists in rule R15. When this revised R15 is fired, the user is first prompted for a rise response. The user is next prompted to indicate how sure he or she is about this response. This degree of certainty becomes the value of the CRISE variable, which is then used to set the certainty factor for the RISE variable.

Suppose the user is three fourths sure about the rise response. The user inputs 75 and this becomes the certainty factor for the RISE value. The inference engine proceeds to calculate a new quota according to the formula in R15. The inference engine also determines a certainty for this NEWQUOTA value, based on the certainty factors of all variables involved in the formula. If the minimum method has been selected for E.CFVA and the product method for E.CFJO, then EFACTOR has a certainty factor of 72 as described earlier. Assume that, with the exception of RISE and EFACTOR, the other variables in the NEWQUOTA formula have 100 certainty factors. Thus the inference engine needs to compute the joint certainty of 100, 72, 100, 100, and 75. As described earlier, the computation method for joint certainties in an expression is controlled by the E.CFJO setting. No matter what this setting is, the three 100 certainty factors do not affect the result. Because the product method has been selected for E.CFJO the joint certainty is 72*75/100 = 54. The inference engine would report a certainty of 54 out of 100 for its new quota recommendation. If the minimum method had been selected for both E.CFJO and E.CFVA, then EFACTOR would have had an 80 certainty factor and the resultant certainty factor for NEWQUOTA would have been 75 (the minimum of 80 and 75).

Remember that the availability of the E.CFJO control allows the expert system developer or user to choose the method that has the most intuitive appeal for a particular application. Selecting the product approach for reasoning about joint certainties is relatively "conservative." For some applications it may result in an understatement of joint certainty levels. On the other hand, the minimum approach is relatively "venturesome" and may result in an overstatement of joint certainties for some applications. The important point is that a tool should allow a choice between these (and other) methods, rather than forcing the inference engine to always employ the same method. Having a choice allows expert systems to be easily tailored to the needs of their respective application areas. It also permits the impacts of different methods on the same rule set to be observed and contrasted by simply changing an environment setting.

THE CERTAINTY OF A RULE ACTION

The foregoing discussion has described how an inference engine can acquire the certainty factor for a variable's value from various integral sources (e.g., via a model execution) and from external sources (e.g., from the expert system's user). It has also described how the certainties of a premise can be combined (via E.CFJO and E.CFCO) in either a joint or confirmative fashion to yield an overall certainty for the premise, how the certainty of a premise affects (via E.CFJO) the certainty factors of variables changed by the conclusion when a rule is fired, and how the certainties of variables in a numeric expression (i.e., a formula) jointly contribute (via E.CFJO) to the certainty of that expression's value. However, none of these topics involve any uncertainties about the rules themselves. They all assume that Jack is completely certain about the reasoning expertise embodied in every rule. What happens if Jack is not fully certain about the "goodness" or "validity" of some rule? Perhaps a rule is usually applicable, but may not be good in some unforeseen circumstances.

Think about rule R6 for example:

```
RULE: R6
  IF: GROWTH >= .04 AND UNEMPLOYMENT <.076
  THEN: ECONOMY = "good"
```

This rule says Jack is certain that if growth and unemployment are at certain levels then the economy should be regarded as good. The validity of this rule itself is absolute. As long as the premise is true, the conclusion is completely valid. However, suppose the premise is true with, say, 72 percent certainty. When the rule is fired, this same certainty is passed along to the conclusion where it is factored into the certainty of the variable that is changed there. As a result, ECONOMY will have a value of "good" with a certainty factor of 72.

Passing an Action's Certainty along to a Variable

Now let's say Jack has some second thoughts about the validity of rule R6. He still feels 90 percent comfortable with it, but realizes that it may not be valid all of the time. To incorporate this uncertainty into the rule set, Jack can use the rule set manager to revise rule R6.

```
RULE: R6
  IF: GROWTH >= .04 AND UNEMPLOYMENT < .076
  THEN: ECONOMY = "good" CF 90
```

This revised R6 indicates that Jack is only 90 percent certain about giving ECONOMY a "good" value when the premise is true. Whenever the revised R6 is fired, the 90 percent certainty about the rule's action is factored into the certainty that results for ECONOMY's "good" value.

Suppose, for example, the inference engine has determined that the premise is true with a certainty of 100. Then when the revised R6 is fired, the certainty of a good economy will be 90. If there had been no CF 90 for the ECONOMY = "good" action, then the certainty of a good economy would have been 100. During a different consultation, suppose the inference engine has determined that the premise is true with a certainty of 70. When the revised R6 is fired, the certainty of a good economy will be based on both 70 (because of uncertainty about the premise) and 90 (because of uncertainty about the action). The inference engine will compute a joint certainty from 70 and 90, using the method indicated by the E.CFVA setting. This becomes the certainty factor for ECONOMY's value. For the minimum method, the joint certainty determined from the premise and action for this variable would be 70. The greater uncertainty about the premise overshadows the mild uncertainty about taking the action. For the product method, the joint certainty would be 63 (70*90/100). The uncertainty about the premise is multiplied by the uncertainty about taking the action, resulting in an even lower joint certainty for the variable.

Different Certainties for Different Actions in a Conclusion

Guru allows Jack to specify a different certainty for each action in a rule's conclusion. For instance, the conclusion of rule R4 might be altered as follows:

```
THEN: EFACTOR = GROWTH/3 CF 95
      LAFACTOR = LOCALADS/120000 CF 88
```

This would tell the inference engine that Jack is 95 percent sure about the validity of taking the first action and 88 percent sure about the second. When the rule is fired, the certainty of EFACTOR is jointly based on the certainty factor of GROWTH, the certainty of the premise, and

95. The certainty factor of LAFACTOR is jointly based on the certainty factor of LOCALADS, the certainty of the premise, and 88.

Variable Degrees of Certainty

All of these examples of specifying a certainty for taking the action of a rule have explicitly stated the certainty. Such certainties can also be indicated implicitly with a variable rather than an integer constant. For example, rule R6 might be stated as:

```
RULE: R6
  IF: GROWTH >= .04 AND UNEMPLOYMENT < .076 AND KNOWN ("CR6")
  THEN: ECONOMY = "good" CF CR6
```

where CR6 is a variable whose value could be established in any of a wide variety of ways. It might be set in the initialization sequence, based on the region of the country, some user input, or the results of performing the ECON model. Or, there may be some new rules added to ADVISOR that determine how certain the inference engine should be about taking the R6 action when its premise is true. This ability to treat certainty factors as variables gives the rule set developer tremendous flexibility relative to tools that force the developer to "hard-wire" constant certainty factors into a rule set.

FIRING MULTIPLE RULES FOR THE SAME VARIABLE VALUE

The ADVISOR rule set contains two rules that can give a "good" value to the ECONOMY variable: R6 and R7. However, the premises of these two rules are specified in such a way that it would be impossible for both of them to be true within a consultation. But consider what can happen if the second condition in R7's premise is eliminated.

```
RULE: R7
  IF: GROWTH >= .02 AND UNEMPLOYMENT < .055
  THEN: ECONOMY = "good" CF 80
```

This revised version of R7 also indicates that Jack is 80 percent sure about the validity of the rule's action when the rule is fired. Along with the previously revised R6:

```
RULE: R6
  IF: GROWTH >= .04 AND UNEMPLOYMENT < .076
  THEN: ECONOMY = "good" CF 90
```

it is now possible that both R6 and R7 could be fired during a consultation. In such a case, the value of ECONOMY is "good," but what is its certainty factor?

Suppose that the initialization sequence for a consultation has given GROWTH a value of .045 with a certainty factor of 85 and UNEMPLOYMENT a value of .05 with a certainty factor of 70. Assume that the minimum method is being used to determine the joint certainty of conjunctions in a premise (i.e., based on the E.CFJO setting). When the inference engine evaluates the premise of R7, it discovers that the premise is true with a certainty of 70. Similarly, it discovers that the premise of R6 is true with a certainty of 70. When R6 is fired, the value of ECONOMY becomes "good" with a certainty factor of 63. This example assumes that E.CFVA is set to use the product method for computing a variable's joint certainty from a rule's premise and action certainties (70 * 90/100). When R7 is fired, the value of ECONOMY now becomes "good" with a certainty of 56 (70 * 80/100). Thus, the certainty for a good economy depends on which rule fired last (as controlled by E.SORD and E.RIGR).

Replacement versus Additive Assignments

Because the actions of rules R6 and R7 involve commonplace assignment statements, the result of the most recently executed statement *replaces* the prior value and certainty for ECONOMY. Though this replacement behavior may be desired for some variables in some expert system applications, a different kind of behavior is probably warranted for the ECONOMY variable. That is, if two rules suggesting a good economy have fired, then the two certainties resulting for ECONOMY should be combined in a confirmative fashion. The resultant certainty factor should be at least as great as the largest of these two. To cause the inference engine to process the ECONOMY variable in this way, Jack would revise the conclusions of R6 and R7 by inserting a + symbol ahead of the = symbol.

```
RULE: R6
  IF: GROWTH >= .04 AND UNEMPLOYMENT < .076
  THEN: ECONOMY += "good" CF 90

RULE: R7
  IF: GROWTH >= .02 AND UNEMPLOYMENT < .055
  THEN: ECONOMY += "good" CF 80
```

The + = indicates that the action is an additive assignment. Rather than replacing the former evidence about a variable's value and certainty, the action provides additional evidence about the variable.

Confirming a Variable's Value

How this additional evidence about a variable is combined with existing evidence in a confirmative fashion is controlled by the E.CFVA setting. The most conservative method is to use the maximum of the existing certainty factor and the just-computed certainty factor. The most venturesome method is to use the probability sum of these two certainty factors—subtracting their product from their sum. Notice that the E.CFVA environment variable controls both the joint and confirmative methods for combining certainties when computing the certainty factor for a variable. Joint certainty for a variable involves the combination *within* a rule based on the premise and action certainties. Confirmative certainty for a variable is concerned with combining joint certainties *across* multiple rules.

Assume that E.CFVA has been set to the product method of computing joint certainties for variables* and the probability sum method of computing confirmative certainties for variables.** Suppose you (i.e., the inference engine) have established that the premise of R6 is true with a certainty of 70, then you fire R6. This gives ECONOMY a "good" value with a certainty of 63 (product of 70 and 90 divided by 100). Suppose you later discover that the premise of R7 is true with a certainty of 70, then you fire R7. In isolation, this rule would tell you to let ECONOMY's value be good with a certainty of 56 (product of 70 and 80 divided by 100). However, because the action involves an additive assignment, you check to see whether ECONOMY already has a "good" value. It does. Therefore, you use the probability sum method to combine the existing certainty factor of 63 with the new certainty of 56:

```
63 + 56 - (63 * 56/100) = 119 - 35.28 =  83.72
```

As a result of firing these two rules, you are now 84 percent sure that the economy is good. This is a greater certainty than either rule can give individually. The rules tend to confirm each other and this is now reflected in the variable's certainty factor.

---

*Not to be confused with E.CFJO, which controls the computation of joint certainties for expressions such as conjunctive premises and arithmetic expressions.

**Not to be confused with E.CFCO, which controls the computation of confirmative certainties for disjunctions of conditions in a premise.

If you had fired R7 before R6, you would produce exactly the same result. If the values of GROWTH and UNEMPLOYMENT had allowed you to fire only one of these rules, then there would have been no confirmative boost in certainty about a good economy. After you fire R6 and R7, there are no further ADVISOR rules that could affect the ECONOMY variable. However, imagine that ADVISOR were expanded to include other rules that could indicate a good economy. As you fire each of these rules after R6 and R7, the certainty of a good economy would tend to grow beyond 84. The amount by which it grows depends on the joint certainty computed for a good economy within the rule being fired. If this certainty is low, then the new evidence for a good economy is weak and 84 increases very little. If the certainty is high, then the new evidence is strong and the certainty factor rapidly approaches 100.

FUZZY VARIABLES

In all of the examples shown to this point, no variable has had more than one value at a time. For instance, the ECONOMY variable could be either unknown, or have a value of "poor," "fair," or "good" at any given point in a consultation. However, it could not be both "fair" and "good" at the same time during a consultation with the ADVISOR rule set shown in Figure 5–1, Chapter 5. In contrast, a human expert who reasons about the economic outlook might be unclear about what that outlook is. The outlook might be fuzzy. At a given moment, the expert might simultaneously think that the outlook is good or fair, each with some degree of certainty. The expert may be equally certain about both values or be more sure about one than the other. The expert uses both of these economic outlooks in subsequent reasoning, yielding two possibilities for the economic factor that will be used to produce new quota advice. Each possible economic factor has its own certainties. Similarly, two possibilities result for the local advertising factor, each with a particular degree of certainty. Ultimately, the expert arrives at two new quota recommendations—each with some appropriate degree of certainty.

How can an inference engine emulate the human expert's ability to reason about fuzzy situations? It must have the capacity to simultaneously keep track of different values for the same variable. It must be able to deal with differing degrees of uncertainty about each of those values. It must be able to incorporate the multiple values and their respective certainty factors into subsequent reasoning activity. Some expert system development tools do not have built-in mechanisms for supporting reasoning about fuzzy situations. Others provide this support. With Guru, it is supported by means of fuzzy variables. Although this book does not delve into Zadeh's fuzzy set theory, it is interesting that a fuzzy variable may be considered to be a fuzzy set [4].

Reasoning with Fuzzy Variables

A fuzzy variable is simply a variable that has more than one value at a time. Each value of a fuzzy variable has its own certainty factor. If a variable has one value, then it becomes fuzzy by assigning an additional value to the variable. This is easily accomplished by using an additive assignment (+ =) action rather than the traditional assignment (=) action. Recall that R6 and R7 were revised to use additive assignment actions. Because both actions resulted in the same value ("good") for ECONOMY, this variable had only one value during a consultation. Now suppose Jack revises R8 by eliminating its second condition and using an additive assignment in its action.

```
RULE: R8
  IF: GROWTH >= .02 AND UNEMPLOYMENT >= .055
      AND UNEMPLOYMENT < .082
  THEN: ECONOMY += "fair" CF 80
```

If this rule is fired, then ECONOMY will have a "fair" value in addition to whatever other known value it may already have. The certainty factor for ECONOMY's "fair" value is automatically computed in the usual way.

Suppose that a particular consultation's initialization sequence has given GROWTH a value of .04 with a 60 certainty factor and UNEMPLOYMENT a value of .06 with a 75 certainty factor. Assume that E.CFJO is set to use the minimum method for calculating the joint certainty of a conjunctive premise. Assume that E.CFVA is set to use the product (within a rule) and probability sum (across rules) methods for combining certainties when determining the certainty factor of a variable's value. Imagine that you are the inference engine.

When you consider the revised R6, you discover that its premise is true with a certainty of 60 (minimum of 60 and 75). You fire R6 to give ECONOMY a "good" value with a certainty of 54 (60 * 90/100). When you consider the revised R7, you see that its premise is false because the unemployment rate exceeds 5.5 percent. When you consider the revised R8, you discover that all three conditions in the premise are satisfied. The certainty of this premise being true is 60 (minimum of 60, 75, and 75). When you fire R8, you give ECONOMY a "fair" value in addition to the "good" value that it already has. The certainty factor for this "fair" value is 48 (60 * 80/100). Thus, the ECONOMY variable now has two values and you are slightly more certain about the "good" value than about the "fair" value.

As the reasoning proceeds, both values of ECONOMY are available for use. For instance, if you now consider rule R3 you will discover that its premise is true with a certainty of 54. When you fire this rule you establish a value for EFACTOR. If you next consider R4, you see that its first condition is true with a certainty of 48. You use the LOCALADS variable description to look up a value for local advertising. As a result, LOCALADS is now known. GROWTH already has a value. Therefore, the premise of R4 is now true with a certainty of 48 (minimum of 48, 100, and 100). If you now fire R4, the value of EFACTOR that resulted from R3 is replaced by the value of GROWTH/3. Replacement is undesirable here because Jack really wants you to explore the implications of both economic outlooks. In other words, EFACTOR should be a fuzzy variable—capable of having multiple values simultaneously.

To achieve the desired reasoning behavior, Jack revises the R3 and R4 actions by inserting the + symbol ahead of the = symbol. As a result, you (the inference engine) know that Jack desires an additive assignment for EFACTOR, rather than a traditional replacement action. Thus, firing R3 and R4 would result in two values for EFACTOR—each with its own certainty. This illustrates a simple, but important, point for rule set developers. A developer should identify which of a rule set's variables should be capable of being fuzzy during a consultation. Wherever a value is assigned to such a variable in rule actions, an additive (+ =) assignment should be specified. In view of the revised R6, R7, and R8 ADVISOR rules, the potential fuzziness of ECONOMY implies that the following variables could also potentially be fuzzy: EFACTOR, LAFACTOR, and NEWQUOTA. Thus, the actions of rules R3, R4, R10, R12, R15, R16, and R17 that result in values for these variables should be additive assignments. For instance, the revised rule R4 would be:

```
RULE: R4
  IF: ECONOMY = "fair" AND KNOWN("LOCALADS") AND KNOWN("GROWTH")
  THEN: EFACTOR+=GROWTH/3;LAFACTOR+=LOCALADS/120000
```

Notice that it would do no harm to employ additive assignments in the actions of rules R9, R5, and R11. However, it is unnecessary for this rule set because the conditions that lead to a poor economy preclude the possibility of simultaneously having any value other than "poor" for ECONOMY.

Reporting the Values and Certainties of a Fuzzy Variable

Suppose you continue the inference started above until you have established two values for the NEWQUOTA variable, each with a particular degree of certainty. You are now ready to take the actions specified in the completion sequence. However, the completion sequence of Figure 5–7, Chapter 5, was not designed to handle the output of multiple values for a fuzzy variable. The completion sequence shown in Figure 6–1 could be used instead. Its commands make use of three of Guru's functions for processing individual values of a fuzzy variable: VALN, CFN, and NUMVAL.

The VALN function provides the nth value of a specified variable, where the order of values is from the one with the highest certainty to the one with the lowest certainty. Similarly, CFN provides the certainty factor of the nth value. The NUMVAL function is used to find out the number of values a specified variable has. Thus, at coordinates 9,5 on the console screen, the inference engine outputs the value of NEWQUOTA having the highest certainty factor. That certainty factor is output on the same line by the CFN function. If NEWQUOTA was assigned more than one value in this consultation, then the second value and its certainty factor are output on line 10.

The logic of Figure 6–1 works well for the revised ADVISOR rule set since NEWQUOTA will never get more than two values. But what if more than two NEWQUOTA values were possible due to further revisions? The completion sequence of Figure 6–2 shows a more general way to handle the output of this fuzzy variable's values. It makes use of Guru's WHILE command to iteratively execute the same output action. Each time this output action is executed, it displays another value and certainty factor of NEWQUOTA on the next line of the screen. This iteration halts as soon as all values of NEWQUOTA have been output to the user. Of course, fuzzy variable values and certainties could be displayed in other ways than those shown here (e.g., via forms or graphs). As described earlier, they are also available for use in nonoutput actions such as spreadsheet processing, procedural modeling, data base management operations, and so on.

FIGURE 6–1 A completion sequence for fuzzy variable output

```
DO:
     CLEAR
     AT 5,1 OUTPUT "Sales Rep:", REP
     AT 6,1 OUTPUT "Product Line:", PROD
     AT 5,20 OUTPUT "Quarter:", QTR
     AT 8,1 OUTPUT "The recommended quota is:"
     AT 9,5 OUTPUT VALN(NEWQUOTA,1) USING "nnnnn", \
       " with a certainty of ", CFN(NEWQUOTA,1) USING "nnn"
     IF NUMVAL(NEWQUOTA) > 1
       THEN AT 10,5 OUTPUT VALN(NEWQUOTA,2) USING "nnnnn", \
         " with a certainty of ", CFN(NEWQUOTA,2) USING "nnn"
     ENDIF
```

FIGURE 6–2   A completion sequence using iteration

```
DO:
      CLEAR
      AT 5,1 OUTPUT "Sales Rep:", REP
      AT 6,1 OUTPUT "Product Line:", PROD
      AT 5,20 OUTPUT "Quarter:", QTR
      AT 8,1 OUTPUT "The recommended quota is:"
      LET I = 1
      WHILE I < = NUMVAL(NEWQUOTA) DO
            AT 8 + I,5 OUTPUT VALN(NEWQUOTA,I) USING "nnnnn", \
                  " with certainty of ", CFN(NEWQUOTA,I) USING "nnn"
      ENDWHILE
```

THRESHOLD OF THE UNKNOWN

When a human expert reasons about a problem, it may happen that the degree of certainty about something is so low that it should be regarded as being unknown. But, what does "low" mean? Where is the dividing line between the known and the unknown? Depending on the nature of an application area, this line could be drawn in different places. For one application, a certainty of 70 might be too low to allow a value to be regarded as being sufficiently known. That is, it should be excluded from the reasoning efforts. For another application, a certainty of 25 might be high enough for a value to be regarded as being known.

In a similar way, an inference engine that processes certainty factors will typically have a threshold of the unknown. If the certainty of a value falls below this threshold, then the value is considered to be unknown. Many inference engines have this threshold "hard wired" into their logic. A typical cutoff is 20, which means that a variable is considered to be unknown if none of its values has a certainty factor in excess of 20. Some inference engines allow a developer to control the level of the uncertainty threshold. For example, the Guru command:

```
LET E.UNKN = 32
```

would set the threshold at 32 rather than its default of 20. This setting could be established prior to consulting a rule set or in a rule set's initialization sequence.

CONCLUSION

The topics of certainty factors and fuzzy variables are extensive. Only a brief overview of some of the basics has been presented here. More detailed explorations of these topics appear in Chapters 10 and 11. It should be kept in mind that an understanding of certainty factors and fuzzy variables is not necessary in order to use an expert system. Furthermore, interesting expert systems can be developed without using such features. However, there are many applications where uncertainty arises. It is therefore valuable that an expert system development tool support the kinds of built-in certainty factor and fuzzy variable capabilities described here. They may not be required for some applications, yet they are always available when needed. Obviously, the degrees of flexibility, power, and convenience that a tool provides for reasoning with uncertainty are also very significant.

EXERCISES

1. What is a certainty factor?
2. In addition to values of variables, what else can have a certainty factor?
3. What are some possible sources of certainty factors?
4. Explain why certainty factors should not be referred to as "probabilities."
5. The two conditions in a conjunctive premise are true with certainties of 60 and 80 respectively. What is the joint certainty for this premise using (a) the product method and (b) the minimum method?
6. Under what two circumstances will the product and minimum methods yield the same joint certainty?
7. Suggest an alternative method for determining joint certainties that is always more venturesome than the product method and always more conservative than the minimum method.
8. Someone suggests that an alternative method for computing a joint certainty factor would be to take the average of the two contributing certainty factors. Discuss this suggestion.
9. The two conditions in a disjunctive premise are true with certainties of 60 and 80 respectively. What is the confirmative certainty for this premise using (a) the maximum method and (b) the probability sum method?
10. Under what two circumstances will the probability sum and maximum methods yield the same confirmative certainty?
11. Suggest an alternative method for determining confirmative certainties that is always more venturesome than the maximum method and always more conservative than the probability sum method.
12. Someone suggests that an alternative method for computing a confirmative certainty would be to take the average of the two contributing certainty factors. Discuss this suggestion.

13. Rule XA has the action:

    ```
    X+=200 CF 70
    ```

    in its conclusion. Rule XB has the action:

    ```
    X+=200 CF 50
    ```

    in its conclusion. Suppose XA is fired with a premise certainty of 90 and then XB is fired with a premise certainty of 80. How certain are we that X has a value of 200 if (a) the minimum and maximum methods are used? (b) The product and maximum methods are used? (c) The most venturesome methods are used? (d) The most conservative methods are used and XB's action is X = 200 CF 50?
14. Why is it important for an inference engine to be able to use different certainty factor algebras?
15. How does a fuzzy variable differ from a traditional variable?
16. Describe a situation where it is valuable to use a fuzzy variable whose values all have a certainty of 100.
17. Why is it important to have functions for working on individual values of a fuzzy variable?
18. Explain what an uncertainty threshold is.
19. How does conventional assignment (i.e., replacement) differ from additive assignment when multiple rules are fired to yield the same value for a variable?

References

1 *Guru Reference Manual*, vol. 1. Lafayette, Ind.: MDBS, Inc., 1985.
2 Shortliffe, E. H. *Computer-Based Medical Consultations: MYCIN.* New York: Elsevier, 1976.
3 Shortliffe, E. H. and B. G. Buchanan. "A Model of Inexact Reasoning in Medicine." *Mathematical Biosciences* 23, 1975.
4 Zadeh, L. A. "Fuzzy Sets." *Information and Control* 8, 1965.

Chapter Seven

Invoking an Inference Engine

Once a rule set exists, a user should be able to ask the inference engine to consult that rule set. There are several important aspects related to this activity of invoking an inference engine. First is the issue of the environment provided for requesting a consultation. Is it a trivial environment, allowing the user to do nothing more than make requests of the inference engine? Or is it a rich environment, allowing a user to intermix such requests with data management, spreadsheet, graphics, and other common decision support requests? Are extensive controls furnished for customizing the environment to suit the user's tastes and needs? What kinds of security mechanisms are there for protecting valuable knowledge from unauthorized disclosure or alteration?

Second is the issue of how a consultation request is actually made. Is it made via a natural language conversation, by selecting desired options presented in menus, by a simple consultation command, or through some special user interface that has been custom built by the expert system developer? Third, what kinds of requests can be made of the inference engine? Beyond the choice of what type of reasoning (forward, reverse, etc.) is to be employed, there are requests that ask the inference engine to explain itself. For instance, when a consultation ends, how can a user ask the inference engine to explain its line of reasoning? How elaborate can the inference engine's responses be?

This chapter examines each of these issues from the standpoint of what is possible today. Once again, examples are based on the KC application scenario and Guru capabilities.

THE CONSULTATION ENVIRONMENT

As explained in Chapter 2, Guru is based on the principle of synergistic integration. It synergistically integrates an extensive expert system component with familiar business-computing components. All of this is available in a single program that serves as an environment for both building and using expert systems. The user environment is of primary interest here. Earlier discussions in this book have suggested some of the ways in which integral business-computing capabilities can be utilized within the consultation of a rule set. This view is now turned inside out to see how the integral consultation capabilities can be exercised within the context of business-computing activities.

In a human decision-making process, the mind provides an environment for exercising various knowledge-processing activities. One such activity is the consultation of experts. This is by no means the only kind of knowledge-processing activity that is possible. And when consultation occurs, it normally happens within the context of other kinds of knowledge processing. Certain activities may stimulate the need for a consultation and the consultation results may make still other activities possible. For instance, as a result of exploring some environmental knowledge, a person may discover that advice is needed about some particular problem. Once the advice is received, it may be incorporated into various calculations, used for selective examination of further environmental knowledge, as a stimulant for seeking additional expert recommendations, treated as an input for analytical modeling, presented in various guises to other persons, and so forth.

The Consultation Context

The important point is that human consultation needs arise and are fulfilled within a rich environment that supports many other varieties of knowledge processing. All of these kinds of knowledge processing (including the capacity to consult experts) are available for use at any time and in any sequence—giving a person great discretion about how to employ them with respect to any particular decision situation. Guru provides expert system users with a similar environment. The user is free to request a consultation whenever he or she deems it appropriate. Such requests can be freely intermixed with requests for any of the other kinds of knowledge processing supported by Guru. The possibilities arising from this flexibility are virtually unlimited.

For example, a KC sales manager might begin an interactive Guru session by working on a spreadsheet for the local advertising budget. By issuing the command:

```
CALC
```

the user could begin filling in a fresh spreadsheet from scratch. Alternatively, if the budgeting spreadsheet had already been built in a previous

Guru session and preserved on a file named BUDGET, then the command:

```
LOAD BUDGET
```

would cause it to be loaded into memory for further processing.

Once the spreadsheet is displayed on the screen, its cells can be defined and redefined.* The cell values can be evaluated as desired for usual "what if" explorations. All of the customary spreadsheet operations are allowed, including border locking, windowing, copying cell definitions from the same or different spreadsheets, row and column insertion and deletion, cell protection, cell formating, modifying column widths, and selective cell printing. In addition, there are many other kinds of capabilities that are extremely powerful, yet virtually unknown in traditional spreadsheet packages such as 1-2-3. There are too many to be fully described here. However, it is worth mentioning a few to give a taste of what is possible in the Guru environment.

There are extensive color controls and special visual effects for both windows and individual cells. For instance, the sales manager may want any budgeted amount exceeding $1,500 to be *automatically* highlighted by giving it a black color against a red background and causing it to blink. All budgeted amounts that do not meet this condition could be, say, white on blue. Any of 56 color combinations can be designated for any cell's highlighted appearance. All highlighting is automatic, without requiring user intervention.

Traditional spreadsheet packages allow a cell to be defined as a constant value or as a formula. The formula typically involves some numeric calculation based on other cells. The synergy of Guru components means that the spreadsheet user can go far beyond constants and formulas when defining a cell. Any command or command sequence can be used in defining a cell. Thus a cell's value can be determined by retrieving it from a data base, by a multivariate statistical calculation, by interacting with the user via graphs and forms, by executing a procedural model, by consulting an expert system, and so on. For instance, the sales manager may want to make use of growth and unemployment projections in the cell formulas used to allocate advertising expenditures. The same ECON model used within the ADVISOR rule set can also be used in a cell definition. The cell would simply be defined as:

```
PERFORM ECON; GROWTH
```

---

*Unlike ordinary spreadsheets, Guru also allows cells to be defined and redefined while the spreadsheet is not visible on the screen!

to indicate that the cell's value is determined by performing the ECON model and using the value of GROWTH. The next cell might simply be defined as:

```
UNEMPLOYMENT
```

to indicate that its value should be the same as that of the UNEMPLOY-MENT variable.

Packing so much power into each cell has far-reaching implications. It enables one cell to handle a task that could require dozens or hundreds of cells in a traditional spreadsheet—if the task were even possible in a traditional spreadsheet. It enables a spreadsheet to be much more concise, without the clutter of uninteresting or intermediate results. It allows a spreadsheet to share many kinds of knowledge that can be represented, maintained, and processed independently of spreadsheet usage. The race among spreadsheet vendors to allow increasingly large spreadsheets becomes almost meaningless. Beyond several thousand cells, the really important question is how much can be done by each individual cell, rather than how much larger can the spreadsheet become. A huge spreadsheet can in no way make up for the absence of real data base management and procedural modeling capabilities.

After working on the local advertising budget, the sales manager wants to selectively retrieve a list of all sales reps whose sales in the fourth quarter for romance books exceeded $8,000. The manager would use the spreadsheet's \BYE command and then issue the CLEAR command to clear the spreadsheet from the screen. Even though it is not presently showing, all of the spreadsheet's cells can be referenced in any subsequent commands. All cell values remain available for immediate use. The manager would now type in the query:

```
SELECT REP, SALES FROM THISYR WHERE QTRNUM = "4",\
 & PROD = "romance" & SALES > 8000
```

Guru would then display the rep names (and their respective sales) for all records in the THISYR table that satisfy the query conditions.

It should be noted that Guru query requests use standard SQL (IBM's Structured Query Language) syntax. A *single* query request is able to extract related data from *multiple* tables. It is able to dynamically edit, sort, group, and statistically analyze the retrieved data as it is output. Because of the synergy of Guru components, there are many query possibilities that are not supported by SQL. For instance, in the above query, "romance" could be replaced by the cell #A19 to achieve the same effect (recall Figure 5–5, Chapter 5). Query output can be displayed on the console screen or routed to a printer. Alternatively, the sales manager could direct Guru to automatically deposit the query results in a spreadsheet, in another data table, in an external disk file (e.g., using a DIF or ASCII format), in a graphics data source, and so on.

Suppose that the above query was asked because the sales manager wants to get fourth-quarter romance quotas for sales reps whose corresponding sales this year exceeded $8,000. In response to the query, Guru provides a listing of these reps. Now, the manager may decide to use the rule set that Jack built to get advice about a new quota for one of the listed sales reps by typing:

```
CONSULT ADVISOR
```

Because the type of reasoning desired is not specified, Guru assumes that reverse reasoning should be used. Because no goal variable is specified, the rule set's default goal (NEWQUOTA) is assumed.

When the consultation is completed and the manager sees the advice Guru has offered, the manager can follow up with any of many possible actions. Suppose the inference engine prompted for a value for the RISE variable. The manager may want to rerun the consultation, but give a different response to the prompt this time to observe the impact on the recommended new quota. This is accomplished by simply typing:

```
CONSULT
```

The inference engine then assumes that the same rule set is to be consulted again. The manager may also want to study the effect of changing some aspect of the advertising budget. As soon as the consultation ends, the manager types:

```
CALC
```

to again bring the spreadsheet into view. The desired change is made to the spreadsheet and Guru recomputes its cell values. The manager uses \BYE to escape from the spreadsheet and again issues the CONSULT command. The modified cell values are now available to the inference engine.

The sales manager may want to generate a memo describing his or her own assessment of what the new quota should be. To do so, the manager types:

```
TEXT "MEMO.TXT"
```

Guru will now begin to accept the text of the memo, which will be preserved in a disk file named MEMO.TXT for subsequent viewing, modification, or printing. The general-purpose text-processing features provided by Guru are well suited to the needs of decision makers for preparing memos, letters, reports, models, and so on.

The manager simply begins typing in the text of the memo. Frequently, a point is reached where the memo should contain a word or number that is the value of a variable. For instance, the manager may want to mention the rep's name, the present sales and quota, the product line, and the recommended new quota. There is no need to type in these values. The manager simply refers to the appropriate variable name and its value automatically appears at the current cursor position in the text. Thus when a point is reached where the rep's name should appear, the manager types the command:

```
\?REP
```

and the value of REP will appear in the text. Suppose the manager wants to prescribe a quota that is $1,583 greater than the quota suggested by the consultation. At this point, the manager enters the command:

```
\?NEWQUOTA + 1583
```

and the result appears in the text of the memo. The ? used here is just a shorthand way of invoking the OUTPUT command introduced earlier. In general, just about any Guru command (including a CONSULT request or a SELECT query) can be directly invoked in the midst of text processing by prefacing it with the backslash (\) symbol. This tells Guru that any outputs displayed by that command should be incorporated into the text.

The foregoing examples are suggestive of the versatility that an expert system user should expect from the environment within which its inference engine is invoked. It should be possible to intermix consultation requests with requests for any of the following types of knowledge processing:

Data base management
(relational and
postrelational)

Ad hoc SQL inquiry

Statistical analysis

Graphics generation

Spreadsheet analysis

Text processing

Remote communications
(terminal emulation and
file transfer)

Customized report
generation

Calculations

Forms management

Procedural modeling

External program execution

A user should be able to intermix these requests on a spur-of-the-moment basis from within a single environment (see Figure 7–1). The creative flow that can so often happen in a decision process should not be interrupted or destroyed by such crude requirements as having to switch among separate programs, produce intermediate files of data, "cut and paste" data values, and so on. The environment should make every effort to stimulate and enhance (i.e., truly support) the flow of a decision process, rather than unnecessarily thwart it.

Environment Controls

Another important consideration for the consultation environment is the extent to which it can be shaped to conform to a user's tastes and needs. Should upper- versus lowercase differences encountered in the comparison of two string values be ignored (e.g., should "romance" be considered as being equal to "Romance")? How many decimal digits should be displayed when a numeric value is output without a picture? What should the foreground and background screen colors be while processing a piece of text? Should a graphics image have different colors than a text screen? Should context-sensitive help information be provided whenever the user makes an error? How big a page margin is desired for printer output? When a graphics image is output on a plotter device, should it be rotated by 90 degrees? What kind of file transfer protocol (e.g., Kermit or XMODEM) should be assumed? Should the underlying commands generated by a natural language request be previewed before executing them? During spreadsheet processing, should there be synchronous window scrolling? There are literally dozens of such questions that can be asked about the environment within which a consultation request can occur.

Conventional expert system development tools typically give little if any control over the answers to such questions. At the opposite extreme is an environment, such as that furnished by Guru, where the controls are too numerous to even enumerate in this short book. Guru supports well over 100 environment variables [2]. Several of these have already been described (e.g., E.DECI, E.SUPD, and E.CFJO). Each environment variable has an initial default setting at the outset of each Guru session. A user can completely ignore these variables if desired— this results in the default environment. Other users may wish to alter the settings to produce a different processing environment. For instance, if automatic statistics generation for each SELECT query's output is not desired, the sales manager might type:

```
LET E.STAT = FALSE
```

FIGURE 7-1 Problem processor supporting many knowledge management abilities and many knowledge representation methods

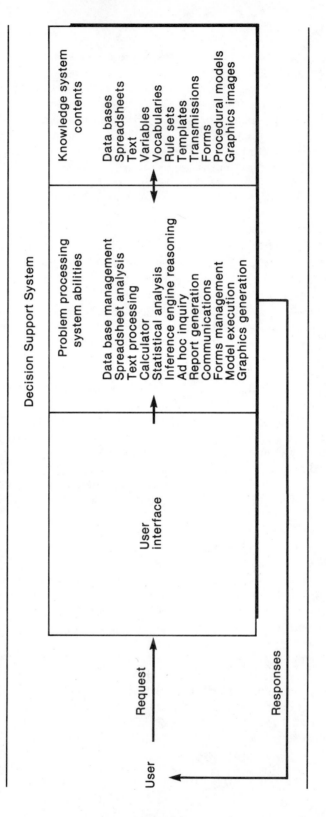

Any of the environment variables can be set in a similar manner whenever desired.

In addition to environment variables, Guru provides about 50 utility variables. Each utility variable begins with the # symbol. These variables are primarily used to customize certain output displays produced by Guru and to monitor the present status of the environment. For instance, #TITLE's value serves as the title Guru uses for query listings and graph displays. The user can change it to any desired value at any time. Another example is #DATE, whose value is automatically set by Guru to be the current date. Similarly, #GOAL's value is always the name of the overall goal (or test) variable of the most recent consultation. The #HOW array always consists of the identifying numbers of rules fired in the most recent consultation, arranged in the order in which they were fired. As with environment variables, there are too many utility variables to even mention all of them here. The main point is that environment and utility variables provide very useful means for tailoring and monitoring the user's processing environment. The user is free to ignore them or to use them as much as desired.

Knowledge Security

Knowledge security is a crucial requirement for most, if not all, business organizations. Knowledge is one of an organization's most important resources. Protecting it from unauthorized disclosure and modification may well be essential for the organization's competitiveness and even survival. Think about the reasoning knowledge that Jack has incorporated into the ADVISOR rule set. There is also procedural knowledge embodied in the ECON model. Data tables such as THISYR contain important knowledge about KC's inner environment. Budgeting spreadsheets contain modeling knowledge (e.g., formulas), as well as derived knowledge (e.g., cell values). What would happen if this knowledge were improperly modified or disclosed to competitors?

Unfortunately, preservation of security is almost entirely ignored by conventional expert systems and tools. While security may not be vital for medical diagnosis, chemical analysis, or geological prospecting, it is a necessity for many business applications. It is instructive to briefly examine some of the kinds of security that are automatically enforced by Guru.

First of all, Guru is able to distinguish between valid and invalid users by means of passwords. When a potential user invokes Guru from the operating system, Guru responds by prompting the prospective user to enter a valid user name and a corresponding password. If the prospective user fails to do so, Guru refuses to accept any requests from that person.

Each valid user has his or her own read and write access privileges. These are simply specified as some subset of the permissible access codes—letters a through p. A read access privilege controls what a user can look at, while a write access privilege governs what the user can modify. Different users can have different, yet overlapping, access privileges. Whenever a user makes a request, Guru itself checks to see whether that user has sufficient clearance. If the user's access privileges are sufficient, then Guru carries out the request. Otherwise, Guru refuses to carry out the request.

Data held in Guru's relational data bases are protected in this way. The protection can be at the table level (e.g., a user is or is not allowed access to THISYR data) or at the level of individual fields (e.g., a user is or is not allowed access to values of the SALES field). For instance, if SALES has an access code of g, then only those users whose access codes include g will be allowed to access SALES values. Because a table exists on an operating system file, it is also necessary to protect the table's data from casual viewing via operating system commands. Guru accomplishes this by automatically encrypting all data as it is stored into a table. Even more elaborate security precautions are available when requests are made for Guru to access data stored in integral MDBS III postrelational data bases [3].

Guru also protects a spreadsheet's cell definitions. This involves much more than the common ability of being able to lock a cell so that its definition is not inadvertantly altered. Because anyone can unlock the cell, such a feature can hardly pass as a serious security mechanism. Much more powerful is the ability to control which users can view a cell's definition and which users can alter its definition. Guru supports such security for blocks of cells or down to the level of individual cells. This allows the procedural knowledge embedded in a spreadsheet to be used by any user, while absolutely protecting it from disclosure to or change by that user.

In a similar vein, the procedural knowledge embodied in a model (e.g., ECON) devised with Guru's integral programming language can be guarded from view. This is accomplished by running the model through a Guru utility program that scrambles the program's instructions in such a way that Guru can still execute them—even though they have a meaningless appearance to the casual observer. As a result, a user can have Guru execute the ECON model, even though the knowledge incorporated in it cannot be seen.

Rule sets are also subject to security. Before a rule set can be consulted, it must be compiled. A compiled rule set's contents are not comprehensible to the casual observer, although they are understood by the inference engine. Rule set compilation also results in significantly faster consultation than can be achieved by working with a textual version of a rule set. When a rule set is built, the developer can specify access codes for it. For instance, Jack might include:

```
ACCESS: c,k
```

prior to the initialization sequence in the ADVISOR rule set. This would mean that Guru will allow only those users with access privileges c or k to consult the rule set. Any user whose access privileges do not include one of these codes will not be allowed to consult the ADVISOR rule set. Built-in security mechanisms such as these should be expected of a consultation environment.

METHODS FOR REQUESTING A CONSULTATION

As noted earlier, there are four major user interface methods: command-oriented, menu-guided, natural language, and customized. These effectively constitute four different approaches to DSS language systems. As shown in Figure 7–2, all may be present in a single decision support system. This enables the system to be conveniently accessed by many different kinds of users, from computer novices to professional systems developers.

Command Invocation of the Inference Engine

Many examples have already been given of the CONSULT command, which can be used to invoke the inference engine. The CONSULT command can be directly used at any time in an interactive session. It can also be used in various indirect ways. It can, for instance, serve as the definition of a spreadsheet cell. Whenever a user requests a spreadsheet recomputation, Guru will carry out the desired consultation within the midst of the recomputation. A CONSULT command can be embedded in the program logic of any procedural model devised with the integral programming language. For example, the ECON model may itself consult an expert system to get advice that helps establish the growth and unemployment projections. This invocation of the inference engine takes place during the execution of ECON, so that the user of ECON may even be unaware that ECON is consulting an expert system.

Another indirect usage of the CONSULT command happens when it is embedded within a rule set. It may appear in the initialization sequence, in a rule's conclusion, in a variable description's find actions, or in the completion sequence. When a user consults an expert system, that expert system can itself consult other expert systems in order to produce the advice that will be reported to the user. The user may be unaware of these additional consultations going on behind the scenes. All of these consultations are processed by the same inference engine.

Menu-Guided Invocation of the Inference Engine

As an alternative to invoking the inference engine with the CONSULT command, a user may prefer to use Guru's menu-guided interface. This

FIGURE 7-2 Alternative interface methods

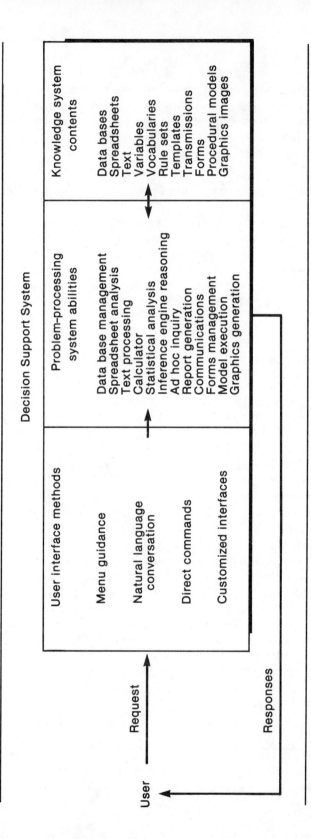

consists of a built-in conglomeration of pop-down menus. The menus have options for expert systems, data management, spreadsheet, graphics, gateway, and other processing options. For instance, after selecting the gateway option, a new window of options pops down on the screen. These include options for executing operating system directives, and running external programs, remote communications, and special executions. By selecting the special executions option, another menu pops down on the screen, and so forth. In general, menu-guided interfaces are appropriate for first-time or casual computer users, even though experienced users find them to be cumbersome and slow relative to a command-oriented interface.

Natural Language Invocation of the Inference Engine

Another interesting interface for novice and casual users involves requesting a consultation by natural language conversation. All the usual natural language capabilities described in Chapter 1 are supported. In addition to data base retrieval, record creation, record modification, spreadsheet access, model execution, statistics calculations, and graphics generation, Guru's integral natural language interface allows users to request a consultation by carrying on a natural language conversation. It should not be long before natural language interfaces progress to the point where they are able to carry out appropriate rule set consultations and model executions that have not been explicitly requested by a user [1].

Customized User Interfaces for Invoking the Inference Engine

The fourth kind of user interface is one whose entire appearance and interaction modes are custom built by the expert system developer. The developer uses Guru's integral programming language as a tool for building such an interface. By executing the resultant program, the flow of a user's interaction with the expert system is governed by logic built into the program. What the user sees on the console screen is also controlled by this interface program. The developer is free to embed any of the following kinds of Guru commands into the program for presenting desired appearances: line-oriented input and output, forms management, graphics generation, and commands using the automatic menu-building function. At the developer's discretion, the interface program can accept user input via keystrokes, mouse manipulation, or function keys.

Notice that all of these are the same facilities that can be embedded in a rule set for governing the user interface *during* a consultation. Here, the focus is on using them to govern the user interface *before* (and after) a consultation. The actual CONSULT commands for invoking the inference engine are embedded in the interface program and are never seen by the user. A simple example is suggestive of the possibilities. Figure 7–3 shows a small interface program written in Guru's structured programming language. By executing this program, the user will be presented with a customized interface for repeatedly invoking the inference engine.

Suppose that a member of KC's information systems department has used Guru's integral text processor to develop the customized interface program of Figure 7–3. This program is distributed to the sales managers on a file named QTA.IPF. Whenever a sales manager wants to consult the ADVISOR rule set within the Guru environment, she or he simply performs the QTA program by typing:

```
PERFORM QTA
```

This causes Guru to execute the program, including one or more of the CONSULT commands that it contains. Thus, the program allows the user to invoke the inference engine without picking options from Guru's built-in menu-guided interface, without having a natural language conversation, and without issuing the CONSULT command directly.

The commands within the Figure 7–3 program are of no interest to the expert system user. However, if you are a developer, then it is worthwhile to examine them in more detail. The program's first three commands set the values of three environment variables. Setting E.LSTR to 50 allows Guru to process string prompts and messages of up to 50 characters. The values of E.BACG and E.FORG respectively control the various background and foreground colors that appear on the screen. The value for each variable consists of five color codes. G denotes green, R denotes red, M indicates magenta, W means white, A represents black, U denotes blue, and so on. In this example, E.BACG's value causes the background color of spreadsheets to be green, of graphics images to be red, of text displays to be magenta, of customized menu options to be red, and of the normal display screen to be black. Similarly, the first code of E.FORG controls the spreadsheet foreground color, the second controls graphics image foregrounds, and so on. In this example, all foregrounds are white, except for menu option foregrounds, which are black.

The next command extends across seven lines. It defines the existence of a form named F1. This form has two color blocks. One covers the entire screen and has a cyan (C) foreground with a blue background. The second color block exists within the first color block, from row 15 through 18 and column 17 through 59. It, too, has a blue background, but its foreground is magenta. In addition to its color blocks, the form is also defined to contain three lines of text located at the indicated positions. Later in the QTA program, this form will be put onto the screen to furnish a backdrop for the menu.

FIGURE 7-3   **A sample interface program that invokes the inference engine**

```
LET E.LSTR = 50
LET E.BACG = "GRMRA"
LET E.FORG = "WWWAW"
FORM F1
      AT 1,1 TO 25,80 PUT "FCBU"
      AT 15,17 TO 18,59 PUT "FMBU"
      AT 2,15 PUT "For which of the following do you want advice?"
      AT 16,18 PUT "Use arrow keys to highlight your choice"
      AT 17,18 PUT "and then press the ENTER key to proceed."
ENDFORM
CLEAR
WANTMORE = TRUE
DIM VAROPT(4)
LET VAROPT(1) = "New Quota"
LET VAROPT(2) = "Economic Outlook"
LET VAROPT(3) = "Local Ad Factor"
LET VAROPT(4) = "Product Factor"
WHILE WANTMORE DO
      PUTFORM F1
      LET CHOICE = MENU(VAROPT,1,4,5,30,2,20,1)
      AT 15,20 OUTPUT "Guru is now thinking about your request."
      TEST CHOICE
                  CASE 1: CONSULT ADVISOR TO SEEK NEWQUOTA
                        CLEAR
                        AT 2,2 OUTPUT "The recommended new quota is:", \
                              NEWQUOTA
                        BREAK
                  CASE 2: CONSULT ADVISOR TO SEEK ECONOMY
                        CLEAR
                        AT 2,2 OUTPUT "The expected economic outlook is", \
                              ECONOMY USING "llll"
                        BREAK
                  CASE 3: CONSULT ADVISOR TO SEEK LAFACTOR
                        CLEAR
                        AT 2,2 OUTPUT "The recommended local ad factor is:", \
                              LAFACTOR USING "d.dd"
                        BREAK
                  CASE 4: CONSULT ADVISOR TO SEEK PFACTOR
                        CLEAR
                        AT 2,2 OUTPUT "The recommended product factor is:", \
                              PFACTOR USING "d.dd"
                        BREAK
                  OTHERWISE:
                              AT 17,20 OUTPUT "Your request is invalid."; CLEAR
      ENDTEST
      AT 4,2 INPUT YN STR USING "u" WITH "Do you want more advice?(Y/N)"
      IF YN NE "Y" THEN WANTMORE = FALSE; ENDIF
      CLEAR
ENDWHILE
RETURN
```

After clearing the screen to give it a black background, the WANT-MORE variable is initialized to TRUE. The program will use this variable to detect when its execution should cease. An array named VAR-OPT is dimensioned to consist of four elements. Values are then assigned to the four elements. These will subsequently be used for processing a customized menu. Now as long as WANTMORE's value remains TRUE, Guru will repeatedly do (i.e., execute) the commands between DO and ENDWHILE. The first of these is to put the F1 form onto the screen. The form's text indicates that the user will be allowed to choose among various types of advice. This is followed by an assignment command that involves Guru's menu-processing function. At this juncture, the user's console screen has the appearance shown in Screen 7 in the color insert.

The MENU function has eight arguments that allow a developer to control what the menu will look like. In this example, values of VAR-OPT's array elements will serve as the menu's options. The second argument (1) indicates that the first of these elements is the default option where the cursor comes to rest as soon as the menu appears on the screen. The next argument (4) indicates that all four elements of VAR-OPT will appear as options in the generated menu. The next two arguments (5 and 30) cause the display of the options to begin on the 5th line of the screen and in the 30th column. The sixth argument (2) causes two blank lines to appear after each row that contains options. The next argument (20) indicates that the background color for each option will occupy up to 20 spaces. The final argument (1) causes the menu options to be arranged in a single column. If this argument had been a 2, then the four options would have appeared in two columns (of two each) instead of the one column shown in Screen 7.

As soon as the customized menu appears on the screen, the user is free to move the cursor to any of the four options. This can be accomplished with control keys, arrow keys, or mouse movement. At any moment, the option presently identified by the cursor is highlighted in reverse video (red on black in this example). When the cursor is resting on the desired option, the user can select it with the return key or a mouse button. An integer corresponding to the chosen option is returned by the MENU function and assigned to the CHOICE variable. If the user chooses the first (New Quota) option, then CHOICE gets 1 as its value. If the second option is chosen, then CHOICE's value becomes 2, and so on. Following an OUTPUT command, Guru will execute the TEST command to carry out the appropriate processing for the user's choice.

The TEST command tests the value of the CHOICE variable against the case numbers. When a match is found, Guru executes the commands specified for that case. Suppose a user chooses the first option. Because the value of CHOICE is 1, Guru will execute the four commands associated with CASE 1. The first of these invokes the inference engine to consult ADVISOR. Reverse reasoning is employed to seek a value for the NEWQUOTA variable. The use of this customized consultation interface assumes that ADVISOR has no completion sequence like that shown in Figure 5–7. When the consultation concludes, the second command in this case clears the screen. The value of NEWQUOTA is then output to the user and Guru breaks out of the TEST to the command following ENDTEST.

Here the user is asked whether further consultation is desired. If the user responds by typing in Y, then the WANTMORE variable's value remains TRUE. This means that the procedure of getting a menu choice and making the proper CONSULT request is repeated. The repetition continues in this fashion until the user responds that no further advice is wanted (by typing N or any key other than Y). When this happens, the WANTMORE variable's value becomes FALSE. The WHILE command's condition therefore has a false value. Processing proceeds to the command following ENDWHILE. In this case it is the RETURN command, which simply means that there is nothing more to perform in the QTA program. At this point the user's PERFORM command to Guru has completed all of its processing. The user is now free to directly invoke another Guru command.

This has been a bare bones example of how a developer might use Guru's integral programming language to devise a customized interface for invoking the inference engine. There is virtually no limit to the variations and elaborations that are possible for customized interfaces. For instance, the interface program in Figure 7–3 could be revised to support the consultation of other rule sets in addition to ADVISOR. It could be modified to give the user a choice between forward and reverse reasoning. Data management, report generation, graphics generation, and other commands could be embedded wherever desired in the procedure. In short, any of the more than 100 different Guru commands for business computing can be incorporated as desired into a customized interface program.

Artificially Intelligent Application Systems

By now, readers who are familiar with developing business application systems will have already noticed the revolutionary implications that software such as Guru has for professional application developers. Guru can serve as a tool for developers to use in building *artificially intelligent application systems*. Developers now have a standard, straightforward way of incorporating reasoning capabilities into the application systems they design and implement. All of the familiar capabilities (programming, data base management, forms management, etc.) traditionally used to build application systems for record-keeping and analytical modeling are provided. But the addition of integral reasoning capabilities is a quantum leap beyond what was heretofore possible in an application system.

Before long, the ability of an application system to consult rule sets will be as ordinary as its ability to retrieve data or execute a procedural model. These consultations can provide advice to the application system's end user. Alternatively, the consultations' advice could be for the application system's own internal use—helping the application system decide what its next activity should be [1]. Business application developers who embrace this new technology will have a decided competitive advantage over those that do not. They will be able to offer highly intelligent application systems for record-keeping and decision support. The positive impacts of such systems on end user productivity and effectiveness will be immense.

THE EXPLANATION ABILITIES

When a person consults a human expert, the resultant advice is, of course, important. It may also be puzzling, surprising, or somewhat less than obvious. In such situations, the expert may be asked to explain the line of reasoning. Explanations may even be desired when the advice is not surprising. There are many reasons for asking the expert for an explanation. For example, an explanation can help the person to assess how reasonable the advice is or to more clearly understand the rationale for the advice. Like human experts, an expert system should be able to explain itself. Software that does not have this ability falls short of the minimum requirements for true expert systems. There are basically two times when an expert system's inference engine is able to explain itself: during a consultation and after a consultation.

Explanations during a Consultation

During a consultation, an inference engine may ask the user for an input of some kind. Before answering, the user may want to know why the question is being asked. The developer of the rule set may have anticipated some such situations, by preceding commands that ask for input with output commands that explain why the ensuing input is being requested. As a result, the inference engine automatically causes the explanation (of why an input is being requested) to be presented to the user before the question is asked. Such an explanation can be as detailed and parameterized as the developer wants it to be. Instead of or in addition to this detailed explanation approach, an inference engine should also be able to make use of an individual rule's reason.

If the user is being prompted because a particular rule is being considered, that rule's reason may help to explain why the user is being prompted. For instance, the inference engine may be in the process of firing rule R15. The user sees the input prompt:

```
Enter estimate of percentage sales increase due to rising interest in scifi ___
```

and wonders why the expert system is asking for this input. If the user presses the control-Y key at this point, the reason for rule R15 is displayed on the console screen.* Of course, the rule set developer has full control over where the reason message will appear on the console screen.

As with most expert system development tools, Guru allows the message to appear line-by-line, beginning on the line following the prompt. However, the developer could also declare a "why" window for a rule set. For instance, Jack might incorporate:

```
WINDOW:
    ROW: 2
    COLUMN: 35
    WIDTH: 40
    DEPTH: 7
    FORG: G
    BACG: A
```

prior to the initialization sequence in the ADVISOR rule set. Whenever a user presses control-Y for this rule set, the "why" window will appear and it will contain the appropriate reason message. In this example, the window begins in column 35 of the second row. It is 40 spaces wide and 7 lines deep. Its background color is black (A) and its contents are green (G). The use of a window such as this is especially important when a rule set uses forms management commands rather than line-oriented input operations.

Explanations after a Consultation

An inference engine must also be able to explain itself after a consultation terminates. How did it reach the advice that it reported? Why did it fire the rules that it fired? In Guru, these questions are answered by the HOW and WHY commands. As with the CONSULT command, these can be directly requested by an end user or they can be embedded at desired points in a customized interface program. Suppose a sales manager invokes the inference engine by typing:

```
CONSULT ADVISOR
```

---

*A non-Guru inference engine may accomplish this in some way other than pressing control-Y.

in order to have it use reverse reasoning in search of a new quota. Remember that there is no need to explicitly specify NEWQUOTA in this command, since NEWQUOTA is already ADVISOR's default goal (see Figure 5–6, Chapter 5). Assume that the user's responses were the same as they were for the reverse reasoning example in Chapter 5.

By the end of the consultation, the inference engine has fired rules R13, R1, R8, R4, and R15, and has calculated a value of 24570 for NEW-QUOTA. As shown in Figure 7–4, the user can type in the HOW command to see how the new quota was determined. The inference engine replies that it was determined by firing rule R15, yielding a new quota of 24570 with a certainty factor of 100. Notice that a descriptive label of "Recommended new quota" appears alongside the variable name. This effect is achieved by incorporating:

```
VARIABLE:NEWQUOTA
    LABEL:Recommended new quota
```

as a variable description in the ADVISOR rule set. For the discussion that follows, assume that the following variable descriptions have also been included in the ADVISOR rule set.

```
VARIABLE:STRONG
    LABEL:Product is strong
VARIABLE:BASE
    LABEL:Base amount
VARIABLE:EFACTOR
    LABEL:Economic factor
VARIABLE:PFACTOR
    LABEL:Product factor
VARIABLE:LAFACTOR
    LABEL:Local advertising factor
VARIABLE:LOCALADS
    LABEL:Local advertising amount
VARIABLE:ECONOMY
    LABEL:Economic outlook
VARIABLE:GROWTH
    LABEL:Anticipated growth rate
```

After seeing that the inference engine fired R15 to achieve a quota recommendation, the user may want to see why R15 was fired. As shown in Figure 7–4, this is accomplished with the WHY command. The WHY command causes Guru to report whether an indicated rule (R15, in this case) has been fired. The rule's reason is then displayed, followed by a portrayal of variables pertinent to the firing of that rule. Notice that variables are mentioned in terms of their descriptive labels, rather

FIGURE 7-4   **Exploring the line of reasoning**

Guru> *HOW*
NEWQUOTA – Recommended new quota
Rule   Value   Certainty
_____

R15   24570   100
Guru> *WHY R15*
Rule R15 (fired)
This is a strong product line. The base amount, economic factor, product factor and
local advertising factor for calculating the new quota are all known. A subjective
assessment of the expected sales increase due to general rising interest in the product is
requested. The new quota is then calculated.

(2) Product is strong	true	cf	100
(3) Base amount	2100	cf	100
(4) Economic factor	.01	cf	100
(5) Product factor	.10	cf	100
(6) Local advertising factor	.01	cf	100

Guru> *HOW 4*
EFACTOR – Economic factor
Rule   Value   Certainty
_____

R4   .01   100
Guru> *WHY R4*
Rule R4 (fired)
When the local economics outlook is fair, the economic factor is one third of the growth
rate and the local advertising factor is 1/120000th of the amount budgeted for local
advertising.

(7) Local advertising amount	1200	cf	100
(8) Economic outlook	fair	cf	100
(9) Anticipated growth rate	.03	cf	100

---

than their actual names. The value and certainty factor for each variable is displayed. The parenthesized number preceding each variable label makes subsequent "howing" very convenient. Suppose that in examining why R15 was fired, the user decides that it would be useful to
know how the economic factor was determined (as a basis for firing
R15). This is accomplished by specifying the corresponding number (4,
in this case) when again executing the HOW command. Guru responds
by explaining that rule R4 was fired in order to produce the .01 economic
factor. The final WHY command in Figure 7–4 asks the inference engine
why rule R4 was fired.

This "howing" and "whying" can proceed for as long as the user desires. The HOW and WHY commands can be freely intermixed with
any other commands, either interactively or indirectly. The entire rea-

soning history of each consultation remains accessible with these two commands until the next consultation begins.

Because a rule set's developer has control over the contents of each rule's reason and each variable's label, the explanations that can be produced by the inference engine can be customized to suit the nature of the application. In some cases, a developer may want rule reasons to be detailed, explicit restatements of the rules' premises and actions. In other cases, it may be undesirable for a rule's reason to be too explicit. Compare, for instance, the reasons of rules R7 and R8 in Figure 5-1, Chapter 5. The former is fairly specific while the latter is not. In general, reasons and labels should be constructed so that they are meaningful to potential users of the expert system, without unnecessarily disclosing reasoning knowledge that should remain hidden (e.g., for security purposes).

CONCLUSION

The environment available for invoking an inference engine is important to both developers and users of expert systems. A consultation environment may range from rudimentary and rigid to powerful and flexible. This chapter has highlighted some of the most important things to examine when evaluating a consultation environment. It has also described the various user interface methods that could be expected to be available within a consultation environment for invoking an inference engine. Especially significant are customized interfaces that allow the creation of artificially intelligent application systems for record-keeping and decision support. Such interfaces are made possible by the synergistic integration of expert system technology and traditional programming capabilities. No matter what interface methods are supported, an expert system's inference engine must be capable of explaining its behavior to a user. Ideally, these explanations should be easily customizable by the expert system developer.

EXERCISES

1. What kinds of capabilities would you expect to find in an AI environment for business computing? Why?
2. Identify various places in a joint human-computer decision-making process where the ability to consult an expert system could be valuable.
3. How are environment variables useful?
4. How are utility variables useful?
5. What is knowledge security and why is it important?

6. Explain how the ability to specify a reason for each rule is useful from a security standpoint.

7. If a rule set has been given access codes k and c, which users will be able to consult that rule set?

8. Identify four distinct interface methods that may be available to a user for requesting a consultation.

9. If a function is not available for the automatic construction and processing of menus, how would a developer produce a customized menu interface?

10. What is necessary in order to build application systems that can reason?

11. What must an expert system be able to explain about itself?

12. Explain the role of a "why" window.

13. Explain the difference between the HOW and WHY aspects of an inference engine's explanation of its line of reasoning.

References

1 Bonczek, R. H.; C. W. Holsapple; and A. B. Whinston. *Foundations of Decision Support Systems.* New York: Academic Press, 1981.

2 *Guru Reference Manual,* vol. 1. Lafayette, Ind.: MDBS, Inc., 1985.

3 *MDBS III Data Base Design Reference Manual.* Lafayette, Ind.: MDBS, Inc., 1981.

Part III

BUILDING A BUSINESS EXPERT SYSTEM

Modern tools carve out new trails.

Chapter Eight

Developing a Rule Set

The five preceding chapters have acquainted you with the basic structure, characteristics, and operation of business expert systems. You now know what kinds of facilities can be expected of tools used to build expert systems and what kinds of features to expect of an environment for expert system consultation. Like Jack, you are able to formally represent a fragment of reasoning knowledge as a rule. In looking at the AD-VISOR rule set or other rule sets, you can understand the reasoning knowledge that has been captured. All of this provides a good background for beginning to think about developing your own rule sets.

The activity of rule set development is perhaps more an art than a science—for the present at least. Practice may well be the best teacher. Nevertheless, there are a number of considerations that, if kept in mind, can greatly facilitate the development process. These considerations are explored in this chapter.

First, there is the issue of how to identify an expert system opportunity. Once such an opportunity is identified, the proposed expert system's objectives should be clearly stated and a plan for meeting those objectives established. Then the actual development of an expert system's rule set can begin. The evolutionary and iterative nature of rule set development can be viewed as forming a development spiral. Each cycle in this spiral consists of seven stages. As these are explored, several rule set construction facilities and techniques not presented in earlier chapters will be introduced.

EXPERT SYSTEM OPPORTUNITIES

Rule set development begins only after an expert system opportunity has been identified. Such opportunities are abundant in most organizations, but managers must develop an "eye" for seeing them. Nearly every person in an organization is (or should be) an expert at playing some role [1] that is important to the organization's viability. In some cases, an expert system

could help the human expert in carrying out particular activities demand-
ed by a role, freeing the person to concentrate on other aspects of that role.
The productivity of both the expert and the expert system's users can increase. To help recognize such situations, it is useful to recall the Chapter 3
discussion of potential benefits offered by expert systems.

The manager should look for problem-solving activities where human experts are in short supply, overburdened, unavailable when needed,
or very expensive. An expert system opportunity may well exist if such
an activity involves reasoning for the purpose of:

- Diagnosing the cause of a situation (e.g., auditing, troubleshooting,
  debugging).

- Prescribing a course of action (e.g., planning, designing, repairing).

- Predicting what will happen (e.g., forecasting, speculating).

- Understanding what is happening (e.g., interpreting, teaching,
  monitoring).

- Governing what is happening (e.g., implementing, controlling,
  managing).

- Evaluating diagnoses, prescriptions, predictions, situations, and
  actions.

Expert system opportunities exist not only where human experts
need relief or need to be replicated; they also exist where human experts
have not yet ventured. For instance, an expert stock trader may be
limited to following a small number of stocks because of the large
amount of time required in making daily or hourly trading decisions
about each one of them. If an expert system were developed, the trader's
expertise could be applied to a larger number of stocks than the trader
could possibly handle personally. The expert system would simply
make the same trading recommendations that the trader would make,
given enough time to do so. In this way, the trader's expertise is highly
leveraged. Thus, managers should be alert for expert system opportunities even where a single human expert has been unsuccessful (e.g., to effectively trade 50 stocks rather than 5).

Of course, reasoning expertise about the problem area must exist or
be capable of being acquired. Otherwise, an expert system's rule set cannot be developed. Furthermore, it must be possible to represent the reasoning knowledge as rules. KC's expert system for quota advice was
built to handle a situation where sufficient expertise (i.e., Jack's) was not
available for all managers at the same time (i.e., year's end). The problem area involved prescribing a course of action (i.e., setting quotas).
The desired reasoning expertise for this problem area existed (i.e.,
Jack's) and could be represented as rules (see Figure 5–1, Chapter 5). As

a result, each sales manager can exploit Jack's expertise while leaving Jack free to pursue his own role within the organization.

Expert system opportunities exist for both small and large problems. A small problem is one that requires only modest effort on the part of a human expert. It typically involves a fairly small number of variables and takes the expert anywhere from a few minutes to an hour to solve. Large problems are those that might require hours, days, or even weeks for an expert to solve. These usually involve many variables. Because rule set development for large problems requires greater development time and expense, an expert system for a small problem will typically have a more immediate impact and payback. Its benefits will be visible more quickly.

The claim is sometimes made that expert systems are justified only for large problems. If an investment has been made in specialized hardware, expensive tools, and a staff specially trained in using exotic languages, then the claim may be warranted. It would seem peculiar to devote such a large investment to handling a modest problem such as establishing sales quotas. But this does *not* mean that expert systems for small or medium problems are economically impractical. On the contrary, these problems are precisely where the greatest expert system opportunities lie. They can be developed rapidly with relatively inexpensive tools running on everyday business computers. Like Jack, the developers do not need any extraordinary training in artificial intelligence topics such as hierarchical frame memory structures, PROLOG's predicate calculus formulations, or LISP's cons, car, and cdr operators. An expert system developer does not need a doctorate or master's degree in artificial intelligence.

Another claim that is oft repeated but that also has little validity is the assertion that expert systems can be reasonably developed for symbolic problem domains, but they are inappropriate for numeric problem domains. The best-known expert systems of the past (MYCIN, DENDRAL, etc.) were definitely nonnumeric in orientation. In the past, conventional tools for developing expert systems have offered little more than some token arithmetic operators. With such a tool, the above claim is true and business expert system possibilities are limited. However, as the ADVISOR rule set suggests, today there is no good reason why problems involving numbers cannot be addressed with expert systems. When human experts reason about a problem, they are free to use numbers whenever and wherever desired. The same is true for modern expert systems. Problems that involve reasoning with numbers and mathematical models are a source of many business expert system opportunities.

Expert systems are not panaceas. On the other hand, their possibilities should not be underestimated. When looking for expert system opportunities it is important to keep an open mind. Candidate problem areas may range from large to small. Some may have a very narrow focus, while others involve a broad class of problems. They invariably involve reasoning and may involve reasoning about uncertain situations. The problems to be solved may be wholly or partially numeric in nature. They may need to be solved frequently or rarely, regularly or sporadically, in bunches or in isolation. The reasoning knowledge applied to the problem area may be stable or it may be undergoing continuing change. Expert systems are particularly appropriate where those who ask for advice also want to explore the line of reasoning that has led to a recommendation. Perhaps the best way to begin looking for expert system opportunities is to identify those areas in an organization where human experts are pressured, overloaded, not always available when needed, unable to take the time to enlarge their expertise, and so on. Also be on the lookout for situations where consultation services are not presently available but could be valuable.

AN ASIDE FOR PROGRAMMERS*

Sometimes persons who have experience in writing programs will ask, Why not develop a program instead of developing a rule set? This is a reasonable question. A program could be written in COBOL or C that has roughly (or even exactly) the same effect as any expert system. Are there, then, really any expert system opportunities as opposed to programming opportunities? This is a commonly asked question, but it confuses the ends (expert systems) with the possible means (program development versus rule set development). Such confusion should be avoided when looking for expert system opportunities.

Just because a problem could be solved with a program does not mean that it is not an expert system opportunity. Nor does it mean that the problem should be solved with a program. Recall from the knowledge management discussion in Chapter 2 that there may be multiple ways to represent and process a particular kind of knowledge. The reasoning knowledge that is essential for an expert system can be represented in a rule set and processed by an inference engine. Alternatively, the same reasoning knowledge can be represented and processed within a program. If you are familiar with programming, then you are well aware that it is very different than the rule set and inference engine characteristics presented in Chapters 3–7.

Trying to create an expert system by writing a program rather than developing a rule set has many drawbacks. First, and most importantly, it requires the developer to be a programmer. In contrast, rule set developers need not be programmers because a rule set is basically nonprocedural rather than algorithmic. The developer simply states reasoning

---

*Readers unfamiliar with programming may want to skip ahead to the next section in this chapter.

facts and leaves to the inference engine the activity of processing them in a correct sequence. Also, the programming alternative tends to mix the reasoning knowledge with the control logic that governs the use of that knowledge—violating the principle of generalized problem processing (recall Chapter 2). This makes the management of reasoning knowledge difficult. The specification and modification of reasoning knowledge represented in a rule set is much more convenient.

Unlike a rule set developer, the programmer must build a reasoning explanation mechanism into the program. If reasoning with uncertainty or fuzzy variables is needed, a programmer must program all the necessary certainty factor calculations and fuzzy variable operations. The program must be devised to allow a user to optionally get explanations for any input prompts. The programmer will also need to build various environmental controls into the program. All of this amounts to reinventing the inference engine "wheel" that is already available to a rule set developer.

The relationship of an expert system development tool to programming is somewhat similar to the relationship of a spreadsheet package to programming. A programmer can certainly write programs to solve the same problems that are handled by a spreadsheet, but why bother? Moreover, persons who are not programmers are able to meet many of their own knowledge management needs with a spreadsheet package, since it provides a very convenient way for viewing, maintaining, and thinking about certain kinds of procedural modeling problems. Similarly, a tool for developing rule sets provides a convenient way for viewing, maintaining, and thinking about reasoning knowledge. On the other hand, neither a spreadsheet package nor an expert system development tool supplants a programming language. Neither would be appropriate for implementing a large-scale optimization algorithm, for example. They simply make it easier to accomplish certain kinds of knowledge management tasks, compared to what would be required with a programming language.

In real-life decision making, the dividing lines between various kinds of knowledge management tasks are not always clear and may even be nonexistent. This is why the synergistic integration embodied in software such as Guru is so significant. If some aspect of a problem area involves a well-known algorithm and another aspect necessitates expert reasoning, both can be accommodated by the same tool within a single decision support system. There is no need to try to represent the algorithm as a set of rules nor to represent reasoning expertise as a sequence of program statements. Each can be handled in the most convenient way and can be used together as desired.

Thus, software offerings such as Guru are *not* "expert system shells" like the stand-alone tools shown in Table 1–3, Chapter 1. They are much more: They are an interesting realization of a class of software referred to as "object-oriented languages" [5]. Such a language gives the developer a way of defining instances of many kinds of objects. These various types of objects include rule sets, programs, variables, arrays, cells, spreadsheets, fields, records, tables, text, graphs, queries, commands, terms, and so forth. The language supplies a collection of operators that allow a developer to process any of these objects in various ways whenever desired. Furthermore, objects are allowed to process (i.e., send messages to) other objects. Object-oriented languages have thus progressed to the point where they subsume rule sets, programming, data base management, spreadsheet analysis, and most other business-computing activities. Traditional distinctions between expert system development and application system development are beginning to vanish. To use such languages effectively, seasoned programmers may need to broaden their perspectives beyond conventional programming techniques.

SEIZING AN EXPERT SYSTEM OPPORTUNITY

Once an expert system opportunity has been identified, there are a few preliminaries to take care of before actual development of the rule set begins. For the most part, these involve the normal managerial actions that precede most projects: specifying objectives and planning how to meet them. For small problems, all of this may be done rather quickly and even informally. For a major development effort, greater detail and formality in accordance with the organization's customary project management methods are usually advisable.

Objectives

From the outset it is a good idea to be clear about what the proposed expert system will and will not do. One way to begin is by characterizing the organizational setting within which the expert system will be used. There should be a clear statement of the expert system's purpose within that setting. What kind of problem will it solve (e.g., giving sales quota advice)? Who will use it (e.g., sales managers)? When will they use it (e.g., at year's end)? What kinds of knowledge will users be able to furnish to the expert system during a consultation (e.g., sales rep names)? How fast must a typical consultation be if it is to be of value to a user? What style of user interface is appropriate? How "good" must the expert system's advice be? Why is the expert system being constructed (e.g., for better, more timely, or less expensive decision support)? What is its expected benefit? In view of these benefits, how much is it reasonable to spend for the expert system's construction and ongoing operation? When must it be ready for operation? Answers to all of these kinds of questions should be included in a statement of objectives. They will form a basis for planning and later evaluation.

Planning

Planning identifies resources that will be needed to construct the desired expert system. It prescribes a flow of actions that will use those resources to meet the objectives. It establishes a budget for the construction project. For small problems, the development plan can be produced quickly. Larger problems typically require greater planning effort.

Resources that are essential for expert system construction include an expert, a developer, a development tool, and a host computer. Each must be selected in light of overall objectives and together they should be compatible with each other. The specific resources should probably be selected in the above order—the expert first, then the developer, the tool, and the host computer.

The chosen expert must be both able and willing to participate in the development process on a continuing basis. Choosing an expert who is uninterested in or feels threatened by the proposed expert system will inevitably result in the failure of the entire project. It must be made clear to the expert that the proposed expert system will contribute to the productivity of co-workers. It may be regarded as an extension of the expert, leveraging his or her expertise and increasing personal productivity. Additional incentives may be needed to ensure expert cooperation. For some projects, a group of experts might be necessary. A book or document could also serve as the source of expertise about a problem area.

Ideally, the developer that is chosen should already have some familiarity with the expert system's problem area. The developer and the expert may very well be the same person. At any rate, they should be capable of maintaining a good working rapport with each other. For large problems, a team of developers may be warranted, allowing parallel development of various aspects of a rule set. Different developers might work on various rule sets that are consulted by a primary rule set. Some developers may work exclusively on the user interface cosmetics, on procedural models used by the rule set, and so forth.

All else being equal, an experienced developer is preferable to an inexperienced one, but the developer may or may not have formal training as a "knowledge engineer." An appreciation of business-computing methods is also very helpful: These methods are just as concerned with the engineering of knowledge as traditional AI techniques. As the foregoing chapters have shown, there is really nothing very mysterious about specifying reasoning knowledge in the form of rules, provided a convenient tool is available and the development activity is approached in an organized way.

Regardless of the extent of training and experience, there are several basic traits that good rule set developers will have. They are talented designers and investigators. They pay attention to details. They are skilled at self-expression, interpersonal relationships, and interviewing techniques. Above all, a good developer has a positive attitude toward learning, with both a willingness and an ability to be an inquisitive, fast-learning student or apprentice of the expert.

Selecting a development tool for the proposed expert system is also an important decision. The tool should fit the developer and the problem area. For instance, if a developer is not adept at PROLOG's logic programming, then a PROLOG-based tool is inappropriate. Or if the problem area involves reasoning with uncertainty, then a tool without built-in facilities for handling uncertainty should be avoided. In practice, it is a good idea to select a development tool that can be used repeatedly for building a variety of expert systems. Purchasing and learning five different tools for five different expert systems is a more expensive and time-consuming proposition than using the same tool for building all five systems. This, of course, implies that the tool should be flexible and versatile. It may well have many features that are not pertinent to a particular expert system development effort, but these features may be essential for later development efforts and enhancements.

Chapter 12 provides a detailed set of guidelines to consider when selecting a general-purpose development tool for business expert systems. Perhaps the most important factor to keep in mind is that the tool should enhance a developer's productivity by providing natural ways of representing knowledge. Regardless of what a developer wants to represent, the ideal tool allows the representation to be accomplished in a direct, straightforward manner. It should not be an obstacle course that tests the developer's ingenuity at overcoming its limitations. It might help to think about whether the tool being considered would be able to conveniently handle the relatively modest quota advisory expert system presented in Chapters 3–7. This example is quite typical of what we should expect to encounter in developing a business expert system.

Finally, a computer for development needs to be selected, including both the hardware and operating system. Obviously, the chosen computer must be one that accommodates the selected development tool. To the extent that it supports other software, it may have additional value beyond the scope of expert system development. It should be remembered that additional units of the development machine (or one that is compatible with it) will need to be installed at every site where the expert system will eventually be used. If a tool is operable on a variety of machines, then the resultant expert system could be used on different computers at different sites.

Having identified the resources that will be used for expert system construction, a plan for using them can begin to take shape. This involves establishing milestones for the development project and setting target times for reaching each of them. The time to develop a rule set depends very much on the nature, size, and scope of the problem area. It also depends heavily on the resources that have been selected. All else being equal, faster development times should result from a powerful and flexible development tool, an actively cooperative expert, a seasoned developer, and so on. The plan of action should be accompanied by a budget for expenditures on resources during the life of the development project. Both the timing and budget for the project should satisfy the objectives specified earlier.

A plan may involve several phases. At the end of each phase, progress in meeting the objectives is evaluated. If the development during a phase is satisfactory, then work proceeds to the next phase. The plan for the next phase may be adjusted or fleshed out in more detail before work actually begins. If a phase is not completed in a satisfactory manner, the plans for subsequent phases will probably need to be substantially revised or the entire project may be terminated.

The initial phase of a plan, especially for a large or expensive project, is usually a feasibility study. The intent is to gain some relatively quick confirmation that the selected resources are indeed workable for constructing an expert system for the target problem area. The centerpiece of this study is a working prototype. This is a bare bones expert system, having a subset of the capabilities envisioned for the full-fledged expert system. In the case of Jack's expert system, a prototype might have been developed first that gave quota recommendations based only on the base amount and product factors. Or the rules shown in Figure 5-1 might be considered as the prototype for a more refined ADVISOR rule set involving still other factors that Jack considers pertinent to giving quota advice.

In any event, the prototype concentrates on some subset of the project's objectives. If this subset cannot be developed in fairly short order, the reason will usually become obvious during the prototyping experience. One or more of the resources will be inadequate for developing the desired expert system; or there will be some mismatch or incompatibility among the selected resources. In such a situation, the selected resources should be reconsidered, and necessary changes made. If it is not feasible to make the needed changes, then the project might be abandoned or its objectives revised to conform with available resources.

Not only is prototype development an inexpensive trial run for highlighting glitches (if any) in the plan, it is an important part of selling the overall development plan to management. Solid managerial backing of the project is essential for eventual success of an expert system. Seeing is believing. Rapid development of a prototype that addresses some interesting subset of the problem area can give fairly compelling evidence that support for the project is warranted. Demonstrations of prototypes should convey a sense of what expert systems are, highlight their potential benefits, and instill confidence in their practicality. Through its suggestion of technical feasibility, a prototype can help gain project approval, but this by itself is usually not sufficient. In addition, the project objectives must be clearly presented. The remaining phase(s) of the plan must be well conceived vis à vis the objectives. Economic feasibility needs to be shown, by detailing why and how the benefits that would result from meeting the objectives justify the costs identified in the plan's budget.

THE DEVELOPMENT PROCESS

Once a plan has been accepted, actual development can begin. There is a typical cycle of activities that recurs repeatedly during the development of a rule set. As shown in Figure 8-1, this cycle consists of several stages: study, problem definition, rule set specification, expert testing, interface construction, user testing, and installation. These stages are the major considerations facing a rule set developer, but they are not engraved in stone. Novice developers may want to follow them fairly closely, while experienced developers can adapt them to suit their own needs and tastes.

Each iteration through the development cycle results in a more complete realization of the expert system than the former iteration. Each iteration may be thought of as corresponding to a phase in the project's overall plan. Even the construction of a prototype will normally consist of an iteration through the development cycle. Thus the development of a rule set tends to be incremental and evolutionary in nature. Put together, repeated iterations through the development cycle form the development spiral shown in Figure 8-2. Each iteration builds and expands on the result of the prior iteration, broadening the rule set's scope and more nearly approaching the overall project objectives. As the spiral grows, these objectives may themselves grow (or change)

FIGURE 8-1   **Stages in a development cycle**

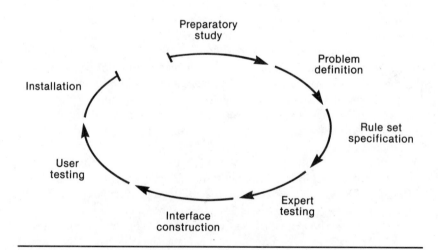

FIGURE 8–2   The development spiral

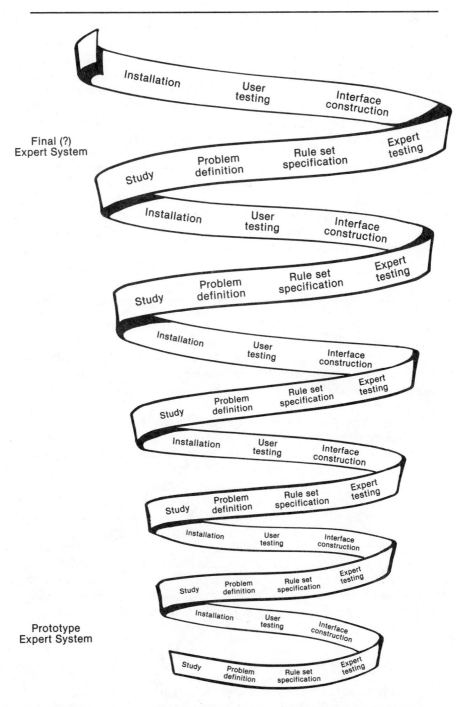

Final (?)
Expert System

Prototype
Expert System

based on what is gleaned from the development experience. Due to the dynamic nature of certain problem areas, a "final" expert system may never be reached: Objectives can be open ended, allowing the expert system to perpetually grow.

Rule set development is a learning process for the developer and should be approached with an experimental, investigating spirit. The developer is out to explore the mind of the expert, to discover what the expert knows, to understand the expert's reasoning behavior. Typically, the expert's reasoning knowledge has not previously been formalized. It exists informally and may never have been systematically scrutinized before—not even by the expert. Therefore rule set development is a process of formalizing the informal, of making the implicit explicit. A developer, then, is a student, a transformer, a designer, and an organizer. He or she grasps the heretofore unseen and gives it a form that is understandable to an inference engine. In developing a rule set, the developer documents expertise. This rule set document is then used by an inference engine in solving problems.

STUDY AND PROBLEM DEFINITION

A developer begins by doing his or her homework. Before interrogating the expert, the developer should get acquainted with the problem area and its terminology. First-hand familiarity with prospective users should also be acquired, as well as an appreciation of the circumstances in which the expert system will be consulted. Finally, the developer should have an understanding of the knowledge representation methods supported by the chosen tool.

After this preparatory study, the next stage in a development cycle is to meet with the expert for the purpose of jointly defining the problem domain that will be addressed. This problem definition must, of course, be consistent with the project's objectives and plan. It should also be quite detailed. It identifies the variable (or variables) that will serve as the expert system's goal. The problem definition provides a very specific characterization of those problems that the expert system should be able to solve. One way to do this is to come up with a representative series of sample consultation problems. These may be actual consultation problems that the expert has previously handled, or hypothetical problems that the expert considers to be typical of those encountered in the problem domain. For the ADVISOR rule set, this could have involved a sampling of specific quota-setting problems from various regions, involving different sales reps and product lines.

RULE SET SPECIFICATION

The problem definition stage will begin to give the developer an appreciation of the kinds of inputs that the expert system will need for reasoning, as well as the kinds of output that should result from the reasoning. The third stage of a development cycle involves the actual specification of rules than can transform inputs into desired outputs. One strategy for accomplishing this is to concentrate on one sample problem at a time. The developer's style and line of questioning should encourage the expert to explain in detail how and why the solution is derived for that problem, in a spirit similar to an expert system user invoking HOW and WHY commands (Chapter 7) to examine the line of reasoning employed during a consultation. The developer then translates the expert's explanations into specifications of the reasoning knowledge (i.e., rules) needed to solve the sample problem. The developer and expert then focus on another sample problem, enlarging and generalizing the existing rule set to handle this new case as well. This continues until the rule set handles all problems defined in the previous stage of the development cycle.

Another strategy would be to specify needed reasoning knowledge without directly considering the samples one after another. Instead, the developer's line of questioning might try to elicit general reasoning principles or patterns from the expert. This reasoning knowledge is general in the sense that it is applicable to the problem domain as a whole. The sample problems drawn from that domain can be used in the developer-expert interchanges to illustrate the general rules that are being explained and specified. This continues until the developer and expert agree that sufficient rules have been specified to handle the defined problem domain.

Interestingly, these two developer strategies for the rule set specification stage mirror two popular approaches to learning within management schools: the case study method and the systemic method. In the former, learning is accomplished by working through specific cases that have been chosen to be representative of common situations. Generalizations to other situations may be made based on what is gleaned from specific cases. In the latter approach to learning, the student works at understanding a system of ideas (e.g., a theory) or techniques (e.g., mathematical modeling) that are generally applicable to numerous situations. For illustration and reinforcement, the relatively abstract system may be examined in the contexts of specific situations. Just as both learning methods can be applied in the same curriculum, a mix of the two specification strategies could be used by the developer. The approach taken will depend on the nature of the problem domain and the inclinations of the developer and expert.

Regardless of whether a developer is working on the rules for a specific sample problem or for the problem domain as a whole, he or she is confronted with the issue of how to pursue an effective line of questioning. What should the developer ask about first? One interrogation strategy might be described as random—posing whatever questions happen to come to mind in the course of discussions with the expert. Such wandering may be fine for getting acquainted with the expert, but is ill advised once serious rule specification work has begun. It is likely to result in gaps and require frequent recoverage of the same ground. A more structured interrogation strategy could conceivably begin in various places. Its first questions might be directed toward acquiring an understanding sufficient for specifying the rule set's initialization sequence. Or it might begin by asking questions that allow the rules to be specified before the initialization or completion sequences.

Discovering the Variables

Of the many possibilities, we will here explore an interrogation strategy that begins with rule set variables. The developer pursues a line of questioning aimed at discovering the variables that will ultimately be referenced by the rules, initialization sequence, and completion sequence. These include goal variables, input variables, and intermediate variables. From the preparatory study and problem definition stages, the developer already has an inkling of the kinds of variables that will be needed. Rather than directly asking the expert to name all variables, the developer asks the expert questions such as: What kinds of things do you like to know about when you begin to ponder a problem? What facts or hypotheses do you try to establish when thinking about a problem? What are the factors that influence how you reason about a problem? Does this factor depend on other factors? If so, which ones?

Each factor that an expert identifies is recorded, as it will most likely become a variable that is referenced in the rule set. For instance, when developing the ADVISOR rule set, Jack may have asked himself what factors he considers when setting a quota.* He would have answered with questions such as: Who is the sales rep? What is the product line? How well did the rep perform last year for this product line? Is the product line strong or weak? How much local advertising is there? What is the economic outlook? Each of these factors led to at least one corresponding variable in the ADVISOR rule set: REP; PROD; QUOTA and SALES; STRONG, WEAK, PFACTOR; LOCALADS; and ECONOMY. Notice that sales rep performance led to the QUOTA and SALES variables, which together characterize performance. Alternatively, a PERFORMANCE variable could have been designated. When Jack then asked himself what an assessment of performance depends on, he would have thought of the two additional factors of quota and sales levels.

It may turn out that not all variables identified in this way will be used in the eventual rule set. Conversely, some additional variables may need to be specified later if the expert has overlooked some factors. In any event, the initial identification of pertinent variables is a good basis

---

*He was both the developer and the expert.

for later talking about and specifying rules. Variables furnish the basic raw materials for actually specifying each rule.

As an expert identifies each factor, the developer invents a corresponding variable name. The name should be reasonably descriptive of the factor described by the expert. No two variables should be given the same name. Before proceeding to the next factor, it is worthwhile to quiz the expert about the nature of the variable. What type of values can it have? What range of values is permissible? From what source(s) could the variable's value be acquired—a data base, a procedural model, a spreadsheet, the user, a remote computer system, a computation, a consultation? That is, where would the expert turn to get its value during a consultation? When is the variable's value established—before a consultation begins, during the initialization, in the course of reasoning, after the reasoning? Is the variable's value usually known to the expert before any reasoning actually happens or might it be unknown? Is the factor (i.e., variable) needed for solving all (or nearly all) problems within the defined problem domain, or is it needed only for some problems but not for others? For practical purposes, does the expert assume that a value for this variable is known with certainty, or does the expert sometimes ascribe some degree of uncertainty to a value? Does the variable always have only one value at a time or does the expert sometimes conceive of it as having several possible values at the same time?

Forms similar to those shown in Figures 8–3 and 8–4 are useful in keeping track of the expert's characterization of each variable. They

FIGURE 8–3   Specification form for a single variable

Variable name: SALES
Description: The amount of a product line actually sold by a rep in particular quarter.
Type of values? ___✓___ Numeric _____ String _____ Logical
Size of values: _____
Range of values: *0-100,000*
Value can be uncertain? ___✓___ No _____ Yes
Maximum values at a time: 1
Source of values? _____ User   _____ Statistical analysis
               ___✓___ Data base   _____ Computational expression
               _____ Spreadsheet   _____ Assignment
               _____ Model   _____ Remote communication
               _____ Consultation _____ External file/external program
Status when reasoning begins? _____ Unknown ___✓___ Known
Value established? ___✓___ Before consultation begins
               _____ During consultation's initialization sequence
               _____ During consultation's reasoning with rules
               _____ During consultation's completion sequence
Depends on other variables? none

FIGURE 8–4   **Specification form for multiple variables**

Variable name	Type N u m	Type S t r	Type L o g	Size	Range	Certainty factor N	Certainty factor Y	Values (max)	User	SpSh	DB	Model
BASE	√				0 to 2000000	√		1				
SALES	√				0 to 200000	√		1			√	
QUOTA	√				0 to 200000	√		1			√	
PFACTOR	√				− .5 to .5	√		1				
LOCALADS	√				0 to 5000	√		1		√		
PROD		√		12	products	√		1	√			
REP		√		10	valid reps	√		1	√			
NEWQUOTA	√				0 to 250000	√		1				
ECONOMY		√		4	good fair poor	√		1				
GROWTH	√				− .5 to .5	√		1				√
STRONG			√			√		1				

Consult	Stat	Comp	Asgn	Comm	Ext	Initial status U	K	Pre	Init	Reas	Comp	Depends on
		✓				✓				✓		SALES QUOTA
							✓		✓			
							✓		✓			
		✓								✓		PROD OLDTITLES NEWTITLES
						✓				✓		
							✓		✓			
							✓		✓			
		✓				✓					✓	BASE EFACTOR LFACTOR WEAK STRONG RISE FALL
			✓			✓						GROWTH UNEMPLOYMENT
							✓		✓			
			✓			✓					✓	PROD

also serve as handy reminders of the kinds of questions a developer should ask the expert for each variable that is invented. As an interesting exercise, the development tool's forms management and data base management facilities could be used to keep track of variables during the development process. Rather than filling in a paper form, the developer would fill in a comparable electronic form on the console screen— with the information being automatically stored in a data base. Alternatively, a tool's facilities for incorporating variable descriptions within a rule set (e.g., within the Guru BUILD command's menu structure) give a somewhat similar effect.

As a further design aid, dependency diagrams such as the one shown in Figure 8–5 can be helpful in visualizing relationships among variables. For instance, this dependency diagram shows that ECONOMY can depend on GROWTH and UNEMPLOYMENT. In turn, ECONOMY can lead to values for EFACTOR and LAFACTOR. To construct a dependency diagram from scratch, it is easiest to begin at the left and work your way to the right. First, write down a variable for a goal factor (e.g., NEWQUOTA) and then ask, "What factors might this goal depend upon?" The answer to this question allows you to write down variables for additional factors (e.g., BASE, EFACTOR, etc.), each pointing to the goal. The process is then repeated for each of the newly specified variables, and so on. In the resulting diagram, each variable that depends on other variables will necessitate one or more rules for establishing its value.

Discovering the Rules

Having reached an understanding of the variables that will be referenced in a rule set, the developer's line of questioning can turn to the rules. The variable specification forms give good clues about what questions should be asked. In Figure 8–4, for instance, notice that the BASE variable's value is set (by a computation) during the reasoning portion of a consultation. In other words, one or more rules will need to be specified to indicate the reasoning an expert uses to establish a value for the BASE variable. From Figure 8–4, the developer should expect the expert's explanation to be contingent on sales and quota levels. The developer transforms the expert's conversational explanations into rules R1 and R2:

```
RULE: R1
  IF: SALES > 1.15 * QUOTA
  THEN: BASE = QUOTA + SALES - 1.15 * QUOTA
  REASON: In cases where the sales for this product
          exceeded the quota by more than 15%, the base
          amount for the new quota is set to the past
          quota plus the excess sales amount.
```

FIGURE 8-5   A dependency diagram for ADVISOR

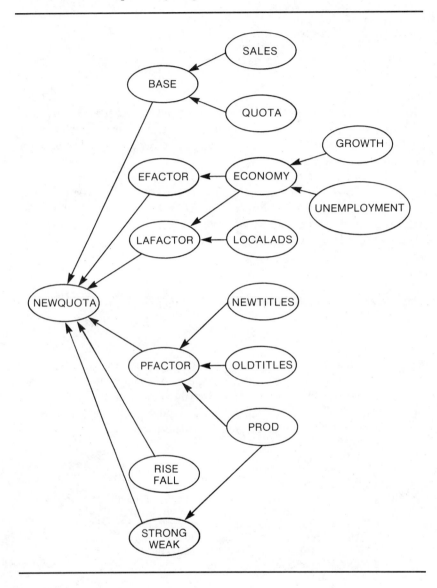

```
RULE: R2
  IF: SALES <= 1.15 * QUOTA
  THEN: BASE = QUOTA
  REASON: The base amount for the new quota is the same as
          the past quota because this product's sales did
          not exceed that past quota by more than 15%.
```

The reason specified with each rule may well be a verbatim or paraphrased rendition of the expert's explanation. This process can be repeated for each variable whose value is to be set during the reasoning portion of a consultation.

In looking at the Reas (reasoning) column under the heading Value set in Figure 8–4, the developer might next ask how the expert reasons about the product factor (PFACTOR). As each rule is specified, the developer should ask the expert whether there are other conclusions implied by the rule's premise. For instance, when the rule:

```
IF: PROD IN [''computer'',''romance'',''scifi'']
THEN: PFACTOR = (NEWTITLES + OLDTITLES)/OLDTITLES - 1
```

is first specified, the developer might ask if there are any other conclusions that can be drawn about the computer, romance, and science fiction product lines. The expert would reply that these are strong, not weak, product lines. The developer would then specify two additional actions in the rule's conclusion, yielding rule R13:

```
RULE: R13
  COMMENT: The premise of this rule will need to be changed when
           additional product lines become strong or when
           the product lines shown are no longer strong.
  IF: PROD IN [''computer'',''romance'',''scifi'']
  THEN: PFACTOR = (NEWTITLES + OLDTITLES)/OLDTITLES - 1
        STRONG = TRUE
        WEAK = FALSE
```

Notice that in addition to its premise and conclusion, this rendition of rule R13 also contains a comment. The developer can optionally specify a comment for any rule in the rule set. Rule comments are ignored by the inference engine and are never seen by end users. A comment is visible only when working on the rule with the rule set manager. It is used to document the rule in some way, such as providing an explanation of why the rule is specified the way it is or of what things to consider if the rule needs to be modified.

When extra actions are put into a conclusion, the developer should recheck the premise with the expert to be sure that its truth is sufficient to imply that *all* of the conclusion's actions be taken. This is clearly the case for R13; but think about how rule R4 might have come into being. Suppose that when the expert explains how the local advertising factor is determined, the rule:

```
IF: ECONOMY = "fair" AND KNOWN("LOCALADS")
THEN: LAFACTOR = LOCALADS/120000
```

is specified by the developer. As a follow-up question, the developer asks whether there are any other implications of a fair economy. The expert replies that the economic factor should be set at one third of the growth rate in such a situation. The developer expands the conclusion to be:

```
THEN: EFACTOR = GROWTH/3;LAFACTOR = LOCALADS/120000
```

However, this conclusion is incorrect unless the premise is also expanded to indicate that the GROWTH variable must be known before the conclusion's actions could be taken. The correct specification is:

```
RULE: R4
  IF: ECONOMY = "fair" AND KNOWN("LOCALADS") AND KNOWN("GROWTH")
  THEN: EFACTOR = GROWTH/3;LAFACTOR = LOCALADS/120000
```

Continuing through the variable specification form in Figure 8–4, a developer would see that the value of LOCALADS is established during a consultation's reasoning. Upon being asked for an explanation of the reasoning that leads to a LOCALADS value, the expert would explain that he or she normally looks up the value in a spreadsheet when it is needed. To look up the value, it is necessary to know who the sales rep is and what the product line is. Thus, the rule:

```
IF: KNOWN("REP") AND KNOWN("PROD")
THEN: REPCOL = LOOKUP(REP,#Y2,#Y13,#Z2)
      LOCALADS = LOOKUP(PROD,#A18,#A31,#(18,REPCOL))
```

might be specified. However, the developer might notice that the premise will always be true because REP and PROD are always known before the reasoning portion of a consultation occurs (see REP and PROD in Figure 8–4). Thus, instead of a rule for establishing the LOCALADS value, the developer could specify the following variable description for LOCALADS:

```
VARIABLE:LOCALADS
FIND: REPCOL = LOOKUP(REP,#Y2,#Y13,#Z2)
      LOCALADS = LOOKUP(PROD,#A18,#A31,#(18,REPCOL))
```

Although both approaches would yield the same consultation result, the latter is preferable because it means fewer rules and therefore faster reasoning. A developer should be alert for rules whose premises are always true and consider eliminating them in favor of variable descriptions in the rule set.

As rules are being specified, the developer should keep in mind that it is perfectly permissible for a rule's actions to involve commands that generate graphs, collect input from the user, retrieve or modify data held in a data base, dial up another computer to acquire needed information, execute a procedural model written with the native programming language, and so forth. External software can also be executed and data from external files can be incorporated into data tables.

For example, there may be an existing program that the expert sometimes runs when reasoning about problems. The program's results are factored into the ultimate advice that the expert gives. Suppose this program is named PRG and is written in FORTRAN. The developer would construct a rule premise identifying conditions under which the expert runs PRG. The conclusion of this rule might contain the commands:

```
THEN: RUN "PRG"
      ATTACH FROM "RESULT.PRG" TO PRGTBL
```

The first command tells the inference engine to execute PRG. Assuming that the program's output is produced on a file named RESULT.PRG, the second command attaches the contents of this file to records existing in the PRGTBL table (if any). Once they are within this table in Guru's data base, the results can be accessed just like the contents of any other table. The ATTACH command assumes the fields defined for PRGTBL conform in type and size with the data held in RESULT.PRG.

By the time the expert has explained the reasoning for each variable whose value can be set after initialization and prior to completion, the developer will have specified the rule set's rules (and variable descriptions, if any). The order in which these rules are specified is irrelevant for consultation purposes. The main point is that they should all be present in the rule set. Some developers may want to elicit the rules in a "top-down" fashion—beginning first with rules that affect the goal variable (e.g., NEWQUOTA), proceeding to rules that affect variables in the premises of rules for the goal, and so forth. Other developers may prefer to discover rules in a "bottom-up" fashion—beginning with rules for variables (e.g., BASE) that depend on other variables whose values are known when reasoning begins, proceeding to rules for variables that depend on other variables for which rules have just been specified, and so forth.

Initialization and Completion Sequences

After the rules have been specified, the developer proceeds to construct the rule set's initialization sequence. Here, all variables that should be unknown before the reasoning begins are explicitly assigned the UN-KNOWN value. Furthermore, appropriate commands should be included for all variables whose values are to be set in the initialization sequence (see the Init (initialization) column under the Value set heading in Figure 8–4). For variables involving input from a user, elaborate prompting and screen cosmetics are unnecessary at this stage of the development cycle. Similarly, when the completion sequence is specified, an elaborate presentation of results is not yet needed. The completion actions are the final aspect of rule set specification.

If the initialization sequence changes the environment settings in some way, it is usually a good idea to first preserve the original settings in some temporary variables. The variables can later be used in the completion sequence to restore the environment to its original state. For example, Jack may want to ensure that no output is routed to the printer during a consultation. All output should be routed to the console screen. These output routings are controlled by the E.OPRN and E.OCON environment variables, respectively. The initialization sequence would contain the commands:

```
TEMP1 = E.OPRN; TEMP2 = E.OCON
E.OPRN = FALSE
E.OCON = TRUE
```

The completion sequence would conclude with the commands:

```
E.OPRN = TEMP1
E.OCON = TEMP2
```

This gives the desired effect during a consultation and leaves the environment unchanged at the end of a consultation.

The rule set can be compiled when the initialization and completion sequences have been specified. Any errors detected by the rule set manager's compiler should be corrected. Any warning messages about possible errors or inconsistencies should also be heeded. Once the rule set is compiled, the expert system will be ready for expert testing.

EXPERT TESTING

In this stage of the development cycle, an expert tests the expertise that has been captured in a rule set. The developer normally sits with the expert during this testing stage. Together they consult the expert system, with the expert critiquing the system's reasoning behavior and advice. They are on the lookout for indications that the rule set may be inaccurate, incomplete, or inconsistent. The sample problems produced in the cycle's problem definition stage should offer a good set of consultation test cases. If the expert agrees that the expert system offers sufficiently good advice and the advice is generated on a sufficiently timely basis, then the developer proceeds to the next stage.* Otherwise, the rule set will need to be modified.

Suppose the expert believes that the expert system's advice is invalid for some consultations. Who is right—the expert or the expert system? What is the cause of this apparent discrepancy between the expert system's advice and the advice that the expert would have given? How can the developer determine where the inference engine began to go off track? Once the answers to these questions are known, the developer can make corrections to the rule set and again work through test cases with the expert. There are at least three techniques that could be used to answer such questions: asking the inference engine for an explanation, automatic tracing of the reasoning process, and customized tracing.

HOW and WHY Review

The first technique makes use of the HOW and WHY commands introduced in Chapter 7 (see Figure 7–4). By using these commands, the developer and expert can examine the line of reasoning that was used for the sample problem. The expert can either agree or disagree with how a particular variable's value was determined or why a particular rule was fired. If there is disagreement, then one or more of the rules may need to be altered. The HOW and WHY commands help identify sources of disagreement and targets for alteration.

Using the HOW command, the expert may see that a rule was fired that should not have been fired. The expert and developer should examine this rule's premise for errors and oversights. The premise may need

---

*Sufficient with respect to project objectives.

to be adjusted by changing its existing conditions or incorporating new conditions into it. For instance, if Jack had forgotten to include the GROWTH $>$ = .04 condition in R6's premise, rule R6 would sometimes fire when it really should not. By seeing that R6 fired when it should not have, Jack is alerted to the fact that its premise is incomplete. The rule set manager is then used to add the omitted condition, yielding the R6 shown in Figure 5–1, Chapter 5.

If the expert believes that the premise is correct, then at least one of the variables in the premise must have received an unexpected value—otherwise, the rule would not have been fired. The WHY command lets the developer and expert see what values of the premise's variables allowed the rule to be fired (see Figure 7–4). To see how a variable with an unexpected value received that value, the HOW command is used for that variable. It shows the rule or rules that led to the unexpected value. One or more of these rules should not have fired, or some additional rule affecting the variable should have fired, or a fired rule's conclusion may have been erroneous or incomplete. The rules should be revised accordingly.

If HOW and WHY review of a consultation detects that the premises of all fired rules are correct, then rule conclusions may be the source of the expert's disagreement. For example, if the conclusion of R16 incorrectly multiplies EFACTOR with LAFACTOR (instead of adding them), then the resultant NEWQUOTA value will not agree with the expert's advice. Here again, HOW and WHY can be used to discover which variable's value does not conform to the expert's expectations. The fired rules' actions that affect that variable should be examined for correctness. There may be an inaccurate calculation, erroneous data base retrieval request, improper model invocation, and so on. If such an error is found, the developer can make the needed corrections with the rule set manager (e.g., changing an erroneous * to a + , yielding the correct R16).

It is possible that a HOW and WHY review will show that all premises and conclusions are correct, even though the expert disagrees with the advice generated for a test case. This is likely due to a failure to recognize some important factor (i.e., variable) that influences the expert's reasoning. For instance, if Jack had forgotten about the UNEMPLOYMENT variable, then unexpected quota advice could have resulted. ECONOMY would have been based only on GROWTH. The developer needs to prompt the expert to identify such an oversight. When the new variable is recognized, it is incorporated into existing rules or new rules. If UNEMPLOYMENT had been originally overlooked, then it would not have appeared in rules R5–R9. Once recognized, it would now be incorporated into those rules as shown in Figure 5–1.

It may be that no additional variables are identified. In such a situation, the developer should prompt the expert for additional fragments of reasoning knowledge (i.e., rules) that may have been overlooked. For example, if rule R2 had been inadvertently omitted from the ADVISOR rule set, then the inference engine would have given an "unknown" recommendation for NEWQUOTA whenever sales did not exceed the quota by more than 15 percent. The expert would, of course, disagree with this advice. In examining the rule set it would be seen that all rules are correct and all important variables have been used in the rules. It would also be seen that NEWQUOTA is given an unknown value because BASE has an unknown value. This should suggest to the developer that an additional rule is needed for assigning known values to BASE. In examining the incomplete rule set, the developer can see that BASE is set only for one possible relationship between sales and quota. By conferring with the expert, the developer would be able to add R2 to the rule set to cover the other possibility.

Automatic Tracing

The HOW and WHY review examines what the inference engine has done. A second technique allows the expert and developer to examine what the inference engine is doing. In other words, the inference engine gives a blow-by-blow account of its activities while the reasoning is taking place. This trace of reasoning behavior appears on the console screen. It portrays the dynamics of reasoning by showing such activities as the selection of a rule for consideration, encounters with unknown variables, and the firing of rules.

Guru allows a developer to control the inference engine's automatic tracing via the E.TRAC environment variable. The value of E.TRAC when reasoning begins (i.e., when initialization is complete) determines how extensive the tracing will be. The possible values are V, C, F, and N. The most extensive tracing is achieved by setting E.TRAC to V. If no tracing is desired, then E.TRAC should be set to N. Automatic tracing is of primary interest during the testing of a rule set's expertise. In fact, if that expertise needs to be hidden from view, then it is important to have a way of disabling the tracing capability after testing is completed. Otherwise, important knowledge about the internals of the reasoning process will be readily available to any user of the expert system. Guru's tracing can be easily disabled for the consultations of a particular expert system by including the command:

```
E.TRAC = "N"
```

in the initialization sequence of the expert system's rule set.

With Guru, automatic tracing is extremely fast, flashing by on the console screen without perceptible pauses. It may be desirable to follow along with the inference engine processing at a more leisurely pace. This can be accomplished by including Guru's WAIT command in the rule set, in each place where you want the inference engine processing to pause. Each time the WAIT command is encountered, processing halts and waits until you press the space bar before resuming. One handy place to put a WAIT command is in the conclusion of a rule. If it is used as the last action in every rule, then the inference engine will wait after each rule is fired. For example, Rule R1 would now be:

```
RULE: R1
  IF: SALES > 1.15 * QUOTA
  THEN: BASE = QUOTA + SALES - 1.15 * QUOTA
        WAIT
```

In this way a developer can slow down the inference engine to suit his or her own preference during the expert-testing stage. Of course, these WAIT commands should be removed at the conclusion of this stage.

Even within the testing stage, a developer may want to switch between real time processing speeds and slow-motion reasoning. The switch is easily accomplished by using the rule set manager to globally modify the characters:

```
WAIT
```

replacing them with:

```
!WAIT
```

throughout the rule set. The exclamation symbol (!) causes Guru to ignore everything that follows it on a line. This change is accomplished in a single operation by either of the Guru rule set managers. A change in the reverse direction (from !WAIT back to WAIT) is also accomplished in a single operation. The WAIT command can appear wherever commands are valid within a rule set. This includes rule actions, variable find actions, the initialization sequence, the completion sequence, and so on.

The inference engine takes a different approach to automatic tracing if a "why" window (recall Chapter 7) has been declared for the rule set. In this case, tracing messages will appear line by line within the window. When the window is full, the inference engine pauses until the space bar is pressed. The inference then proceeds until the window is again filled, and so forth until the consultation concludes.

Customized Tracing

There may be certain aspects of reasoning with a particular rule set that are not covered by the built-in tracing mechanism. For instance, more elaborate reporting of rule firing may be desired. This customized tracing is handled very easily with the OUTPUT command. Suppose that a developer wants the inference engine to display the values of BASE, QUOTA, and SALES as soon as rule R1 fires. This is accomplished by inserting an OUTPUT command into R1's conclusion:

```
RULE: R1
  IF: SALES > 1.15 * QUOTA
  THEN: BASE = QUOTA + SALES - 1.15 * QUOTA
        OUTPUT "Sales:",SALES," Quota:", QUOTA," Base:",BASE
        WAIT
```

The OUTPUT command can be used in a similar way to produce customized tracing messages during the execution of an initialization or completion sequence, or of any rule conclusion's actions, or any variable's find actions.

There is yet another place where OUTPUT commands for tracing can be used. We have seen that each rule can be declared to have a premise, a conclusion, and a reason. Any rule can also be given a sequence of preactions. This is simply a sequence of one or more Guru commands (e.g., OUTPUT, WAIT) that the inference engine will automatically execute as soon as the rule is selected for consideration. The preaction sequence is not restricted to OUTPUT and WAIT commands. Like the rule's conclusion (a *re*action sequence), the preactions consist of any Guru commands. Because a rule's preactions are carried out before an attempt is made to evaluate the premise, using OUTPUT and/or WAIT there gives a way to generate customized messages and/or a pause as soon as a rule is selected for consideration.

When specifying a Guru rule, the word READY (as in "ready-aim-fire") denotes the beginning of a preaction sequence. As an example, rule R3 might be expanded to be:

```
RULE: R3
  READY: OUTPUT "Now about to consider R3."
         OUTPUT "Will attempt to set EFACTOR."
         OUTPUT "ECONOMY must be good to fire."
         OUTPUT "GROWTH  must be known to fire."
         WAIT
  IF: ECONOMY = "good" AND KNOWN("GROWTH")
  THEN: EFACTOR = GROWTH
  REASON: When the local economic outlook is good, the
          economic factor is equal to the economy's
          anticipated growth rate.
```

In addition to their use in tracing the flow of reasoning, preactions can also be a valuable aspect of the reasoning itself [2]. They give the developer a convenient way to be sure that certain actions are always taken before a given rule's premise is evaluated.

Saving and Using Stored Test Cases

The three techniques of HOW/WHY review, automatic tracing, and customized tracing are all helpful when testing the correctness of an expert system's reasoning behavior. Any or all of them can be employed for each test case that is examined. In situations where there are many test cases or when the testing of each sample problem requires a considerable amount of user input, it is worthwhile to be able to save the input values of each case. This should be done in such a way that the input does not have to be reentered directly to the inference engine each time a case is tested. It should also be possible to pick any one of these stored cases for individual testing or to iterate through the entire series of sample problems. In other words, it is important to be able to conveniently manage the test cases.

Because of the built-in data base management system, this is very easy with Guru. The developer defines a data table having a field for each kind of data that needs to be input by the expert system's user. Interactive table definition is accomplished with the DEFINE command. The developer then uses the CREATE command to interactively create one record in this table for each of the test cases. Each record consists of the values that a user would type in response to the expert system's prompts (e.g., such as those produced by INPUT statements in the rule set). An example of such a table constructed for the ADVISOR rule set is shown in Figure 8–6. This table is named SMPL and consists of six fields—one for each of the five INPUT statement variables existing in ADVISOR (see Figure 5–5, Chapter 5) and one called ID, which is used to uniquely identify the individual sample problems.

To make use of this table during the testing stage, the rule set manager would be used to change the Figure 5–5 initialization sequence to

FIGURE 8–6   Sample problems table

SMPL

ID	REP	PROD	QTR	OLDTITLE	NEWTITLE
1	Toby	romance	3	100	10
2	Kim	computer	1	57	12
3	Kris	reference	2	203	18
4	Kevin	photo	2	13	1
5	Kerry	scifi	3	93	8
6	Toby	sports	2	23	3

the one shown in Figure 8–7. Notice that each of the original INPUT commands has been prefaced with an exclamation symbol. Thus their five prompts will not appear when the rule set is tested. Instead, the inference engine will execute only one INPUT command, which prompts the developer for the identifier of the desired test case. As long as the response consists of a valid identifier, the inference engine will obtain the values of REP, PROD, QTR, OLDTITLE, and NEWTITLE from the corresponding record in the SMPL table. The inference engine then proceeds to reason about this sample problem. If a nonexistent identifier is entered, then a record corresponding to it cannot be found and the INPUT command prompting for a sample identifier is again executed.*

Speeding Up the Consultations

When rule set testing has progressed to the point where the expert agrees that it provides sufficiently good advice, the developer should examine

FIGURE 8–7   Initialization sequence for testing purposes

```
INITIAL:
     LET E.LSTR = 50; LET E.SUPD = TRUE
     !INPUT REP STR WITH "What is the sales rep's name?"
     !INPUT PROD STR WITH "Enter product line:"
     !INPUT QTR STR USING "n" WITH "Enter quarter:"
     !INPUT OLDTITLE NUM WITH "How many oldtitles for " + TRIM(PROD) + "?"
     !INPUT NEWTITLE NUM WITH "How many new titles?"
     IF NOT INUSE("THISYR") THEN USE THISYR; ENDIF
     #FOUND = FALSE
     IF NOT INUSE ("SMPL") THEN USE SMPL;ENDIF
     WHILE NOT #FOUND DO
          INPUT SID NUM WITH "Enter sample ID:" USING ddd
          OBTAIN RECORD FROM SMPL FOR SMPL.ID = SID
     ENDWHILE
     OBTAIN RECORD FROM THISYR FOR REPNAME = SMPL.REP & \
        PRODNAME = SMPL.PROD & QTRNUM = SMPL.QTR
     PERFORM ECON
     ECONOMY = UNKNOWN; EFACTOR = UNKNOWN
     LOCALADS = UNKNOWN; LAFACTOR = UNKNOWN;
     PFACTOR = UNKNOWN
     BASE = UNKNOWN; STRONG = UNKNOWN; WEAK = UNKNOWN
     NEWQUOTA = UNKNOWN
GOAL:
     NEWQUOTA
```

*If you use the initial release of Guru, every rule set reference to a field must be qualified by that field's table name (e.g., OLDTITLE and SALES should be changed to SMPL.OLDTITLE and THISYR.SALES in the ADVISOR rules).

the expert system from a performance viewpoint. Does testing show that the expert system meets the project's processing speed objectives? Have both forward and reverse reasoning speeds been tested—with the fastest one being compared to the objectives? A developer can try to speed up consultations in any of three ways: changing the inference environment, modifying the rule set, and converting to a different computer or inference engine.

The first is the least expensive, since it often does not require even a recompilation of the rule set. Several kinds of environment controls were briefly discussed in earlier chapters and they are dealt with in more detail in Chapters 9, 10, 11, and 12. Because they affect the inference engine's reasoning behavior, they can affect consultation speeds. For example, a developer can test the effects of different E.SORD settings on sample problems, noting which selection order for competing candidate rules yields the fastest consultation. A major benefit of such environment variables is that they can be used to tune the inference engine's performance for a particular rule set. They may even be used to set the environment depending on the specific problem being posed for a consultation. Indeed, an extra rule set could be specified that, when consulted, would determine the best environment settings to use when solving a specific problem with the original rule set. This new rule set would probably be invoked by consulting it from within the initialization sequence of the original rule set.

Just as environment settings can influence expert system performance, the rule set contents can also affect consultation speed. In general, a small number of rules will yield faster reasoning than a large number of rules. A tool that provides a rich assortment of knowledge representation methods permits more concise, parsimonious rule sets than less sophisticated tools; but regardless of what tool is being used, the developer should consider whether there is a way to reduce the number of rules in a rule set. For instance, if two rules have the same premise, then the developer may collapse them into a single rule having that premise together with a conclusion formed from the conclusions of the two original rules. Rules can also be collapsed if the premise of one is a special case of or subordinate to the premise of the other.

There is yet another general approach to reducing the number of rules. Consider the rules R1 and R2.

```
RULE: R1
  IF: SALES > 1.15*QUOTA
  THEN: BASE = QUOTA + SALES - 1.15 * QUOTA
  REASON: In cases where the sales for this product exceeded
          the quota by more than 15% the base amount for
          the new quota is set to the past quota plus the
          excess sales amount.
```

```
RULE: R2
  IF: SALES <= 1.15 * QUOTA
  THEN: BASE = QUOTA
  REASON: The base amount for new quota is the same as the
          past quota because this product's sales did not
          exceed that past quota by more than 15%.
```

Notice that together they cover all possibilities for the possible relationships between sales and a quota. There is an easy way to combine them into a single rule that is equivalent from a reasoning viewpoint. The new rule is:

```
RULE: RSQ
  IF: KNOWN("SALES") AND KNOWN("QUOTA")
  THEN: IF SALES <= 1.15 * QUOTA THEN BASE = QUOTA
          ELSE BASE = QUOTA + SALES - 1.15 * QUOTA
        ENDIF
  REASON: If sales do not exceed the quota by more than
          15%, then the base amount is the same as the
          past quota; otherwise the base amount is set to
          the past quota plus the excess sales amount.
```

Replacing rules R1 and R2 with RSQ would result in the same advice, while giving the inference engine one less rule to consider.

In addition to rule reduction, a developer should consider the actions appearing in the initialization sequence. Generally, actions that establish values of variables that are not frequently needed in consultations should be removed from the initialization sequence. Instead, they should appear in a variable description (or rule conclusion). If the initialization sequence executes a model (e.g., the ECON program in ADVISOR), it may be prudent to remove that action from the initialization sequence. The alternative is to preexecute the model and have it store its results where they are accessible to the inference engine (e.g., in a data table or spreadsheet). This can lead to faster consultations if the model is large and the same model results are used repeatedly by many consultations. On the other hand, it yields slower overall processing if different results are needed from an interactive model by different consultations.

No matter where an action appears in a rule set, the developer should ensure that it is accomplished in the fastest way possible. For instance, one common action involves the retrieval of a record from a data table. With data base management facilities like those of Guru, there are various commands available for record retrieval. For large tables, indexed retrieval (with the PLUCK command) is the fastest approach and should therefore be used instead of other retrieval methods (e.g., the OBTAIN command).

When performance gains through environment controls and rule set alterations are insufficient to meet project objectives, the performance objectives should be reevaluated and possibly revised. If actual performance still falls short, more drastic measures may need to be taken to enhance the expert system's performance. One possibility is to acquire a new, faster computer that still supports the development tool (and therefore, its rule set). Another possibility is to acquire a different development tool and restate the rule set in a form that can be processed by its inference engine. On the same computer, there is no guarantee this new rendition of the expert system will be faster than the earlier one. However, when thinking about acquiring a new development tool, there are a couple of fairly safe generalizations. All else being equal, support of rule set compilation results in faster consultations. Second, implementation of an inference engine in a language like assembler or C results in faster consultations than implementing the same inference engine in an interpretive language or a high-level language like Pascal.

There is one final point to always keep in mind when changes are made for the purpose of speeding up consultation performance. The changes must be made in a way that does not alter consultation results produced by the original rule set. To this end, the new expert system should again be tested for correctness after efficiency adjustments have been made and before proceeding to the stage of interface construction.

INTERFACE CONSTRUCTION

At this point in a development cycle, the necessary reasoning knowledge has been correctly captured in a rule set. However, little attention has been paid to the ergonomics of the expert system's user interface. While concentrating on getting the rules right, a developer normally does not want to bother with constructing an elaborate user interface at the same time. For this reason, the initial user interface built into a rule set typically consists of line-oriented INPUT and OUTPUT statements. The prompts and messages generated by these commands may be cursory or skeletal in nature—sufficient for interaction during expert testing, but not appropriate for end users of the expert system. At the very least, these will need to be made palatable for end users.

What is an appropriate user interface? The answer to this question depends on both user tastes and the facilities provided by the development tool for interface construction. Chapter 5 described the main kinds of facilities a tool might provide for customized user interfaces: line-oriented input/output, forms management, menu processing, function key definition, and combinations of these. The latter will be used in place of or in addition to the existing INPUT and OUTPUT commands. The project objectives may be detailed enough to prescribe the exact nature of the interface. If they are not, the expert may be able to provide further guidance based on prior interaction with prospective users. But the best source for details (e.g., wording, colors, screen layout) about a suitable interface is the expert system's ultimate user. As a useful starting point, the developer can pose alternate interface styles to the user for reactions and suggestions. Rapid modification of screen designs (e.g., with the PAINT command in Guru) while the user looks on can greatly accelerate the interface construction activity.

In addition to that aspect of the user interface that is built into the rule set, there is also the interface used for invoking the inference engine. The developer might simply allow the user to request a consultation with the native command language, natural language, or menus provided for inference-engine invocation. As explained in Chapter 7, another option is to construct a customized interface for making consultation requests. Here again, it is worthwhile to have the user actively involved in deciding the characteristics of this custom interface.

Another part of the user interface that a developer may wish to customize is the operation of the postconsultation explanation ability. As described in Chapter 7, a bona fide inference engine will have built-in HOW and WHY capabilities that allow users to explore the line of reasoning employed in a consultation. A developer can customize these standard explanation abilities to some extent by controlling the textual description that makes up each rule's reason in the rule set. With tools such as Guru, a developer can construct more specialized explanation abilities in addition to the standard HOW and WHY commands. In the case of Guru, this is accomplished by #HOW, an array whose elements are automatically set by the inference engine to indicate the sequence of rules fired in the consultation.

For example, if #HOW has elements of 13, 1, 8, 4, and 15, then the inference engine fired the 13th rule first, the 1st rule second, the 8th rule third, the 4th rule fourth and finally the 15th rule last. Because the inference engine sets the #HOW elements as soon as the reasoning portion of a consultation ends, the rule set's completion sequence can be designed to use the #HOW elements. Thus, in addition to reporting consultation results, a completion sequence can also report on the sequence of rules that were fired. Special actions can be carried out if a particular rule happens to have been fired. For instance, including:

```
I = 1
WHILE I <= #HCNT DO
    IF #HOW(I) NE 13 THEN I = I+1
        ELSE PLOT % PIE FROM NEWTITLE,OLDTITLE
            BREAK
    ENDIF
ENDWHILE
```

in the completion section will generate a percentage pie graph comparing the number of new titles to old titles if the 13th rule was fired during the consultation. The #HCNT utility variable's value is automatically set by the inference engine to indicate how many rules were fired during the consultation. Another common way to use #HOW in the completion sequence is to look up and print information held in spreadsheet rows or records corresponding to each rule that was fired.

The remaining activity in constructing a user interface consists of devising documentation for the user. This documentation should, of course, provide a clear explanation of the expert system's purpose, scope, and operation. Practice consultation sessions should be included to give the user a first-hand feel for the expert system's capabilities. The documentation can be in the form of manuals and/or on-line descriptions.

USER TESTING

Once the user interface has been constructed, the expert system is ready for user testing. The same series of sample problems that were used in expert testing may again be used here. The purpose of this testing is not to check the advice that is given, but rather the way in which it is requested, presented, and explained. The documentation is also being tested in these final trial runs of the expert system. User reactions to the expert system should be closely monitored by the developer (and expert, if possible) to ascertain what aspects of the user interface need adjustment. If the user was involved in the prior interface construction phase, these adjustments should normally be relatively minor.

INSTALLATION

After any needed adjustments are made in the user-testing stage, the developer is ready for the final stage of a development cycle: installation. This involves the introduction of the expert system into the workplace where it is consulted as desired by end users. During the installation stage, these users are instructed about how to invoke the inference engine, what kinds of inputs they may need to provide, and how to correctly interpret or apply consultation results. All of the conventional wisdom about successfully introducing technological change into an organization is valid when installing an expert system [3].

Installation can be followed by another cycle—one turn higher on the development spiral. For a developer, this means that the learning process continues. Taking the existing expert system as the starting point, the developer studies the problem area in greater depth or breadth, defines an expanded set of problems that the new expert system will address, specifies and tests its rule set, constructs and tests its interface, installs it, and proceeds to the next cycle in the development spiral.

CONCLUSION

Opportunities for building business expert systems abound for both small and large problems. In each case, the expert system is built by developing its rule set. The planning that precedes rule set development is much like the planning that would precede any project of comparable magnitude within the organization. The development process itself follows an evolutionary spiral composed of development cycles. Each cycle picks up where the last ended, building on the prior rule set. For a developer, the spiral represents a continuing education process in which more and more of an expert's reasoning knowledge is discovered and formalized in the rule set. Here, each development cycle was presented in terms of seven consecutive stages. Other characterizations of a development cycle (involving differnt stages or sequences) may be equally valuable. Many aspects of traditional systems analysis and project management can be applied to the development of expert systems.

Rule set development is a process of discovery and documentation. Research is under way (e.g.,[4]) to find ways of automating various aspects of the process. It would not be surprising to eventually see expert systems that can assist in this process—that is, an expert system that "picks the mind" of a human expert in order to build new expert systems. Until that time comes, the topics discussed in this chapter should serve as reminders to business expert system developers of issues to consider during the development process. They should also spark research into knowledge acquisition techniques and principles.

EXERCISES

1. What must be true in order for expert system opportunities to exist for small problems?
2. What is the single most important factor influencing the expert system development process?

3. Once an expert system opportunity has been identified and before a plan for its development is devised, what crucial managerial action must take place?

4. Identify the resources required for developing an expert system and indicate the order in which they should be selected.

5. What kinds of personality traits will a good rule set developer have?

6. Discuss the value of a prototype.

7. Suggest a sequence of activities that will constitute a development cycle.

8. What is the advantage of discovering a rule set's variables prior to discovering its rules?

9. What is the purpose of a rule's comment?

10. If an initialization sequence resets the values of environment variables, why is it a good idea to have the initialization sequence first save the original values of these variables?

11. What is a rule preaction and how might it be usefully applied?

12. Describe three techniques that can be used to check out an expert system's reasoning behavior.

13. In some quarters there is a tendency to judge the magnitude of an expert system in terms of how many rules it has. Explain the flaw in this viewpoint.

14. What is the advantage of avoiding an unnecessarily large number of rules in a rule set?

15. What are the drawbacks of collapsing too many rules into a single rule?

16. In what ways is #HOW valuable to a rule set developer?

17. Explain how to construct an initialization or completion sequence in such a way that its behavior can be easily altered without changing the rule set.

18. How can a developer specify a rule's conclusion in such a way that the effect of firing that rule can be altered from one consultation to the next without requiring a recompilation of the rule set?

References

1   Bonczek, R. H.; C. W. Holsapple; and A. B. Whinston. *Foundations of Decision Support Systems.* New York: Academic Press, 1981.

2   Holsapple, C. W.; K. Tam; and A. B. Whinston. "The Synergistic Integration of Expert System Technology with Conventional Knowledge Manage-

ment Facilities." In *Symposium on the Impact of Microcomputers on Operations Research.* Denver: March 1985

3 Lucas, H. *The Analysis, Design and Implementation of Information Systems.* New York: McGraw-Hill, 1976.

4 Mitchell, T. M.; P. E. Utgoff; and R. B. Banerji. "Learning Problem Solving Heuristics by Experimentation" in *Machine Learning: An Artificial Intelligence Approach,* eds. R. Michalski; J. Carbonnel; T. Mitchell. Palo Alto, California: Tioga Press, 1983.

5 Stefik, M. and D. G. Bobrow. "Object-Oriented Programming: Themes and Variations." *AI Magazine,* Winter, 1986.

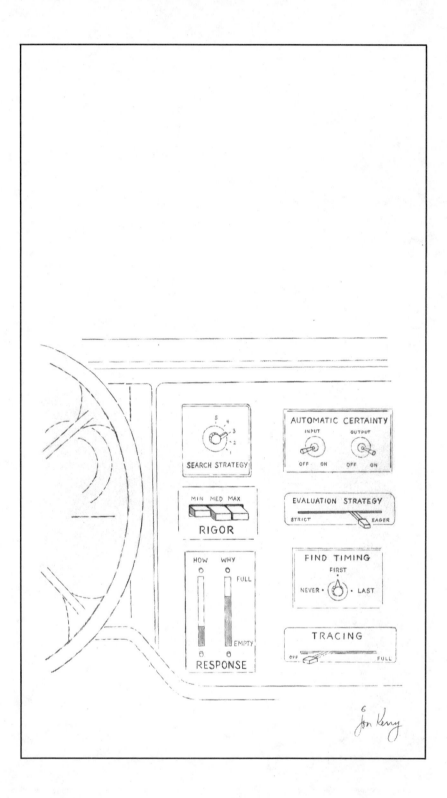

Chapter Nine

Reasoning Controls

The development cycle presented in Chapter 8 concentrates on the construction of a rule set. The advice generated by an expert system is heavily dependent on the rule set that has been developed, but it is also dependent on the way in which the inference engine reasons with that rule set. Two different inference engines, both performing forward (or reverse) reasoning for the same problem and using the same rule set, could carry out different lines of reasoning and/or produce different advice. The line of reasoning pursued by one may yield a faster consultation than the other. The advice given by one may be closer to human advice than that of the other. These differences exist when the two inference engines use two distinct variations of forward (or reverse) reasoning. Additional inference engines could use still other reasoning variations.

Ideally, an experienced developer might like to test the effects of each one on the rule set. The developer could then choose the inference engine that gives the best advice in the shortest amount of time. For different rule sets or different experts the choice could be different. The choice could even be different for different problems that use the same rule set. Of course, the developer typically does not have multiple inference engines to choose from when testing a rule set. However, the same benefit can be achieved from a single inference engine if it has built-in variability. By setting a few of the engine's reasoning controls, a developer can adjust the inference engine to exhibit any of many distinct variations of forward (or reverse) reasoning.

This chapter discusses several controls that govern the exact nature of an inference engine's reasoning behavior. One controls how rigorous the inference engine will be as it considers rules. Another control determines the order in which the inference engine selects rules for consideration. There is also the issue of what strategy to employ when trying to evaluate a premise. Yet another reasoning control deals with when (if at all) the inference engine executes any find actions defined for an unknown variable. Together, such controls allow an inference engine to display a multiplicity of reasoning behaviors. By simply setting the controls as desired, an experienced developer can choose the reasoning behavior that he or she deems to be most appropriate for the rule set, problem, and situation. Each of these kinds of controls is examined within the Guru context [1]. Relatively inexperienced developers can ignore all of the optional settings and stick with the inference engine's default setting for each control.

REASONING RIGOR

A human expert may reason about a problem in a very meticulous and exhaustive way, rigorously using all reasoning knowledge at his or her disposal in arriving at a recommendation. On other occasions that same expert may put less effort into solving a problem, halting as soon as some advice can be offered. Thus, the expert expends minimal effort and does not rigorously apply all available reasoning knowledge. The person requesting advice may not have the time to wait for fully rigorous reasoning, may not have the money to pay for it, or may need only rough advice. The degree of reasoning rigor that is needed, desired, or permitted depends on the situation surrounding a consultation session. Both the advice that is offered and the speed with which it is produced depend, in turn, on the degree of rigor.

It is not unreasonable to expect an expert system to be capable of emulating the human capacity for reasoning with varying degrees of rigor. This means that there should be some way of controlling how rigorous an inference engine is during a consultation. During one consultation it may exhaustively use all pertinent rules in arriving at a recommendation. In the very next consultation with the same rule set, the inference engine could stop as soon as the goal variable has a known value—even though further reasoning may have produced a different value for that variable. Absolute expert system rigor may not be needed or desired in all situations.

In the case of Guru's inference engine, reasoning rigor is controlled by the value of the E.RIGR environment variable. The possible settings range from A (absolute rigor) to M (minimal rigor). The exact effects of these environment settings naturally depend on whether forward or reverse reasoning has been requested. The Chapter 5 descriptions of both kinds of reasoning assumed that E.RIGR was set to A.

Forward Reasoning Rigor

When forward reasoning is requested, E.RIGR controls when the inference engine will stop considering further rules. Remember that forward reasoning begins by checking the first rule's premise. If it is true, the rule is fired. If the premise is either false or unknown, the rule is not fired and the inference engine proceeds to check the next rule's premise. The inference engine considers rules one after another in this manner, possibly iterating through the rule set's rules many times, until it has been rigorous enough in its efforts to establish a value for the goal variable. The meaning of "rigorous enough" is governed by the E.RIGR value. When the reasoning stops, the rule set's completion sequence is executed.

If E.RIGR has a value of A when the reasoning begins, then the inference engine repeatedly iterates through the rule set's rules. In each iteration it checks the premise of every rule that has not yet fired. Thus in the second and subsequent iterations, it considers every rule whose premise was formerly found to be false or unknown. If any of these now has a true premise, then it is fired. These iterations through the rule set continue until an iteration occurs in which no rule is fired. At that point, the inference engine has done all that it can possibly do. It has gleaned all that it can about the effects of the presented problem. These effects can now be reported to the user. The inference engine has been absolutely rigorous in its forward reasoning.

At the opposite extreme is minimal rigor. When E.RIGR is given a value of M, the inference engine stops considering rules as soon as the goal variable has a known value.* This may occur before there has been even one full iteration through the rule set or it may involve multiple iterations. At any rate, this setting always results in fewer rule considerations. It will therefore always yield faster reasoning than the setting for absolute rigor. It may or may not produce the same value for the goal variable and other variables reported via the rule set's completion sequence.

In the case of the ADVISOR rules of Figure 5–1, Chapter 5, minimal rigor will always yield the same value as absolute rigor for the NEW-QUOTA goal. This is because the rules for establishing a NEWQUOTA value happen to be mutually exclusive. If one of them fires, then it is assured that none of the others will fire. On the other hand, if a rule set contains multiple rules that could possibly fire for determining a value for the same variable, then absolute rigor and minimal rigor can give different values to the variable. This is because absolute rigor will consider all of those rules and fire all that are appropriate, while minimal rigor may consider and fire only one of them.

Between the two extremes is a compromise. By giving E.RIGR a value of C, the inference engine goes beyond minimal rigor but stops short of absolute rigor. This setting is like minimal rigor, except the inference engine continues to consider every unfired rule that could affect the goal variable if it were fired. If such a rule's premise is true, then the rule is fired. If the premise is false or unknown, then the inference engine will not consider this rule again in the current consultation. Typically, this compromise approach to reasoning rigor will cause the inference engine

---

*A value is known if its certainty factor exceeds the E.UNKN setting (default of 20).

to consider more rules (i.e., take more time) than minimal rigor, but fewer rules (i.e., less time) than absolute rigor. If rules are not mutually exclusive, the compromise could yield different variable values than either minimal or absolute reasoning.

To observe the processing differences between various degrees of rigor, a developer can pick a sample problem and use the automatic tracing mechanism to see how far the inference engine goes for each. No matter what degree of rigor is chosen, the usual HOW and WHY review will indicate the line of reasoning employed. Suppose a user consults the ADVISOR rule set with the command:

```
CONSULT ADVISOR TO TEST BASE
```

in order to get advice about the base amount. If E.RIGR's value is A, then the reasoning would go through all the same iterations as:

```
CONSULT ADVISOR TO TEST
```

with the rule set's default goal of NEWQUOTA. On the other hand, if E.RIGR's value is M, then the reasoning would consider no more than two rules. Rule R1's premise is checked first. If it is true, then R1 is fired and the completion sequence is executed. Otherwise, R2's premise will be true, R2 will be fired, and the completion sequence will then be executed. In other words, the inference engine's tracing and postconsultation explanations will be quite different depending on the degree of rigor. Though the resultant value for BASE will be the same regardless of E.RIGR, the values of other variables will be different. For instance, absolute rigor will give NEWQUOTA a known value while minimal rigor leaves its value as unknown.

Reverse Reasoning Rigor

When reverse reasoning is requested, E.RIGR controls how exhaustive the inference engine will be in considering the candidate rules for determining the value of an unknown variable. Remember that at various times during reverse reasoning, the inference engine will identify candidate rules for establishing the value of an unknown variable. A candidate rule is one whose action could possibly change the variable's value if it were fired. Therefore, E.RIGR controls how much effort the inference engine expends in attempting to establish an unknown variable's value. The same degree of rigor is applied to each unknown variable encountered during reverse reasoning.

If E.RIGR has a value of A when reverse reasoning begins, the inference engine will consider all candidate rules identified for an unknown variable. A candidate rule is considered by checking its premise. If the premise is true, the rule is fired and the next candidate rule is considered. If it is false, the rule is not fired and the next candidate rule is considered. If the premise is unknown, further reverse reasoning occurs in order to determine whether the premise is true or false, with the rule then being fired or not fired accordingly. This continues until all candidates rules for an unknown variable have been considered. Thus the inference engine has been absolutely rigorous in its reverse reasoning.

At the opposite extreme, E.RIGR can be given a value of M to indicate that minimal rigor should be used when considering an unknown variable's candidate rules. This means the inference engine will stop considering the variable's candidate rules as soon as the unknown variable is given a known value (that is, known with a certainty factor that exceeds E.UNKN). In other words, as soon as a candidate rule fires to establish a known value for the variable, the inference engine declares a cease fire for that variable and goes on to another unknown variable (if any). Because it never considers more rules than absolute rigor, reasoning with minimal rigor will always be at least as fast as the more exhaustive approach. Minimal rigor may or may not produce the same value as absolute rigor for an unknown variable.

In the case of the ADVISOR rules of Figure 5–1, as with forward reasoning, both approaches always yield the same values for unknown variables. This is because the candidate rules for establishing any unknown variable's value happen to be mutually exclusive. If one of the candidate rules fires, none of the others can. However, if a rule set contains multiple rules whose actions could change a variable's value and whose premises could all be true, then absolute rigor and minimal rigor can yield different values for the variable. This is because absolute rigor will consider all candidate rules and fire those whose premises can be determined to be true, while minimal rigor may consider and fire only one of them.

As with forward reasoning, there is a compromise between the two extremes in reverse reasoning rigor. By giving E.RIGR a value of C, the inference engine goes beyond minimal rigor for an unknown variable, but stops short of absolute rigor. This setting is like minimal rigor, except the inference engine continues to examine each remaining candidate rule. If its premise is true, the rule is fired. If its premise is false or unknown, the inference engine proceeds to the next candidate rule and so forth until all candidate rules have been examined. This differs from absolute rigor in that no reverse reasoning will occur in an attempt to ascertain values of unknown variables in premises of residual candidate rules. Typically, the compromise approach causes an inference engine to consider more rules (i.e., take more time) than minimal rigor, but fewer rules (i.e., less time) than absolute rigor. If candidate rules are not mutually exclusive, the compromise could yield a different value for the unknown variable than either minimal or absolute reasoning rigor.

To observe the processing differences between various degrees of rigor, a developer can pick a sample problem and use the automatic tracing mechanism to compare how far the inference engine goes when working on unknown variables. Regardless of the rigor setting, a HOW and WHY review will show the extent of the reasoning employed. Suppose a user consults the ADVISOR rule set with the command:

```
CONSULT ADVISOR
```

This causes reverse reasoning for the rule set's default goal of NEW-QUOTA. Thus NEWQUOTA will be one of the unknown variables encountered by the inference engine. From Figure 5-1, it is clear that the inference engine will identify three candidate rules (R15, R16, and R17) for NEWQUOTA. If E.RIGR's value is A, the inference engine will consider each one of them, complete with reverse reasoning for all unknowns in the premise of each. On the other hand, suppose E.RIGR's value is M. If reverse reasoning determines that the premise of R15 is true, then R15 is fired and the remaining two candidate rules are ignored. If R15 cannot be fired, then R16 is considered and is fired if reverse reasoning finds that its premise is true. Rule R17 is ignored unless R16 did not fire, in which case it is considered as a way for establishing a NEWQUOTA value. As with forward reasoning, minimal rigor is the most efficient choice when reverse reasoning with the ADVISOR rule set.

RULE SELECTION ORDER

As an inference engine reasons about a particular problem, it must select and process the rules in some order. The order in which rules are examined can affect both the speed with which advice is generated and the actual nature of the advice. At any moment during the reasoning, there will be one or more rules competing for the inference engine's attention. All prior discussion of reasoning processes has assumed that the competing rules are considered according to their relative positions in the rule set. However, other selection orders are also possible.

In the case of forward reasoning, the group of competing rules consists of all unfired rules that have not yet been considered in the present iteration. When the first iteration begins, all rules are competing for consideration. Which one should be considered first, which one second, and so forth? As each subsequent iteration begins, the number of competing rules diminishes because some rules have been fired in the prior iteration. Regardless of which iteration it is in and which degree of rigor is being used, an inference engine examines competing rules according to a specific selection order.

In the case of reverse reasoning, the currently competing rules are all of the unconsidered rules that are candidates for establishing an unknown variable's value. When the inference engine begins working on an unknown variable, all of the variable's candidate rules are competing for consideration. Which one should be considered first, which one second, and so forth? Regardless of which unknown variable is being worked on and which degree of rigor is being used, an inference engine examines the competing candidate rules according to a specific selection order.

The selection order that Guru's inference engine employs during a particular consultation is controlled by the value of E.SORD. Because so many (over 50) selection orders are possible, the desired order is represented by a sequence of one or more codes. Each code denotes a particular selection criterion. If more than one code is specified for E.SORD, the first takes highest precedence. The second takes next highest precedence, and so on. Before reasoning begins, E.SORD can be set to any one of the code sequences enumerated in Table 9–1. Each represents one of the distinct selection strategies supported by Guru's inference engine.

During the expert-testing stage of a development cycle, a developer is free to experiment with different selection strategies by simply changing the value of E.SORD before invoking the inference engine. If the rule set does not contain multiple rules that can all fire in a consultation and can all change the value of the same variable, then the chosen selection strategy will not affect the consultation results or efficiency—provided absolute rigor is employed. If the reasoning is less rigorous, different selection orders can yield different reasoning speeds and, in the case of forward reasoning, different variable values as well. If a rule set contains multiple rules whose conclusions could change the same variable and whose premises are not mutually exclusive, then the value of that variable is sensitive to the selection order. The main point of all of this is that the developer can use a selection order mechanism to adjust the reasoning behavior for a particular problem or rule set. The adjustment may be for the purpose of more nearly replicating the advice a human expert would give or for the purpose of optimizing reasoning speeds.

There are too many selection strategies to fully discuss here, so the descriptions that follow concentrate on the six primary selection criteria that correspond to the six single-code possibilities for E.SORD:

- F: Select the competing rule closest to the first rule in the rule set, then the next closest competing rule, and so on.

- P: Select the competing rule with the highest priority, then the one with the next highest priority, and so on.

- C: Select the competing rule with the cheapest action, then the one with the next cheapest action, and so on.

- U: Select the competing rule with the fewest unknown variables in its premise, then the one with the next fewest unknowns, and so on.

TABLE 9-1 Distinct selection order possibilities

F (first)			
P (prioritize)	PH	PHC	PHCU
		PHR	
		PHU	PHUC
	PC	PCH	PCHU
		PCR	
		PCU	PCUH
	PR		
	PU	PUH	PUHC
		PUR	
		PUC	PUCH
C (cheapest)	CH	CHP	CHPU
		CHR	
		CHU	CHUP
	CP	CPH	CPHU
		CPR	
		CPU	CPUH
	CU	CUH	CUHP
		CUR	
		CUP	CUPH
	CR		
U (unknown)	UH	UHC	UHCP
		UHR	
		UHP	UHPC
	UC	UCH	UCHP
		UCR	
		UCP	UCPH
	UP	UPH	UPHC
		UPR	
		UPC	UPCH
	UR		
H (highest)	HC	HCP	HCPU
		HCR	
		HCU	HCUP
	HR		
	HP	HPC	HPCU
		HPR	
		HPU	HPUC
	HU	HUC	HUCP
		HUP	HUPC
		HUR	
R (random)			

- H: Select the competing rule whose actions would give the highest certainty to the unknown variable, then the one with the next highest certainty, and so on.

- R: Select competing rules in a random order.

The remaining (multicode) strategies shown in Table 9-1 are simply combinations of two or more of these criteria.

The First (F) Criterion

If E.SORD has a value of F, competing rules will be selected according to their relative order in the rule set. Rule names do not in any way affect selection order. For instance, suppose rule R2 has been specified prior to rule R1 in the ADVISOR rule set. When these two rules are competing, the inference engine will select R2 for consideration before R1. Such a rearrangement would be preferable if Jack happens to know that for most consultations the sales will not exceed the quota by more than 15 percent. With minimal reasoning rigor, this means that most consultations will be faster because they do not need to consider rule R1 whose premise will be more often false than true.

This same technique of rule arrangement can be usefully applied throughout a rule set. As rules for determining a variable's value are elicited from an expert, the developer can ask which are most and least likely to be needed. The rules are then arranged accordingly—most likely to least likely. Even if E.SORD has some value other than F (which is its default), such an arrangement can still be worthwhile. This is because the relative order of rules in a rule set is the ultimate tie-breaker. Whenever the selection strategy indicated by E.SORD results in a tie between two competing rules, the rule that appears closest to the start of the rule set is selected.

The Priority (P) Criterion

If E.SORD has a value of P, then the selection order among competing rules is determined by rule priorities. When a rule is being specified, the developer can give it a priority. As an example, rule R1 might be specified as:

```
RULE: R1
  PRIORITY: 70
  IF: SALES > 1.15*QUOTA
  THEN: BASE = QUOTA + SALES - 1.15 * QUOTA
  REASON: In cases where the sales for this product exceeded
          the quota by more than 15%, the base amount for
          the new quota is set to the past quota plus the
          excess sales amount.
```

If the priority selection criterion is in force and R1 is a candidate rule, then R1 will be selected before other candidate rules having lower priorities and after those with higher priorities. As explained earlier, if some

other rule also has a priority of 70, then the priority tie is broken by selecting the one that appears nearest the start of the rule set.

Any rule can be given any priority in the range from 0 through 100.
If no priority has been explicitly specified for a rule, then the rule set
manager automatically gives it a priority of 50. Generally, a rule's priority is easier to change than the rule's relative position in a rule set. Rule
prioritization gives a handy way of forcing one competing rule to be
considered before another. Sometimes an expert will describe two rules,
both of which can affect the same variable, and make the additional
comment that one must be considered before the other. This is easily accomplished by giving that rule a higher priority than the other rule and
setting E.SORD to yield a prioritized selection order.

The Cost (C) Criterion

In reasoning about a problem, it is not unusual for a human expert to
postpone expensive actions as long as possible. It may turn out that a
solution can be reached before a costly action has to be taken, resulting
in savings of time and effort. The same effect can be achieved in inference engine reasoning by letting E.SORD have a value of C. This causes
the least costly competing rule to be selected first, then the second
cheapest competing rule, and so on. When less than absolute rigor is
employed, this selection order can affect the inference engine's reasoning speed and advice—just as it does for the human expert.

The rule set developer has full discretion over specifying the relative
costs of rules. A rule's cost reflects the developer's assessment of how expensive it would be to take the rule's preactions, test its premise, and/or
carry out its conclusion if the premise happens to be true. Suppose rules
R1 and R2 of Figure 5–1 are revised to have both priorities and costs.

```
RULE: R1
  PRIORITY: 70
  COST: 15
  IF: SALES > 1.15 * QUOTA
  THEN: BASE = QUOTA + SALES - 1.15 * QUOTA

RULE: R2
  PRIORITY: 60
  COST: 10
  IF: SALES <= 1.15 * QUOTA
  THEN: BASE = QUOTA
```

Jack has given rule R1 a somewhat higher cost than R2 because its conclusion involves greater computational effort. If E.SORD's value is P,

rule R1 will be selected before R2 when the two rules compete. However, if E.SORD's value is C, rule R2 is selected before R1 because of its lower cost. A rule's relative cost can be anywhere from 0 through 100.

The Unknown (U) Criterion

When confronted with several competing rules, a plausible strategy is to select the one with the fewest unknown variables in its premise. If one of the rules has no unknown variables in its premise, the truth or falseness can be determined very rapidly. It will take longer to make this determination for a rule with one unknown variable in its premise. If there are 10 unknown variables, even more time and effort are required. By focusing first on rules about which the least is unknown, an inference engine may be able to achieve a faster reasoning speed—provided the degree of rigor is less than absolute. This kind of selection order results if E.SORD's value is U when reasoning begins.

The Highest (H) Certainty Criterion

Another possible selection strategy is to first choose the competing rule whose action involving the unknown variable has the highest certainty.* The next highest is chosen second and so forth. In the event of minimal rigor, the rule that is able to make the greatest contribution to the variable value's certainty is fired. This strategy is only of interest when certainty factors appear in actions of at least some of the rule set's rules.

Consider the revised versions of rules R6 and R7 that were discussed in Chapter 6:

```
RULE: R6
  IF: GROWTH >= .04 AND UNEMPLOYMENT < .076
  THEN: ECONOMY = "good" CF 90

RULE: R7
  IF: GROWTH >= .02 AND UNEMPLOYMENT < .055
  THEN: ECONOMY = "good" CF 80
```

When the ECONOMY variable is unknown, these are competing rules. If E.SORD has a value of H, then R6 will be selected for consideration before R7. This is because the 90 certainty factor in R6's action for changing the value of ECONOMY exceeds the corresponding certainty factor of 80 in R7's conclusion.

---

*In the case of forward reasoning, this "unknown variable" is of course the goal or requested test variable.

The Random (R) Criterion

If the value of E.SORD is R as reasoning begins, the inference engine will make random selections from among competing rules. This means that the inference engine will very likely consider rules in a different order in separate consultations involving exactly the same problem. While this may mimic the way in which some human experts reason, it is probably advisable only when reasoning is completely rigorous and the developer is indifferent about the selection order.

Combining Selection Criteria

As Table 9–1 shows, the six selection codes can be combined in various ways to yield additional selection orders. Basically, these give alternatives to using the rule set order to break ties. For instance:

```
E.SORD = "PC"
```

will cause the inference engine to select from among competing rules in a similar way to:

```
E.SORD = "P"
```

The difference is that when two competing rules have the same priority, PC breaks the tie by selecting the rule having the cheapest cost. Remember, the P by itself breaks a tie by selecting the rule positioned nearest the start of the rule set.

Even with two rule selection criteria, there may still be a tie. Any of the three-code permutations appearing in Table 9–1 can be used to control how such a tie is broken. For instance, it is broken based on the fewest number of unknown variables if the third code in E.SORD's value is a U (as in PCU). This can be carried a step further, by assigning a sequence of four selection codes to E.SORD. If there is still a tie even after the inference engine has tried four selection criteria, then the tie is broken based on the order of the tied rules in the rule set.

PREMISE EVALUATION STRATEGY

Think of yourself as an inference engine engaged in reverse reasoning. You have just selected some rule for consideration. Having carried out its preactions (if any), you are now ready to check its premise. You notice that the premise cannot be immediately evaluated as either true or false because it has several unknown variables. You realize that a value needs to be determined for at least one (and perhaps all) of these unknown variables before you can evaluate the premise as being either true or false. You will use reverse reasoning to establish values for one or more of the unknown variables. But which unknown variable will you work on first, second, and so on? Will you work on getting values for all of the unknowns, or only some of them? When will you actually test the premise to try to see whether it is true or false? These are some of the issues facing an inference engine as it endeavors to evaluate the selected rule's premise. Guru's inference engine allows a developer to furnish the answers to these questions.

Sequence of Unknowns

Unknowns in a premise are normally processed from left to right, unless some other sequence is desired. A different sequence can be specified in the rule's definition with a NEEDS clause. For instance, rule R16 could be defined as:

```
RULE: R16
  IF: WEAK AND KNOWN("BASE") AND KNOWN("EFACTOR")
      AND KNOWN("PFACTOR") AND KNOWN("LAFACTOR")
  NEEDS: BASE,PFACTOR,EFACTOR,LAFACTOR,WEAK
  THEN: INPUT FALL NUM WITH\
        "Enter percent sales decrease due to falling interest in "\
        + PROD
        NEWQUOTA=BASE*(1+EFACTOR+LAFACTOR+PFACTOR-FALL/100)
```

Here, the NEEDS clause will cause the inference engine to work on BASE first, then PFACTOR, and so on. In general, a NEEDS clause can be specified for any rule, should include all premise variables that could be unknown, and can sequence those variables in any order.* Thus, the developer can easily control which unknown variable is the first one subjected to reverse reasoning, which one is next, and so on.

Think about a premise composed of multiple conditions connected by the AND operator. For such a premise, the developer might position the conditions that are least likely to be true at the beginning of the premise. In other words, if one of the conditions in this premise turns out to be false, we would like the inference engine to discover that fact

---

*Specifying a NEEDS clause for every rule will probably yield faster rule set compilation because it allows the compiler to spend less effort in figuring out what variables might need to be tested when the premise is evaluated.

as soon as possible. Once a condition is found to be false, the inference engine knows that the entire premise must be false. Values will not need to be found for any unknown variables that remain in the premise's other conditions. This yields faster processing than a situation where all of the premise's unknown variables are worked on before the very last condition in the premise is discovered to be false.

A reverse strategy for sequencing conditions (and therefore variables) in a premise should be used when they are connected by the OR operator. As soon as any condition is found to be true, the overall premise is known to be true—regardless of whether the remaining conditions are true, false, or unknown. This suggests that the developer should sequence OR conditions from the one that is most likely to be true with minimal reverse reasoning effort to the one that is least likely to be true while requiring maximal reverse reasoning effort. The possible exception to this strategy occurs when certainty factors exist for the premise's variables. In such a situation, stopping with the first true condition may very well result in a different overall certainty factor for the premise than an alternative strategy of determining the certainty factors of all true conditions in the premise.

Timing

The foregoing discussion suggests three distinct approaches to timing the testing of a premise. These correspond to the three possible settings for Guru's E.TRYP environment variable: E (eager), P (patient), and S (strict). An E setting causes the inference engine to evaluate the premise's conditions each time one of its unknown variables becomes known via reverse reasoning. If this evaluation of conditions provides sufficient evidence to make the premise either true or false, testing of the premise halts and the rule is fired or not fired accordingly. The P setting for E.TRYP involves a more prolonged strategy in which the inference engine does not try to evaluate the premise until it has made an attempt to establish a value for each of the premise's unknown variables. If E.TRYP's value is S, the inference engine proceeds to work on each unknown variable until it either cannot establish a value for one of them or has established values for all of them. In the former case, the premise remains unknown, so the rule does not fire. In the latter case, the premise is then evaluated and the rule is fired if it is true. In either case, processing proceeds to the next candidate rule.

Which of these E.TRYP settings should be chosen for consulting a particular rule set? The answer depends on what kinds of premises will need to be tested. It is fair to say that no one strategy for testing premises is "best" for all kinds of premises. Suppose, for instance, that variables in the conjunctive (i.e., ANDed) premises of rules in Figure 5–1 have been arranged so that the variables most likely to be unknown appear at the left of their respective premises. A good choice for E.TRYP would then be S. However, this is not such a good strategy for rules R9 and R12, whose premises contain OR operators. If their conditions are organized from the most to least likely to be true, then the E strategy would be preferable to S.

It is easy to make exceptions to the E.TRYP strategy by specifying the testing strategy that should be used for individual rules. For instance, rule R9 might be specified in the rule set as:

```
RULE: R9
  TEST:E
  IF: GROWTH < .02 OR UNEMPLOYMENT >= .082
  THEN: ECONOMY = "poor"
```

As a result, the inference engine will ignore E.TRYP whenever rule R9's premise is being checked. For R9, it will use the E premise-testing strategy regardless of E.TRYP's value. That same testing strategy could be specified for R12 in a similar fashion.

A few general observations on picking efficient and appropriate testing strategies for individual rules can be offered. If a premise has only one condition, or multiple conditions not involving the OR operator, and with unknowns loaded toward the beginning of the premise, then the S premise-testing strategy is a decent choice. On the other hand, if conditions most likely to be false are positioned toward the beginning of the premise, the E strategy may give faster processing. When a premise has multiple conditions involving the OR operator, and certainty factors do not dip below 100, the E strategy is normally best. Lower certainty factors would suggest that the P strategy be employed if the developer wants to incorporate as much as possible into the premise's overall certainty factor. A developer is free to depart from these guidelines as warranted by the idiosyncratic nature of a particular rule, by the effort to make the inference engine produce advice that more closely mirrors the human expert's recommendations, or by efficiency considerations.

WORKING ON AN UNKNOWN VARIABLE

Once again, think of yourself as an inference engine engaged in reverse reasoning. In the course of evaluating the premise of some selected rule, you encounter an unknown variable. You know that there may be two approaches to establishing its value (recall Chapter 5). You could use reverse reasoning, which begins by identifying candidate rules for the unknown variable and endeavors to fire at least one of them. Or if the rule set contains a variable description for the unknown variable, you could carry out the actions specified in that description. Which approach should you take?

Guru's inference engine will first attempt to establish the variable's value by reverse reasoning. If it is successful, processing for the premise proceeds. However, if reverse reasoning is unable to infer a value, the inference engine executes the variable's find actions (if any exist) before proceeding. This strategy can be easily altered by changing the E.WHN environment variable's value from its default of L. Rather than executing find actions as a last resort, the developer may decide that the inference engine should execute an unknown variable's find actions first. Only if they do not make the variable known will the inference engine attempt reverse reasoning for that unknown variable. The value of E.WHN should be set to F if this alternative strategy is desired.

Because the execution of find actions is typically less time consuming than reverse reasoning, the F setting for E.WHN may result in faster reasoning. On the other hand, it may give a different consultation result than the last resort strategy when both the find actions and reverse reasoning could potentially establish values for the variable. The developer is free to choose either approach for a particular consultation, depending on the desired effect. There is one other E.WHN setting that could be used: By giving E.WHN a value of N, the developer causes the inference engine to never execute any variable's find actions during a consultation.

It is common for the developer to want some variables to be handled in one way (e.g., find actions as a first resort) while others are to be handled in a different way (e.g., find actions as a last resort). In such a situation, each variable description can contain an indication of when its find actions are to be executed. For example, the variable description:

```
VARIABLE: LOCALADS
   WHEN: F
   FIND: REPCOL=LOOKUP(REP,#Y2,#Y13,#Z2)
         LOCALADS=LOOKUP(PROD,#A18,#A31,#(18,REPCOL))
```

forces the inference engine to always execute the find actions as a first resort when working on LOCALADS. Thus, the value of E.WHN is ignored when trying to establish a value for LOCALADS. Screen 8 in the color insert shows how this timing for LOCALADS would appear through the menu interface for rule set management.

SETTING THE REASONING CONTROLS

The E.RIGR, E.SORD, E.TRYP, and E.WHN variables give considerable latitude for adjusting an inference engine's reasoning behavior. One final issue is when should these controls be set. During the expert-testing stage of a development cycle, they are probably set interactively by the developer as opposed to being set by actions within the rule set's initialization sequence. This allows the developer to easily study the effects of different settings without necessitating recompilation of the rule set. For instance, Jack may want to examine the effects of minimal versus complete rigor for some particular problem. He would enter:

```
E.RIGR = "M"
CONSULT ADVISOR TO TEST BASE
```

to see the effects of minimal rigor and then:

```
E.RIGR = "A"
CONSULT ADVISOR TO TEST BASE
```

to explore the effects of absolute rigor.

As the user interface is being constructed, the reasoning controls should be incorporated into the rule set's initialization sequence. This guarantees that the inference engine will obey those specific settings, rather than the "chance" values the environment variables may happen to have prior to the consultation request. A user of the expert system should not be expected to know about the E.RIGR, E.SORD, E.TRYP, or E.WHN environment variables.

Settings for the reasoning controls can be "hardwired" into the initialization sequence. By including the commands:

```
E.RIGR = "M"
E.SORD = "PU"
E.TRYP = "E"
E.WHN  = "F"
```

in the initialization sequence, the indicated settings will control the reasoning for every consultation of the rule set. As an alternative to "hardwiring" the settings, a developer may wish to make some of them conditional or even prompt the user as a basis for determining the reasoning controls. For example, the commands:

```
INPUT RIGOR STR WITH "Do you need a quick answer? (Y/N)"
IF RIGOR="Y" THEN LET E.RIGR="M"
     ELSE LET E.RIGR="A"
ENDIF
```

might be incorporated into the initialization sequence. Of course, prompts should insulate the user from terms such as *inference rigor, selection order, premise testing,* and *find actions.*

CONCLUSION

Forward and reverse reasoning are two fundamentally different approaches to reasoning. Within each approach, many variations are possible. There are many kinds of reverse reasoning and many kinds of forward reasoning. Because no single kind of reasoning is best in all situations, skilled developers find it valuable to have mechanisms for easily adjusting an inference engine's exact reasoning behavior so it can differ from one consultation to another and from one rule set to another. Such adjustments can help the developer build an expert system whose advice more closely resembles that of the human expert. They can also allow the developer to tune the inference engine in the interests of maximizing consultation speeds.

Aspects of reasoning that can be adjusted include the degree of reasoning rigor, the selection order for considering competing rules, the testing strategy employed for premise evaluation, and the timing of reverse reasoning for unknown variables. These can be adjusted from one consultation to the next by simply changing the values of environment variables. The latter two controls are also meaningful on a rule-by-rule and variable-by-variable basis, respectively. It is possible to set the reasoning controls prior to a consultation or have them set by the inference engine whenever it executes the rule set's initialization sequence. The two chapters that follow discuss additional reasoning controls that pertain specifically to reasoning with uncertainty and with fuzzy variables.

EXERCISES

1. What is a reasoning control?
2. Why should an inference engine provide an assortment of reasoning controls?
3. What kinds of reasoning controls might an inference engine reasonably be expected to support?
4. Why might the rigor setting affect the solution derived by the inference engine?
5. Describe a situation where priorities are a worthwhile selection criterion.
6. What role does a rule's NEEDS clause play?

7. Describe three distinct strategies for trying to evaluate a premise that contains unknown variables.

8. What premise-testing strategy should usually be avoided for a disjunctive premise involving certainty factors below 100? Why?

9. What is the advantage of being able to specify different testing strategies for different rules?

10. Explain the role of E.WHN and how it can be overridden.

11. Someone claims that the availability of many environment variables makes the development process more difficult and complex than it would otherwise be. Explain why this claim is incorrect. Explain why the exact opposite is true.

Reference

1 *Guru Reference Manual*, vol. 1. Lafayette, Ind.: MDBS, Inc. 1985.

Brace yourselves—we're cutting through the uncertainty zone.

Chapter Ten

Certainty Factor Algebras

It is a fact of nature that people are not always certain about all of the knowledge they use. Human experts are able to work with various uncertainties when they reason about problems. There may be uncertainty about the precise nature of the problem, about the factors involved in reasoning about that problem, or about some of the reasoning knowledge itself. All of these are taken into account in arriving at some advice for the problem. Examples of various sources of uncertainty were discussed in Chapter 6. In a rule set, such uncertainties can be represented as certainty factors. Inference engine techniques for processing certainty factors during the reasoning process were also introduced in Chapter 6.

An inference engine must use a particular certainty factor algebra when it derives a new certainty factor from existing certainty factors. This algebra is merely a mathematical convention that determines how the new certainty factor is computed. Several examples of alternative algebras (e.g., the minimum versus the product methods) were introduced in Chapter 6. The alternatives are now examined in more detail. Some inference engines do not allow a choice among different certainty factor algebras. They are akin to a human expert that is able to think in only one way, regardless of the problem being faced. Nevertheless, it is still worthwhile for a developer to understand the single algebra that is employed.

Many human experts tend to be more adaptable. Their methods of dealing with uncertainty will differ, depending on the situation. In one situation, an expert may be daring about the way in which uncertainties are combined. For another problem, the expert may be risk averse. In yet another context, the expert's handling of uncertainty may fall between these extremes. In order to approximate this adaptability, an inference engine should have certainty factor controls. The different settings for these controls correspond to different certainty factor algebras.

In the Guru environment, these controls are the E.CFJO, E.CFCO, and E.CFVA environment variables [2]. The former two govern the certainty factor algebras that the inference engine will use in computing the certainties of expressions that it evaluates. The setting of the third environment variable indicates what algebra to use when computing the certainty factor of a variable. Three other environment variables related to certainty factors are also discussed in this chapter. They are E.UNKN, E.ICF, and E.OCF.

If a rule set does not involve any explicit certainty factors (i.e., everything has a certainty of 100), then the settings of certainty controls are of no interest. Inexperienced rule set developers will probably be unconcerned about alternative settings and just stay with the standard default values for the certainty controls. However as experience grows, alternative settings may be fruitfully explored during the expert-testing stage of a development cycle. This is accomplished by simply altering environment variable values prior to successive consultations with a sample problem. The settings can be examined from the standpoint of which causes the inference engine to generate advice that most closely replicates the expert's advice.

THRESHOLD OF THE UNKNOWN

When are we certain enough about a value to consider it to be known? If the value of a premise variable has a certainty factor of 12 out of 100, should the inference engine regard that variable as being known for purposes of premise evaluation? Or should the inference engine regard the variable's value as being unknown because of the "low" certainty? Is 12 really a "low" degree of certainty? What about a certainty factor of 22, 32, or 82? Might not they also be viewed as too low to regard the variable as being known? The answer to all of these questions is that it depends on the nature of the problem and how the human expert characterizes uncertainties.

As explained in Chapter 6, the point where a certainty factor becomes too low to regard the variable's value as being known is called the unknown threshold. Some inference engines give a developer no control over the level of this threshold. For instance, if the level is fixed at 20, the developer will need to keep it in mind when eliciting certainties from an expert. The developer will need to revise these certainties in cases where the expert regards 20 as being a fairly high degree of certainty within the context of a particular problem area. In other words, the expert and developer must conform to an unknown threshold that is arbitrarily fixed.

Other inference engines permit a developer to set the unknown threshold at any desired level. In other words, the inference engine can conform to the expert's and developer's way of characterizing certainties for a particular problem area. The Guru E.UNKN variable is an illustration of this kind of certainty control. Its value can be changed to any number between 1 and 100 at any time before the actual reasoning within a consultation begins. Thus, the effects of alternative E.UNKN settings on reasoning behavior can be readily examined during the expert-testing stage of a development cycle.

CERTAINTY FACTORS FOR EXPRESSION

The inference engine for a business expert system is apt to encounter many expressions during a consultation. Some of these expressions are likely to be numeric, such as 1.15*QUOTA. Others will most certainly be simple logical expressions, such as GROWTH > = .04 or SALES > 1.15*QUOTA. In earlier chapters each of these has been referred to as a condition.* Notice that a condition can itself contain a numeric expression. Conditions can be connected by Boolean operators (e.g., AND, OR, XOR) to form compound logical expressions such as GROWTH > = .04 AND UNEMPLOYMENT < .076. The premise of every rule is a logical expression. String expressions such as TRIM(REP) may also be encountered.

Whenever it encounters an expression, the inference engine will try to evaluate it using the values of the variables involved. If a numeric expression can be evaluated, then its value is a number. Similarly, a string expression will have a string of text as its value. A logical expression will evaluate to either TRUE or FALSE. In situations where a numeric, string, or logical expression cannot be successfully evaluated, its value is said to be unknown. If the inference engine's evaluation is successful, then the expression's value is known with a specific degree of certainty. This certainty depends on three things. First, there are the certainty factors of the variables' values that were used in evaluating the expression. Second, there are the kinds of operators (e.g., +, *, >, =, AND, OR) specified in the expression. Third, there is the certainty factor algebra that is employed.

Two controls exist for selecting the algebra used by the inference engine for computing certainty factors of expression. Bear in mind that an expression *value* is always computed according to the operators and is unaffected by individual certainties of variables in the expression. Those certainties are combined to yield a certainty factor for the expression's value.** For numeric expressions, string expressions, conditions, and logical expressions involving AND or XOR, the E.CFJO controls the joint certainty factor algebra that is used. For a logical expression of the form:

---

*Simple logical expressions are also sometimes called relational expressions because they often involve a relationship (e.g., greater than, equality, inclusion) between two terms. The >, =, IN, and similar symbols are examples of relational operators.

**If that certainty factor falls below the unknown threshold indicated by E.UNKN's setting, then the expression's value is regarded as being unknown.

```
condition-1 OR condition-2
```

the certainties of condition-1 and condition-2 are combined in a confirmative fashion, according to the algebra indicated by the E.CFCO setting.

Joint Certainty Factor Algebras

As the examples in Chapter 6 have shown, there are several kinds of expressions that are susceptible to joint certainty factor computation. These can be summarized as shown in Table 10–1. In each instance, there is at least one variable in the expression. If there is only one variable, then the certainty factor for the expression's value will be the same as that of the variable. This is because each constant (e.g., 2, 3, 50, "good") has a certainty factor of 100. For instance, if LOCALADS has a certainty factor of 57, it makes sense that the value of LOCALADS/1000 should also have a certainty factor of 57—no matter what certainty factor algebra is selected.

When an expression of the kind shown in Table 10–1 involves multiple variables, their certainty factors need to be combined to produce a joint certainty factor for the expression's value. The algebra used for computing joint certainties of expressions is controlled by the value of E.CFJO. The permissible settings for this environment variable are M, P, A, and B. Each setting corresponds to one of the four joint certainty

TABLE 10–1 Expressions having joint certainties

Types of expression	*Examples*
Numeric	LOCALADS/1000 MIN(GROWTH, .085-UNEMPLOYMENT) I + J + 2 (28 + X) ** 3 SQRT((QOH − 50)/5) REVENUE − EXPENSE
String	TRIM(FNAME) + " " + LNAME TRIM(STREET) + " " + TRIM(CITY) + " " + STATE + " " + ZIP "This is the report for " + REP
Condition	GROWTH > = .02 PROD IN ["computer", "romance", "scifi"] EOQ < SQRT((QOH − 50)/5) ECONOMY = "good"
Logical (compound)	ECONOMY = "good" AND KNOWN ("GROWTH") GROWTH > = .04 AND UNEMPLOYMENT < .076 GROWTH > = .02 AND GROWTH < .04 AND UNEMPLOYMENT > = .055

algebras described below.* Each description refers to x and y, where these simply denote two certainty factors that are being combined in a joint fashion.

Minimum method (**E.CFJO** = "**M**"). When the minimum method is selected, the joint certainty of an expression is:

```
MIN(x,y)
```

Inference engines that do not support multiple algebras for joint certainty computation typically use this method. This method is also Guru's default setting for E.CFJO.

Consider the expression:

```
GROWTH >= .04 AND UNEMPLOYMENT < .076
```

and assume that both conditions are true—the first with a certainty factor of 90 and the second with a certainty factor of 60. What is the joint certainty of this expression's TRUE value? It is MIN(90,60) = 60. The rationale is that a chain is only as strong as its weakest link. If we are 90 percent sure that growth is at least 4 percent and 60 percent sure that the unemployment rate is under 7.6 percent, then we cannot be more than 60 percent sure that *both* conditions will hold.

As a second example consider the expression:

```
REVENUE-EXPENSE
```

and assume REVENUE's value has a certainty factor of 50 while there is a certainty factor of 70 for the EXPENSE value. What joint certainty should be attributed to the difference between revenues and expenses? It is MIN (50,70) = 50. If we're half sure about revenues and 70 percent sure about expenses, the minimum method says that we should not be more than half sure about the difference between them.

Product method (**E.CFJO** = "**P**"). When the product method is being used, the joint certainty of an expression is:

```
(x*y)/100
```

The product method is more conservative than the minimum method. The product will always be less than or equal to the minimum. In thinking about the minimum method, one cannot deny that a chain is no stronger than its weakest link. But is it even as strong as its weakest

---

*The M and P settings have also been described in Chapter 6.

link? The product method answers no. It says that both uncertainties should be reflected in the joint certainty.

Once again consider the expression:

```
GROWTH >= .04 AND UNEMPLOYMENT < .076
```

assuming 90 and 60 certainty factors respectively for the two conditions. What is the joint certainty factor? With the product method it is $(90*60)/100 = 54$, which is less than what the minimum method would yield. Unlike the minimum method, this algebra argues that both uncertainties should contribute to the overall degree of certainty.

Suppose that the 90 certainty factor is replaced by 80. The product philosophy says we should be less certain about the expression's value; the joint certainty would be $(80*60)/100 = 48$. In contrast, the minimum method would still give a joint certainty of $MIN(80,60) = 60$, even though there is now less certainty about one of the conditions. In fact, the first condition's certainty factor could fluctuate from 60 to 100 without affecting the minimum method's joint certainty. With the product method, each shift upward or downward in x or y yields a corresponding shift in the joint certainty. Notice that if the first certainty shifted all the way to 100, the product method would yield the same result as the minimum method: $(100*60)/100 = 60$. As another example, again consider the expression:

```
REVENUE-EXPENSE
```

assuming certainty factors of 50 and 70 respectively for the two variables. With the product method, the joint certainty computed for the difference will be $(50*70)/100 = 35$. Once again both certainty factors contribute to a joint certainty that is less than either of them.

In thinking about which joint certainty algebra to adopt for a particular problem area, a developer may find it useful to ask the expert about which of the two methods matches his or her own way of jointly combining uncertainties. This can be done by way of a few examples drawn from expressions specified in the rule set. For each, the developer can ask whether the expert deems a minimum or product more reasonable. Or the developer could ask what joint certainty the expert would invent and then check to see whether it is closer to the minimum or the product. The two remaining joint certainty methods accommodate experts whose reasoning falls between these extremes.

Average method (E.CFJO = "A"). When the average method is employed, the joint certainty of an expression is:

```
(MIN(x,y)+(x*y)/100)/2
```

If neither the minimum nor product methods seems to fit the expert or problem area, then the average method offers a compromise between the two. For the growth/unemployment example, it yields a joint certainty of:

```
(MIN(90,60)+(90*60)/100)/2=(60+54)/2=57
```

For the revenue/expense example, the average method produces a joint certainty of:

```
(MIN(50,70)+(50*70)/100)/2=(50+35)/2=42.5
```

which is half way between the minimum of 50 and the product of 35. When more than two certainty factors must be combined to get the overall joint certainty of an expression, the average method is sensitive to the order in which the certainty factors are combined. Neither the minimum nor product method has this property. If z is a third certainty factor for the expression, then the minimum computation is:

```
MIN(MIN(x,y),z)
```

The x, y, and z can be rearranged in any order within this formula without affecting the resultant joint certainty. Similarly, the joint certainty that results from the product:

```
(((x*y)/100)*z)/100
```

is the same regardless of the order in which x, y, and z are used in the computation.

In contrast, the average method computation of:

```
((MIN(MIN(x,y)+(x*y)/100)/2,z)+(((MIN(x,y)+(x*y)/100)/2)*z)/100)/2
```

is likely to produce a different joint certainty factor than:

```
((MIN(MIN(z,y)+(z*y)/100)2,x)+(((MIN(z,y)+(z*y)/100)/2)*x)/100)/2
```

However, the average method's result will always be between those that would have resulted from the minimum and product methods—regardless of the order in which multiple certainty factors happen to be combined. If desired, this order could be controlled somewhat by the developer through the left-to-right arrangement of variables in the expression.

TABLE 10-2   Comparison of joint certainty factor algebras

Individual certainty factors		Joint certainty factor			
x	*y*	*Minimum*	*Product*	*Average*	*Bonczek-Eagin*
x	0	0	0	0	0
90	20	20	18	19	19.8
80	20	20	16	18	19.2
70	20	20	14	17	18.2
60	20	20	12	16	16.8
50	20	20	10	15	15
40	20	20	8	14	12.8
30	20	20	6	13	10.2
20	20	20	4	12	7.2
10	20	10	2	6	3.6
90	50	50	45	47.5	49.5
80	50	50	40	45	48
70	50	50	35	42.5	45.5
60	50	50	30	40	42
50	50	50	25	37.5	37.5
40	50	40	20	30	30
30	50	30	15	22.5	22.5
20	50	20	10	15	15
10	50	10	5	7.5	7.5
90	80	80	72	76	79.2
80	80	80	64	72	76.8
70	80	70	56	63	67.2
60	80	60	48	54	57.6
50	80	50	40	45	48
40	80	40	32	36	38.4
30	80	30	24	27	28.8
20	80	20	16	18	19.2
10	80	10	8	9	9.6
x	100	x	x	x	x

Bonczek-Eagin method (E.CFJO = "B"). When this method is employed, the joint certainty of an expression is:

```
(x*y/100)*(2-MAX(x,y)/100)
```

Like the average method, the Bonczek-Eagin method always yields a joint certainty factor that is between the product and minimum.* However, it tends to be more skewed toward one of these extremes, based on

*In the Guru documentation this is referred to as the "balance" method [1].

the magnitudes of x and y. Table 10-2 shows how this method differs from the average, depending on how large the largest participating certainty factor is.

If the largest of the two certainty factors exceeds 50, then the joint certainty tends to be more optimistic (closer to the minimum) than the average. The closer MAX(x,y) comes to 100, the closer the joint certainty comes to being identical to the daring minimum method. On the other hand, if the largest of the two certainty factors has not even reached 50, then the joint certainty tends to be more reserved (closer to the product) than the average. The closer MAX(x,y) comes to 0, the closer the joint certainty comes to being identical to the product method. In cases where the larger of the two certainty factors is 50, the Bonczek-Eagin method yields the same result as the average method.

The comparative effects of E.CFJO's setting on joint certainty factors can be visualized graphically as shown in Figure 10-1. Each graph is based on a different E.CFJO setting and shows how the joint certainty (vertical axis) is affected as x varies from 0 to 100 while y is held fixed at 45. Notice that both the average and Bonczek-Eagin methods fall between the minimum and product extremes. The Bonczek-Eagin method yields a smoother curve than the average method.

FIGURE 10-1   Comparison of joint certainty algebras

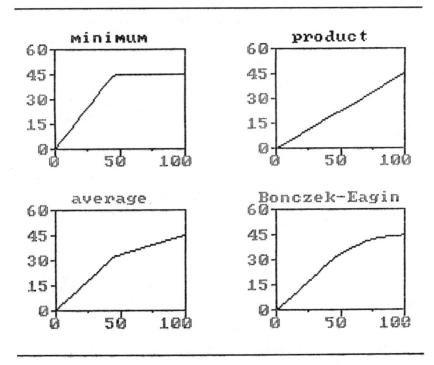

Confirmative Certainty Factor Algebras

The result of a joint certainty factor computation is never greater than the lowest contributing certainty factor. Though such computations are applicable to many kinds of expressions, there is one type of expression where they would be inappropriate. Consider the logical expression:

```
GROWTH < .02 OR UNEMPLOYMENT >= .082
```

Here, the two conditions are connected by the OR operator rather than the AND operator. Suppose the first condition is true with a certainty factor of 90 and the second condition is true with a certainty of 40. What should the overall certainty about the truth of this expression be?

If the inference engine attempted to combine 90 and 40 with one of the joint certainty computations, the result would be somewhere from 36 to 40. Such a result would be peculiar. Unlike the AND operator, both conditions do not need to be true in order for the entire OR expression to be true. If both conditions in an OR expression are true, then they actually reinforce and confirm each other. That is, the overall certainty of the expression should not be less than either of the individual certainty factors.

In the above example, the confirmative certainty would not be less than 90. The first condition makes us 90 percent sure about the expression's truth. Because the second condition is additional positive evidence, it most certainly should not detract from the confirmative certainty. In fact, it may even increase that certainty beyond 90. The algebra used for computing confirmative certainties of expressions is controlled by the value of E.CFCO. Like E.CFJO, the permissible settings for this environment variable are M, P, A, and B. However, the mathematics of each is different from the corresponding E.CFJO setting. Each E.CFCO setting identifies one of the four confirmative certainty factor algebras described below.* Each description refers to x and y, where these simply denote two certainty factors that are being combined in a confirmative fashion.

Maximum method (E.CFCO = "M"). When the maximum method is selected, the confirmative certainty of the expression is:

```
MAX(x,y)
```

In the foregoing example, the maximum method would cause the inference engine to compute a confirmative certainty of MAX(90,40) = 90. The rationale is that the overall evidence should be at least as strong as

---

*The M and P settings have also been described in Chapter 6.

the strongest piece of evidence. But the maximum method stops at the lowest, most risk-averse point by making the confirmative certainty identical to the highest individual certainty—it does not venture beyond.

The Guru default value for E.CFCO is M. Inference engines that do not support multiple confirmative certainty algebras are normally "hardwired" with the probability sum method. The same effect can be achieved in Guru by setting E.CFCO to be P.

Probability sum method (**E.CFCO** = "**P**"). When the probability sum method is being used, the confirmative certainty of an expression is:

```
(x+y) - (x*y)/100
```

This method is more venturesome than the maximum method. The probability sum will always be at least as large as the maximum. In thinking about the maximum, one cannot deny that the overall certainty should be at least as large as the maximum contributing certainty. But shouldn't it be even greater? The probability sum answers yes. It says that both uncertainties should be reflected in the confirmative certainty.

Once again consider the expression:

```
GROWTH < .02 OR UNEMPLOYMENT >= .082
```

assuming 90 and 40 certainty factors respectively for the two conditions' TRUE values. What is the confirmative certainty factor? According to the probability sum method it is $(90 + 40) - (90*40/100) = 94$, which is larger than the maximum method would yield. Unlike the maximum method, this approach argues that both uncertainties should contribute to the overall degree of certainty.

Suppose that the 40 certainty factor is replaced by 10. The probability sum philosophy says we should be less certain than with 40; the confirmative certainty would be $(90 + 10) - (90*10/100) = 91$, which is less than the 94. In contrast, the maximum method would still give a confirmative certainty of $MAX(90,10) = 90$, even though there is now less certainty about one of the pieces of evidence. In fact, the second condition's certainty factor could fluctuate from 0 to 90 without affecting the maximum method's joint certainty. With the probability sum method, each shift upward or downward in x or y yields a corresponding shift in the confirmative certainty.

In thinking about which confirmative certainty algebra to adopt for a particular problem area, the developer may want to quiz the expert in a similar way to the approach used when deciding on an E.CFJO setting. The only difference is that the example expressions involve conditions connected by the OR operator. The two remaining confirmative certainty methods accommodate experts whose reasoning falls between the maximum and probability sum extremes.

Average method (E.CFCO = "A"). When the average method is employed, the confirmative certainty of an expression is:

```
(MAX(x,y) + (x+y) - (x*y)/100)/2
```

The average method offers a compromise between the conservative maximum method and the venturesome probability sum method. For the above example, it yields a confirmative certainty of:

```
(MAX(90,40) + (90 + 40) - (90 * 40)/100)/2
= (90 + 130 - 36)/2 = 92
```

which is half way between the maximum of 90 and the probability sum of 94.

As with an E.CFJO setting of A, the average confirmative method is sensitive to the order in which certainties are combined when there are more than two of them. However, the average confirmative method's result will always be between the results of the maximum and probability sum methods—regardless of the order in which multiple certainty factors happen to be combined.

Bonczek-Eagin method (E.CFCO = "B"). When this E.CFCO setting is in force*, the confirmative certainty of an expression is:

```
MAX(x,y) + ((x*y)/100*(1 - MAX(x,y)/100))
```

Like the average method, the Bonczek-Eagin method always yields a confirmative certainty factor that is between the maximum and probability sum. However, it tends to be more skewed toward one of these extremes, based on the magnitudes of x and y. Table 10–3 shows how this method differs from the average.

As long as one of the certainty factors exceeds 50, the Bonczek-Eagin confirmative certainty tends to be more "optimistic" (closer to the probability sum) than the average. In other words, high incremental evidence is given more prominence than it would be given with the average method. However, it is still given less weight than would accrue to it if

---

*The original release of Guru did not employ the Bonczek-Eagin method when E.CFCO had this setting. It used an alternative computation that always yielded results bounded by the maximum and probability sum. Subsequent Guru releases use the Bonczek-Eagin method for the "B" setting of E.CFCO.

TABLE 10-3   Comparison of confirmative certainty factor algebras

Individual certainty factors		Joint certainty factor			
x	*y*	*Maximum*	*Probability sum*	*Average*	*Bonczek-Eagin*
x	0	x	x	x	x
90	20	90	92	91	91.8
80	20	80	84	82	83.2
70	20	70	76	73	74.2
60	20	60	68	64	64.8
50	20	50	60	55	55
40	20	40	52	46	44.8
30	20	30	44	37	34.2
20	20	20	36	28	23.2
10	20	20	28	24	21.6
90	50	90	95	92.5	94.5
80	50	80	90	85	88
70	50	70	85	77.5	80.5
60	50	60	80	70	72
50	50	50	75	62.5	62.5
40	50	50	70	60	60
30	50	50	65	57.5	57.5
20	50	50	60	55	55
10	50	50	55	52.5	52.5
90	80	90	98	94	97.2
80	80	80	96	88	92.8
70	80	80	94	87	91.2
60	80	80	92	86	89.6
50	80	80	90	85	88
40	80	80	88	84	86.4
30	80	80	86	83	84.8
20	80	80	84	82	83.2
10	80	80	82	81	81.6
x	100	100	100	100	100

the probability sum method were being used. If one certainty factor is less than or equal to 50 and the other (incremental evidence) involves a certainty factor of 50, the Bonczek-Eagin confirmative certainty is identical to the average confirmative certainty. If both certainty factors are low (less than 50), the confirmative certainty will be closer to the maximum than it is to the probability sum, but it will still exceed the maximum. Thus the Bonczek-Eagin method emphasizes the effect of large added evidence more than the average method does, but not as much as the maximum method, which discounts that evidence entirely. Figure 10-2 compares the four confirmative certainty algebras. Each graph

FIGURE 10-2   Comparison of confirmative certainty algebras

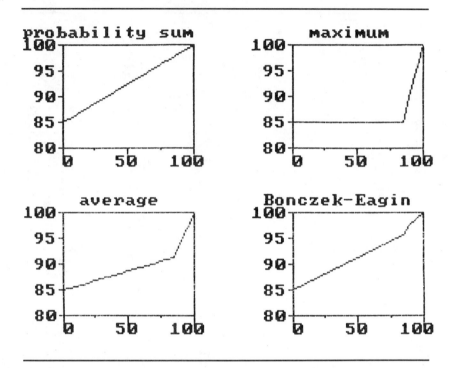

shows how the confirmative certainty (vertical axis) is affected as x (horizontal axis) varies from 0 to 100 while y is held fixed at 85.

CERTAINTY FACTORS FOR VARIABLES

In order to deal with uncertainty, an inference engine must be able to do more than compute certainties for expressions appearing in premises and actions. It must also be able to compute certainty factors for variables' values. Chapter 6 showed how the initial certainty factors for some variables may be established by assignment commands in a rule set's initialization sequence, find actions, or rule actions. Examples included:

```
LET RISE = RISE CF CRISE
LAFACTOR = LOCALADS/120000 CF 88
ECONOMY = "good" CF CR6
```

where CRISE and CR6 were themselves variables whose values became certainty factors for RISE and ECONOMY values, respectively. Remember that the certainty assigned to a variable with such commands could have come from many sources—the user, a procedural model, a statistical analysis of selected data base contents, the expert, and so forth.

The examples in Chapter 6 also showed that the ultimate certainty factor for a variable's value is influenced by rules that have fired, provided those rules contain actions that produce that value. Thus, the certainty of a good economy is influenced by all fired rules whose actions assign a "good" value to the ECONOMY variable. What is the nature of this influence? This question is answered by the certainty factor algebra employed for computing the certainties of variables' values. Some inference engines support only one algebra, which may or may not allow the developer to build an expert system that closely emulates a human expert's results when reasoning with uncertainty. It all depends on the specific expert and the nature of the problem area. Other inference engines support multiple built-in algebras for computing the certainty of a variable's value. During the expert-testing stage of development, these alternatives can be explored to find the one that is most suitable for the particular expert system being constructed. In the case of Guru, this is accomplished by setting the E.CFVA environment variable to any of its 16 possible values.

No matter what algebra is in effect for computing the certainty factor of a variable value, there are two basic aspects to the computation. First, there is a computation for each fired rule whose action assigns the value to the variable. Each such computation involves combining certainty factors that exist within a rule. Each results in an intrarule certainty factor for the variable value. The second aspect is pertinent only when two or more fired rules have actions that produce the same value for a variable. In such cases, there will be two or more intrarule certainties for the same variable value. Thus the second computational aspect involves combining these intrarule certainties to get a single certainty factor for the variable value. This is the interrule certainty factor.

Each permissible setting for E.CFVA consists of two codes. The first identifies the interrule computation method. It can be M, P, A, or B. The second indicates which intrarule computation should be used by the inference engine. It too can be M, P, A, or B. Therefore, 16 different settings exist for E.CFVA, each denoting a different approach to computing the certainty factor of a variable value. To describe each possibility in detail is beyond the scope of this book (see Guru Reference Manual [2] for details). Besides, each one is simply a coupling of two of the methods presented earlier in this chapter. For instance, the setting of:

```
E.CFVA = "PM"
```

means that the certainty factor of a variable value will be computed by taking the probability sum (P) of the intrarule minimums (M). Similarly, a

TABLE 10-4   Sixteen certainty algebras for variable values

E.CFVA codes	Interrule computation	Intrarule computation
MM	Maximum	Minimum
MP	Maximum	Product
MA	Maximum	Average (joint)
MB	Maximum	Bonczek-Eagin (joint)
PM	Probability sum	Minimum
PP	Probability sum	Product
PA	Probability sum	Average (joint)
PB	Probability sum	Bonczek-Eagin (joint)
AM	Average (confirmative)	Minimum
AP	Average (confirmative)	Product
AA	Average (confirmative)	Average (joint)
AB	Average (confirmative)	Bonczek-Eagin (joint)
BM	Bonczek-Eagin (confirmative)	Minimum
BP	Bonczek-Eagin (confirmative)	Product
BA	Bonczek-Eagin (confirmative)	Average (joint)
BB	Bonczek-Eagin (confirmative)	Bonczek-Eagin (joint)

setting of PP causes the inference engine to take the probability sum (first P) of the intrarule products (second P). All possibilities are enumerated in Table 10–4.

Intrarule Certainty

The calculation of a variable value's certainty within a rule depends on the certainty of the rule's premise and the certainty of the expression value that is assigned to the variable in the rule's conclusion. In general, the inference engine will see:

```
IF: premise
THEN: action-1
      action-2
         .
         .
         .
      Z = expression
         .
         .
         .
      action-n
```

when it needs to compute an intrarule certainty for the variable Z based on the premise certainty and expression certainty. Earlier in this chapter it was shown how the premise and expression certainty calculations are themselves based on E.CFJO and/or E.CFCO settings.*

Suppose that the premise certainty has been calculated to be 30 and the expression value's certainty has been calculated to be 60. What should the intrarule certainty of Z be? What kinds of computational methods might be reasonable, joint or confirmative? If one of the confirmative methods were used, the certainty for Z's value would be at least 60 (maximum) and perhaps as high as 72 (probability sum). This would be like saying that we're 30 percent sure that the premise is true and 60 percent sure about the expression's value, therefore we should be 60 to 72 percent sure about the value assigned to Z. This kind of reasoning is clearly undesirable. The certainties of the expression's value and the premise cannot be considered as confirming each other. Neither adds evidence to the other.

Therefore, an intrarule certainty is considered to be the joint result of the premise certainty and an expression certainty. If we're 30 percent sure that the premise is true, then we can't reasonably be more than 30 percent sure about the value of Z, even when we are 100 percent sure about the value of the expression. And if the expression certainty factor is only 60, then perhaps our certainty about Z should be even lower. What calculation should be carried out to get the intrarule certainty for a variable? Inference engines that do not give any choice in this matter typically use a product method. This is Guru's default setting. As Table 10–4 shows, other settings for the second E.CFVA code are M, A, and B (for the minimum, joint average, and joint Bonczek-Eagin methods, respectively).

The computations are exactly like those presented earlier for determining the joint certainty of an expression value. The only difference is that, for an intrarule variable certainty, x is the certainty factor of the rule's premise and y is the certainty factor of an expression in the rule's conclusion. Notice that it is perfectly permissible to set E.CFJO and E.CFVA to cause the inference engine to use the same or different joint certainty methods. For instance, joint certainties for expressions might use the average method, while intrarule certainties for variables are computed with the minimum method. This flexibility gives a developer considerable latitude for matching each expert's way of dealing with uncertainty.

----

*Remember that a premise is just a certain kind of expression (i.e., a logical expression).

Interrule Certainty

Sometimes there will be only one rule that fires to give a variable a specific value. In such a case, the intrarule certainty for that variable value will serve as the value's final certainty factor. At other times, several rules may have fired, with each yielding its own intrarule certainty for the same variable value. These need to be combined in some way to produce the value's ultimate certainty factor. Clearly, this combining of the intrarule certainties should occur in a confirmative fashion. The final certainty factor for the value should be at least as great as its largest intrarule certainty. The lesser intrarule certainties are simply additional evidence in favor of this particular value.

Inference engines that do not give a choice of how to combine intrarule certainties typically use a product sum computation. This also happens to be Guru's default setting. As Table 10–4 shows, other settings for the first E.CFVA code are M, A, and B (for the maximum, confirmative average, and confirmative Bonczek-Eagin methods, respectively). For example, the command:

```
LET E.CFVA = "AM"
```

would change the setting from its PP default to AM. This new setting would cause the inference engine to compute each variable value's certainty factor by taking the confirmative average of its intrarule certainty minimums.

The confirmative computations for a variable are exactly like those presented earlier for expressions. The only difference is that, for computing an interrule variable certainty, x and y are intrarule certainties. It is permissible to set E.CFCO and E.CFVA to cause the inference engine to use the same or different confirmative certainty methods. For example, confirmative certainties for expressions might be set to the conservative maximum method, while interrule certainties for variables are computed with the liberal probability sum method.

Putting It All Together

To see how all of these controls work together, assume that GROWTH has a value of .05 with a certainty of 60 and UNEMPLOYMENT has a value of .05 with a certainty of 50. Suppose, the following two rules exist in the rule set:

```
RULE: R6
  IF: GROWTH >= .04 AND UNEMPLOYMENT < .076
  THEN: ECONOMY += "good" CF 90
RULE: R7
  IF: GROWTH >= .02 AND UNEMPLOYMENT < .055
  THEN: ECONOMY += "good" CF 80
```

When a consultation begins, assume the environment variables have been set as follows:

```
E.UNKN = 10
E.CFJO = "A"
E.CFCO = "B"
E.CFVA = "MP"
```

How certain will the inference engine be that the economy is good? The premise for R6 is true with a certainty of:

```
(MIN(50,60) + (50 * 60/100))/2 = (50 + 30)/2 = 40
```

The joint certainty of this logical expression's truth would have been 50 for an E.CFJO setting of M, or 30 for an E.CFJO setting of P. Similarly, the premise for R7 is true with a certainty of 40. When rule R6 is fired, ECONOMY is given a "good" value with an intrarule certainty of:

```
(40 * 90)/100 = 36
```

The product computation is used because the E.CFVA setting for intrarule certainties happens to be P. Similarly, when R7 fires, its premise certainty of 40 and the action's expression certainty of 80 are combined via a product computation to yield an intrarule certainty of:

```
(40 * 80)/100 = 32
```

E.CFVA's first code of M indicates that the maximum intrarule certainty for a good economy should be used as the interrule certainty factor. Thus, the inference engine is MAX(36,32) = 36 percent certain that ECONOMY has a "good" value. Notice that the setting of E.CFCO was irrelevant, since no expression involved the OR operator.

Now suppose the certainty factor controls are changed to reflect a much more daring approach to reasoning about uncertainties:

```
E.CFJO = "M"
E.CFVA = "PM"
```

What certainty factor would result for ECONOMY's "good" value? The premise certainties are based on E.CFJO's minimum setting. They would therefore be MIN(50,60) = 50 and MIN(50,60) = 50 for rules R6 and R7, respectively. Because E.CFVA is set to PM, the intrarule certainties would also be minimums—resulting in MIN(50,90) = 50 and MIN(50,80) = 50 for rules R6 and R7, respectively. These two intrarule certainties would then be combined in a probability sum to yield a final certainty of $(50 + 50) - (50 * 50/100) = 75$ for a good economy.

Going to the opposite extreme, a conservative attitude toward combining uncertainties would be reflected in the settings:

```
E.CFJO = "P"
E.CFVA = "MP"
```

The E.CFJO setting would cause each premise's certainty to be computed as $(50*60)/100 = 30$. Because E.CFVA is set to MP, the intrarule certainties for rules would be based on the product computation. This yields $(30*90)/100 = 27$ and $(30*80)/100 = 24$ for rules R6 and R7, respectively. The maximum interrule certainty computation then results in a certainty factor of $MAX(27,24) = 27$ for ECONOMY's "good" value.

Peaceful Coexistence

The setting of E.CFVA indicates what certainty algebra the inference engine will use for each variable that is processed during a consultation. But what if the expert tends to be cautious (e.g., MP) about designating the certainty for one variable, venturesome (e.g., PM) for another variable, and in between these extremes (e.g., AA) for a third variable? Can these different attitudes all coexist within a single consultation? Can the reasoning about uncertainty be fine-tuned on a variable-by-variable basis?

To accommodate different attitudes for different variables, the developer should be provided with a means for specifying what algebra to use for each variable. In a Guru rule set, for instance, this is accomplished with the variable descriptions. The type of algebra to be used when assessing the certainty for a particular variable can be specified directly in that variable's description. For example, the variable description:

```
VARIABLE: ECONOMY
   LABEL: Economic Outlook
   TYPE: PA
```

will cause the inference engine to always use the PA algebra when computing the interrule and intrarule certainties for values of the ECONOMY variable—regardless of the current setting of E.CFVA. Any variable description can optionally include the TYPE clause with any of the 16 two-character codes shown in Table 10–4. This flexibility adds another dimension to the developer's world of controlling how an inference engine reasons about uncertainties.

DEVELOPER AIDS

While developing an expert system that deals with uncertainty, there are some additional aids that a developer might expect to see. As noted above, the ability to alter certainty factor settings *outside* of the rule set itself makes it relatively easy to test the effects of different certainty algebras on the advice that is generated. There is no need to alter and re-compile the rule set itself before it can be consulted with different certainty algebras. The exception (in Guru, at least) is the case of certainty computations for a variable that has an algebra explicitly prescribed for it within the rule set. Other developer aids include automatic certainty input and output, interactive experimentation with certainty algebras, and facilities for devising customized algebras.

Automatic Certainty Input and Output

As the developer works at specifying a rule set, it is important that he or she not be bothered with elaborate input and output specifications, which can be quite distracting at this stage of a development cycle. What is needed is a quick way to specify intelligible input or output operations within a rule set. Once the rule set is adequate for reasoning purposes, its user interface can be made more elaborate and polished. For instance, is there a more concise way to input a value for the RISE variable and a related certainty factor than the Chapter 6 approach of:

```
INPUT RISE NUM WITH "Enter rise estimate for " + PROD
INPUT CRISE NUM USING "nnn" WITH\
 "On a scale of 0 to 100, how sure are you?"
LET RISE = RISE CF CRISE
```

where the third command uses the CRISE input to establish a certainty factor for RISE's value? The answer is yes.

There is an environment variable named E.ICF that can be set to cause an automatic certainty factor prompt and assignment for every INPUT statement. Suppose the command:

```
E.ICF = TRUE
```

has been issued prior to a consultation request or in a rule set's initialization sequence. Instead of constructing the three commands shown above, the developer would simply specify:

```
INPUT RISE NUM WITH "Enter rise estimate for " + PROD
```

to get the same net effect without even thinking about a CRISE variable. Suppose PROD's present value is "scifi." When the inference engine executes this INPUT command, the user is prompted to enter a value for RISE:

```
Enter rise estimate for scifi ___
```

As soon as it is entered, the inference engine automatically prompts the user for an associated certainty factor. Whatever certainty is entered becomes the certainty factor for the value of RISE.

Similarly, there is an E.OCF environment variable that can be set to cause each output of a variable's value to be accompanied automatically by a display of the value's certainty factor. If E.OCF has been set to TRUE, then the Chapter 6 command:

```
AT 8,1 OUTPUT "The recommended new quota is: ",\
 NEWQUOTA USING "nnnnn", " with a certainty of ",\
 HICF(NEWQUOTA) USING "nnn", " out of 100"
```

can be replaced by:

```
AT 8,1 OUTPUT "The recommended new quota is: ", NEWQUOTA
```

in order to see both the value of NEWQUOTA and its certainty factor. Later, as the user interface is being constructed, E.ICF and E.OCF would probably be set back to FALSE and more elaborate input and output presentation approaches would be built into the rule set.

Interactive Exploration of Certainty Factor Algebras

Another developer aid associated with certainty factors is the ability to interactively examine the effects of a certainty factor setting—outside the context of a consultation. For instance, the developer might want to examine the effects of various E.CFJO settings on the certainty of the expression A + SQRT(B). The following commands might be entered interactively:

```
E.OCF = TRUE
A = 10 CF 60
B = 25 CF 80
E.CFJO = "M"
```

Now to see the expression's value and that value's certainty via the minimum method, the developer would interactively enter:

```
?A + SQRT(B)
```

and Guru responds:

```
15.00 with certainty 60
```

To compare this to the joint average method, the developer would next type:

```
E.CFJO = "A"
?A + SQRT(B)
```

and Guru responds:

```
15.00 with certainty 54
```

This could then be compared with the Bonczek-Eagin method by typing:

```
E.CFJO = "B"
?A + SQRT(B)
```

to see the response of:

```
15.00 with certainty 57
```

These kinds of interactive expression evaluations and certainty factor computations give a quick way to examine the effects of different algebras.

The effects can also be studied graphically, by plotting the function line implied by a calculation method. For instance, Figures 10–1 and 10–2 are two Guru graphics screens each of which was output to a printer. In addition to having several graphs on the same screen, plotted lines can also be superimposed on a single graph. Suppose x and y are two certainty factors. For a particular y, how does the joint certainty change as x increases? The answer, of course, depends on the joint computation formula. To plot the joint certainties for the joint average with a y of, say, 45, the following commands would be entered interactively:

```
E.DECI = 0
RANGE UP FROM 0 TO 50
RANGE ACROSS FROM 0 TO 100
Y = 45
PLOT FUNCTION =(MIN(X,Y)+(X*Y/100))/2
```

The first command sets an environment variable to 0, so no decimal digits will appear in numbers along the graph axes. The next two commands set the ranges for the vertical and horizontal axes of subsequent graphs. The fourth command gives y a value of 45. The PLOT command tells Guru to plot the joint average function, varying the values on the x (horizontal) axis. As shown in Figure 10–3, the result is a plot of the joint certainty for a y of 45, with x varying from 0 to 100.

How would the plot differ if the minimum method had been used instead? To find out, the command:

```
PLOT ONTOP FUNCTION = MIN(X,Y)
```

would be entered. This superimposes the minimum curve on the same screen that was previously generated to show the joint average curve. The printed rendition appears in Figure 10–4. For comparison purposes, third and fourth lines could also be superimposed via the interactive commands:

FIGURE 10–3   Plot of the joint average for y = 45

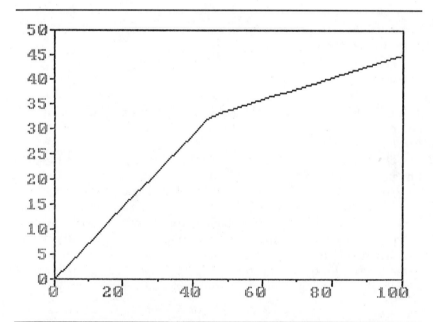

FIGURE 10-4 Superimposed plot of the minimum for y = 45

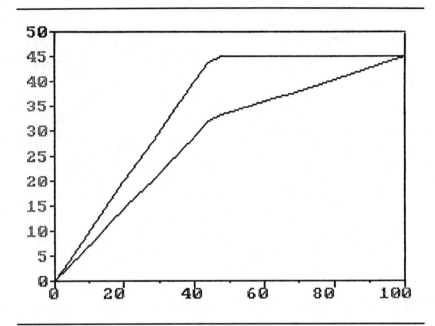

```
PLOT ONTOP FUNCTION =X*Y/100
PLOT ONTOP FUNCTION =(X*Y/100)*(2-MAX(X,Y)/100)
```

As shown in Figures 10–5 and 10–6, these superimpose curves for the product and Bonczek-Eagin methods, respectively.

Confirmative certainty methods can be compared in a similar fashion. Figure 10–7 shows the four curves of Figure 10–2 superimposed on a single large graph. Side-by-side comparisons such as the one in Figure 10–8 are also possible. Other interesting comparisons might involve joint versus confirmative certainty curves (e.g., Figure 10–9) or contrasting curves for each of several different y values, while holding the certainty algebra constant.

Customized Certainty Algebras

It may happen that none of an inference engine's built-in certainty factor algebras is deemed appropriate for building a particular expert system. This would be rare when using a development tool that supports many alternative methods. With Guru, for instance, there are 16 distinct methods for handling expression certainties (four joint times four confirmative methods). Similarly, there are 16 distinct methods for handling variable certainties, each of which can be chosen on a variable-by-

FIGURE 10-5   Superimposed plot of the product for y = 45

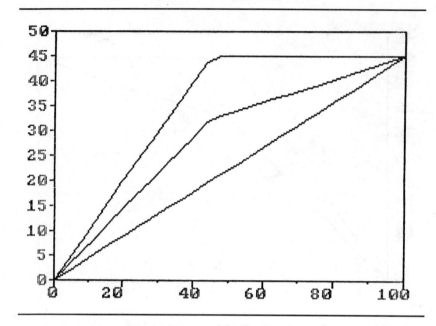

FIGURE 10-6   Comparison of the four joint certainty methods for y = 45

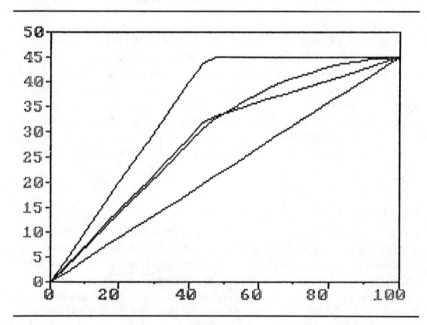

FIGURE 10-7   Comparison of the four confirmative certainty methods for
y = 85

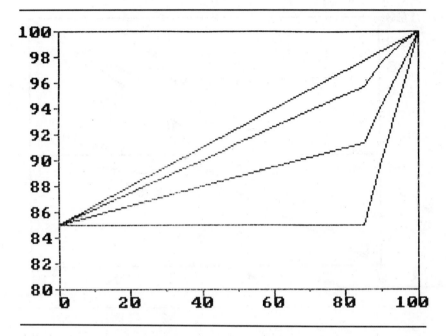

FIGURE 10-8   Joint average versus Bonczek-Eagin for y = 45

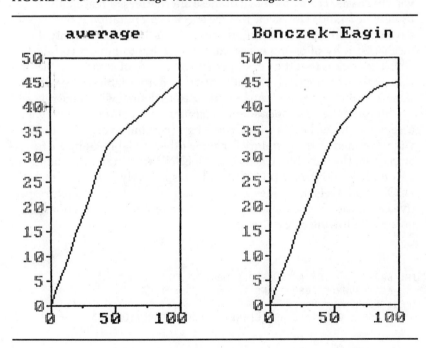

FIGURE 10-9   Joint versus confirmative certainty curves for y = 45

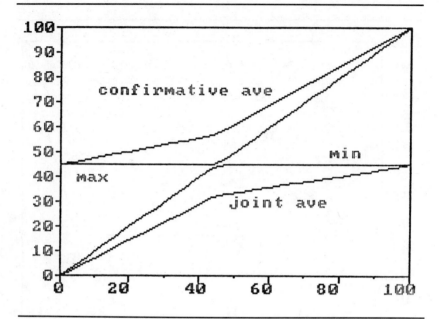

variable basis. From among all of these alternatives, a reasonable fit can usually be found. However, if some special computation is desired, the developer can ignore the inference engine's built-in certainty factor mechanisms by allowing every variable's value to have a certainty of 100. The trick is that the developer will make use of some variables in a rule set to keep track of certainties about other variables. The values of these "certainty variables" can be computed as desired within the rule set.

Suppose the developer adopts a naming convention that every variable whose name begins with CF will be a "certainty variable." Its value will be treated as the certainty for some other variable. Suppose for example that the variables CFGRO and CFUNE are certainty variables for GROWTH and UNEMPLOYMENT, respectively. Assume that the ECON model sets the values of CFGRO and CFUNE to reflect its respective certainties about the growth and unemployment predictions. Suppose the following rule is fired:

```
IF: GROWTH >= .04 AND UNEMPLOYMENT < .076
    AND KNOWN("CFGRO") AND KNOWN("CFUNE")
THEN: ECONOMY = "good"
    CFE = 2*(MIN(CFGRO,CFUNE)+(CFGRO*CFUNE/100))/3
```

The CFE variable for holding ECONOMY's certainty would be calculated from the CFGRO and CFUNE values. Notice that the computation used in this example is similar to the built-in joint average method. The difference is that the resultant certainty is two thirds rather than one half of the distance from the product to the minimum.

This customization of certainty calculations could be used throughout a rule set, giving the developer complete freedom in controlling how certainties will be combined during a consultation. At the end of a consultation, the CFNEW variable's value would indicate the inference engine's certainty about the value of NEWQUOTA. Thus the rule set's completion sequence might contain the command:

```
OUTPUT "Recommended new quota is:",\
 NEWQUOTA, " with certainty ", CFNEW
```

in order to report both the new quota and its certainty to the user. Interestingly, this use of "certainty variables" could be intermixed with built-in certainty factor mechanisms in the same rule set. This would allow "certainty variables" themselves to have certainty factors or the use of built-in facilities where possible and customized certainty computations elsewhere.

CONCLUSION

To accommodate the need to reason with uncertainties, an inference engine can have built-in mechanisms for making automatic certainty factor computations. Such computations are needed both at the time of an expression evaluation and at the time that a variable's value is established (e.g., due to a rule firing). Some inference engines have a single, fixed approach to making such computations [3]. Others support multiple built-in certainty factor algebras. They provide various controls that can be set as desired to govern how the inference engine reasons with uncertainty. This flexibility means that the developer can adjust the inference engine to produce certainty results that resemble those of the expert.

It is fair to say that all experts do not reason about uncertainty in the same way. Even the same expert may handle uncertainty differently in different circumstances. This chapter has presented a healthy assortment of certainty factor algebras that should meet most of the needs of business expert system developers. In some cases statistical methods may be useful in reasoning with uncertainty[1]. As with the reasoning controls discussed in Chapter 9, the certainty control settings could be "hardwired" in to a rule set's initialization sequence, conditionally set in the initialization sequence (e.g., based on the particular problem being posed or on who the user is), or set by asking the user what philosophy (e.g., daring, risk-averse, compromising) to employ. Certainties produced during a consultation can be reported to the user in any of a variety of ways, with developer-determined descriptions and even with graphs. The desired presentation of certainty results is controlled by commands in the rule set's completion sequence.

EXERCISES

1. What is a certainty algebra?
2. What is the human analog for an inference engine that does not support multiple certainty algebras?
3. How can the unknown threshold be raised or lowered for different problems?
4. On what factors does the certainty of an expression's values depend?
5. For what kinds of expressions is a joint certainty computation appropriate?
6. For what kinds of expressions is a confirmative certainty computation appropriate?
7. Suppose we are 70 percent certain that X has a value of 12 and 80 percent sure that Y has a value of 100. What is the value of the expression $X + Y$ and how sure are we about this value for each of the joint certainty algebra methods?
8. Under what circumstances is the average or Bonczek-Eagin method appropriate for joint certainty computation?
9. Suppose the inference engine has determined that $A > B$ with a certainty of 30 and that $B = C$ with a certainty of 60. What is the value of the premise $A > B$ OR $B = C$ and how sure is the inference engine about this value for each of the confirmative certainty algebra methods?
10. Explain why the confirmative average and Bonczek-Eagin methods can be regarded as compromises between the maximum and probability sum methods.
11. Regardless of the algebra being used, what are the two basic aspects of computing a variable's certainty factor?
12. What is the most conservative approach to determining a variable's certainty?
13. What is the least conservative approach to determining a variable's certainty?
14. How is it possible to allow different certainty factor algebras to be used for different variables within a single consultation? What is the value of such a capability?

References

1 Duda, R. O.; P. E. Hart; and N. J. Nilsson. "Subjective Bayesian Methods for Rule-Based Inference Systems." *Proceedings of the National Computer Conference*, 1976.

2 *Guru Reference Manual*, vol. 1. Lafayette, Ind.: MDBS, Inc. 1985.

3 Shortliffe, E. H. *Computer-Based Medical Consultations: MYCIN*. New York: Elsevier, 1976.

What kind of animal is this—a duck or a rabbit?

It's both—just like a fuzzy variable.

Chapter Eleven

Manipulating Fuzzy Variables

Often, a human expert is confronted with the task of making some sense out of a fuzzy situation. One or more of the factors involved in the reasoning process is unclear or out of focus, in the sense that it has simultaneously several plausible appearances. The economic outlook may appear to be both good and fair at the same time—each with a certain degree of plausibility. Chapter 6 showed how a rule set could be devised to accommodate multiple values for a single variable simultaneously. This, of course, depends on having an inference engine that is able to track and propagate a variable's multiple values (and their respective certainties) during the reasoning process. This manipulation of fuzzy variables can be considered to be an implementation of some aspects of fuzzy set theory [2], [3].

Recall from Chapter 6 that additive assignments(+ =), rather than replacement assignments (=), allow the inference engine to accumulate evidence about the value(s) of a variable and the associated certainty factor(s). This chapter delves into the manipulation of fuzzy variables in more detail. It shows how multiple values can be assigned to a single variable in a single command—with each getting its own certainty factor. Such a command could be invoked either inside or outside of a rule set's conclusions. In addition, the topic of fuzzy expressions is examined. Finally, controls are described for adjusting the manner in which an inference engine processes fuzzy variables.

ASSIGNING MULTIPLE VALUES TO A VARIABLE

Examples in Chapter 6 showed that an inference engine can assign the same value to a single variable twice, combining the two intrarule certainties in a confirmative fashion. The inference engine could also assign two different values to a single variable as the result of firing two rules that lead to different conclusions about that variable. In both cases, an additive (+ =) assignment was requested in the rule actions.

In the latter case, the variable became fuzzy as a result of firing two rules. There is a more direct way to give a variable multiple values, either inside or outside the context of a rule set.

Assignment Prior to Reasoning

Recall that the ECON model was specified in Guru's procedural (i.e., programming) language. One purpose of ECON is to establish a value for the GROWTH variable. But what if the economists happen to have three acceptable ways of estimating growth, each of which can give a different growth rate? Is it possible for ECON to establish three values for the GROWTH variable and ascribe some degree of acceptability (i.e., certainty) to each? Not only is it possible, the command for doing so is simple.

Suppose the ECON program contains three algorithms. The growth estimate for the first ends up in a variable named, say, EST1, and has been found to be fairly reliable 80 percent of the time. The second algorithm produces its estimate in a variable named EST2. Historically, the results of this forecasting approach have been "in the ballpark" 7 times out of 10. The third estimate is held in EST3. An associated reliability measure is also determined by the third algorithm and deposited in a variable named CFEST3.

How can the inference engine make use of all three ways for estimating growth? One answer is to actually have three ECON models, one for each algorithm. Each would equate its estimate to the GROWTH variable. Only one of the three models would be made accessible to the inference engine during any particular consultation. By switching among the three algorithms in three separate consultations, an end user would be able to see the effects of three different growth estimates on the new quota advice. This can be cumbersome since it takes three times as many consultations as using just one algorithm for projecting growth.

There is an alternative that will not take any additional consultations. Let all three algorithms exist in ECON as described above and at the end of the commands in ECON, include one extra command:

```
GROWTH += {EST1 CF 80,EST2 CF 70, EST3 CF CFEST3}
```

This makes GROWTH into a fuzzy variable having three values. One is the first algorithm's estimate and it has a certainty factor of 80. Another is the second algorithm's estimate with a 70 certainty factor. Finally, there is the third algorithm's estimate with a certainty dictated by the value of CFEST3. If pertinent assignment statements in conclusions of ADVISOR rules are changed to additive assignments, then each consultation will simultaneously reason with all three growth estimates. Using the completion sequence of Figure 6-2, Chapter 6, all of the multiple new quota recommendations (and their certainties) are reported to the user. Thus, the implications of multiple scenarios for a given problem can be examined via a single consultation.

Assignment within a Rule's Conclusion

During the expert-testing stage of a development cycle, Jack reconsiders rule R6. This rule was originally stated as:

```
RULE: R6
  IF: GROWTH >= .04 AND UNEMPLOYMENT < .076
  THEN: ECONOMY = "good"
```

But Jack now wants to refine this piece of reasoning knowledge. Though it is usually the case that the economy is good for the indicated growth and unemployment levels, Jack realizes that sometimes the economy will be only fair for those levels—and occasionally even poor. To capture this realization in the rule set, he alters R6 to make ECONOMY into a fuzzy variable.

```
RULE: R6
  IF: GROWTH >= .04 AND UNEMPLOYMENT < .076
  THEN: ECONOMY += {"good" CF 95, "fair" CF 30, "poor" CF 10}
```

If R6 fires, then ECONOMY will have all three values. The certainty for each value is computed just like the certainty of a single-valued variable—based on its intrarule certainty and its interrule certainty (if any). As usual, the computation method is controlled by the E.CFVA setting, unless it is overridden with a TEST clause in ECONOMY's variable description.

Now think of yourself as the inference engine, considering whether to fire rule R6. Suppose that the ECON program yielded values of .04, .05, and .03 for the GROWTH variable, with respective certainty factors of 80, 70, and 50. Suppose it also produces a value of .07 for UNEMPLOYMENT with a certainty factor of 90. Should you fire R6 and, if so, what would be the intrarule certainties for each of ECONOMY's three values? To answer this question you must first determine whether the premise of R6 is true. If it is true, you will need to combine your certainty about the premise's truth with the certainty of each value assigned to ECONOMY. You will then have the three intrarule certainties for the three values of ECONOMY.

Looking at the first condition in R6's premise, is it true that GROWTH is at least .04? Because GROWTH is fuzzy, the condition that contains it is a fuzzy expression. In general, if an expression contains one or more fuzzy variables, then the expression itself is probably fuzzy. When you evaluate a fuzzy expression, you will likely end up with more than one value, each with its own certainty factor. In the case of:

```
GROWTH >= .04
```

you will end up with two values for the expression—namely, TRUE and FALSE. This is because two of GROWTH's values (.04 and .05) make the expression true, while the other GROWTH value (.03) makes it false.

How certain are you that the condition is true and how certain are you that it is false? Think about the FALSE value first. There is only one GROWTH value (.03) that results in a FALSE value for the expression. Because .03 has a certainty factor of 50 and no other uncertainty is involved in the expression, you are 50 percent sure that the condition is false. Now the certainties (80 and 70) for the other GROWTH values need to be combined to find out how sure you are that the condition is true. Clearly, these should be combined in a confirmative fashion. Since both .04 and .05 yield a TRUE value, the certainty factor for TRUE should be at least as large as the largest of the certainties for the two GROWTH values. As usual, E.CFCO's setting controls how the confirmative certainty will be computed. Suppose it is set to P (probability sum). You then compute that the certainty for the condition's TRUE value is $80 + 70 - 80 * 70/100 = 94$.

The second condition in the premise is evaluated in the usual way, resulting in a TRUE value with a certainty of 90. Because both conditions are true, the premise as a whole is true. Your certainty about the truth of the premise is computed from the certainties (94 and 90) about the truth of its two conditions. If E.CFJO is set to the minimum method, this yields a certainty factor of 90 for the truth of the premise. The unknown threshold of E.UNKN is probably set well below 90, so you fire rule R6.

Firing rule R6 results in three values for the ECONOMY variable: "good," "fair," and "poor." The intrarule certainty that you attribute to each value is computed from the premise's certainty and the certainty factor specified for that value in the rule's conclusion. Because E.CFJO is set to the minimum method, the intrarule certainty for "good" is MIN(90,95) = 90, for "fair" is MIN(90,30) = 30, and for "poor" is MIN(90,10) = 10. Thus, you have evaluated a premise containing a fuzzy variable, fired the rule, and computed the certainty factor for each value of the conclusion's fuzzy variable. Fuzzy variables are handled in this same manner throughout an inference engine's reasoning activities.

As a brief aside, it is interesting to note that the premise containing a fuzzy GROWTH:

```
GROWTH >= .04 AND UNEMPLOYMENT < .076
```

is logically equivalent to the nonfuzzy expression:

```
(G1 >= .04 OR G2 >= .04 OR G3 >= .04) AND UNEMPLOYMENT < .076
```

where G1 has a value of .04 with certainty 80, G2 has a value of .05 with a certainty of 70, and G3 has a value of .03 with certainty of 50. That is, both evaluate to TRUE with the same certainty factor (90 in this case). Notice that in neither case does the 50 percent certainty that growth is less than .04 detract from the truth of the premise.

  If desired, the developer could construct R6 in such a way that the certainty of falseness for the premise influences the intrarule certainties for ECONOMY's values when the rule is fired. For instance, Jack might restate R6 as:

```
RULE: R6
  READY: LET ENOUGHGROWTH = GROWTH>=.04
  IF: ENOUGHGROWTH AND UNEMPLOYMENT < .076
  THEN: IF MORETRUE(ENOUGHGROWTH) THEN D = 0
         ELSE D = CFV(ENOUGHGROWTH, FALSE) * .1
       ENDIF
       ECONOMY += {"good" CF 95-D,"fair" CF 30-D,"poor" CF 10-D}
```

The preaction results in a fuzzy logical variable called ENOUGH-GROWTH. It is given a value of TRUE with certainty 94 and a value of FALSE with a certainty of 50. The premise is still discovered to be true with a certainty of 90.

  In the rule's actions, the MORETRUE and CFV functions appear. The first of these tests the certainties of ENOUGHGROWTH's TRUE and FALSE values to see whether the certainty of truth exceeds the certainty of falseness. If it does, then no deduction will be made (D = 0) when the certainties of ECONOMY's values are computed. However, if ENOUGHGROWTH is not more true than false, a deduction is calculated (with the CFV function) that is equal to one tenth of the certainty factor for ENOUGHGROWTH's FALSE value. This deduction is used to adjust each of the three certainties for ECONOMY prior to the intrarule certainty computations, by subtracting it from 95, 30, and 10. The important point of this example is not the formula used to compute D nor the manner in which D is used to adjust some certainties. These could be varied in a multitude of ways. The important point is that a developer is able to construct rules that treat individual certainties of a fuzzy variable's values in specially customized ways. This is made possible by built-in functions such as MORETRUE and CFV, which allow a rule (or procedural model, spreadsheet cell, interactive command, etc.) to reference individual fuzzy variables and their certainties. Guru's built-in functions for this purpose are enumerated in Table 11–1.

Subtractive Assignments

The action of the rule:

```
RULE: R6
  IF: GROWTH >= .04 AND UNEMPLOYMENT < .076
  THEN: ECONOMY += {"good" CF 95, "fair" CF 30, "poor" CF 10}
```

illustrates how to give multiple values to a variable. But what if we need to remove one of a fuzzy variable's values or reduce its certainty? This is

TABLE 11–1   Built-in functions for fuzzy variable manipulation

Function	Arguments	Function value
CFN(v,n)	v: Variable name	The nth highest certainty factor existing for the values of v.
	n: Number or numeric expression	
CFV(v,e)	v: Variable name	The certainty factor for the value of v that matches the value of e.
	e: Expression whose value matches one of the values of v.	
HICF(v)	v: Variable name	The highest certainty factor existing for any of the values of v.
HIVAL(v)	v: Variable name	The value of v having the highest certainty factor.
KNOWN(v)	v: Variable name	TRUE if any value of v has a certainty factor that exceeds E.UNKN.
LOCF(v)	v: Variable name	The lowest certainty factor existing for any of the values of v.
LOVAL(v)	v: Variable name	The value of v having the lowest certainty factor.
MORETRUE(l)	l: Logical expression	TRUE if the certainty that l is true exceeds the certainty that it is false.
NUMVAL(v)	v:Variable name	The number of values that presently exist for v.
VALN(v,n)	v: Variable name	The value of v having the nth highest certainty factor.
	n: Number or numeric expression	
WAVE(v)	v: Name of a variable having numeric values	The weighted average of the values of v, where each value is weighted by its certainty factor.

accomplished by the opposite of additive assignment—namely, subtractive assignment. Subtractive assignment is indicated by including a minus sign immediately prior to an equal sign (i.e., $-=$).

As Jack ponders rule R6, he recognizes that there is a growth rate beyond which he is sure that the economy cannot be poor. If this is .05, then he wants "poor" to no longer be a value of ECONOMY. There are several ways to represent this reasoning knowledge in the rule set. One is to create an additional rule such as:

```
RULE: RSUB
  PRIORITY: 40
  IF: GROWTH >= .05 AND KNOWN ("ECONOMY")
  THEN: ECONOMY -= "poor"
```

This tells the inference engine to eliminate ECONOMY's "poor" value when GROWTH has a value(s) of at least .05 and ECONOMY has one or more known values.* The rule is given a lower priority than rule R6's default priority of 50. By setting the E.SORD control to P, Jack ensures that RSUB will not be considered before R6. If it were, then there is the possibility that R6 could add the "poor" value back into the fuzzy ECONOMY—making it fuzzier than it should be.

The same effect could be achieved more efficiently without RSUB by altering R6 as follows:

```
RULE: R6
  IF: GROWTH >= .04 AND UNEMPLOYMENT < .076
  THEN: ECONOMY += {"good" CF 95, "fair" CF 30, "poor" CF 10}
        IF GROWTH >= .05 THEN ECONOMY -= "poor"; ENDIF
```

The subtraction of "poor" could even be conditioned by the degree of certainty that growth is at least 5 percent. For example, Jack might want to remove the "poor" value only if there is at least a 70 percent certainty about achieving this level of growth. To do so, the rule's conclusion would be restated as:

```
  THEN: ECONOMY += {"good" CF 95, "fair" CF 30, "poor" CF 10}
        HIGROWTH = GROWTH>=.05
        IF CFV(HIGROWTH,TRUE) >= 70 THEN ECONOMY -= "poor"
        ENDIF
```

Here, the CFV function is used to get the certainty that HIGROWTH has a TRUE value, where HIGROWTH is a fuzzy variable with TRUE and FALSE values.

---

*If an attempt is made to remove a value from a variable that has no values, a diagnostic message (e.g., "Undefined name: ECONOMY") results.

Now as Jack continues to ponder rule R6, he decides that if the growth is high, then the certainty about a fair economy also should be reduced. Furthermore, he reasons that the certainty of ECONOMY's "good" value should be increased in such a situation. To accomplish this, he uses the rule set manager to revise R6:

```
RULE: R6
  IF: GROWTH >= .04 AND UNEMPLOYMENT < .076
  THEN: ECONOMY += {"good" CF 95, "fair" CF 30, "poor" CF 10}
        IF GROWTH >= .05 THEN
          ECONOMY -= "poor"
          ECONOMY -= "fair" CF 80
          ECONOMY += "good" CF 20
        ENDIF
```

The second subtractive assignment command within the conclusion's IF statement indicates that Jack is 80 percent sure about getting rid of ECONOMY's "fair" value when growth is high. When the inference engine fires R6, it checks to see whether the growth is at least 5 percent. Because GROWTH is a fuzzy variable (values of .04, .05, and .03, with certainties of 80, 70, and 50), the expression:

```
GROWTH >= .05
```

will have both a FALSE value and a TRUE value. One GROWTH value (.05) makes the expression TRUE with a certainty of 70. Thus, "poor" is eliminated from ECONOMY's values and the certainty of the "fair" value needs to be diminished.

To reduce a value's certainty during a subtractive assignment, the inference engine takes the complement of the certainty factor that is specified in the assignment.* The complement is then combined in a joint fashion with the value's existing certainty. In this example, the complement is $100 - 80 = 20$. Because E.CFJO is set to the minimum method, combining 20 and 30 yields a new certainty of 20 for ECONOMY's "fair" value. If the product method were being used, the certainty for "fair" would have been much lower. In any event, the final certainty that R6's actions yield for "fair" can then be combined with the premise certainty to determine the intrarule certainty of a fair economy.

Notice that as higher certainty levels are specified in a subtractive assignment, the resultant certainty decreases and vice versa. If 89 had replaced 80 in the above example, the subtraction would have resulted in a certainty of 11 rather than 20. The certainty factor that is specified is an indicator of how sure an inference engine should be about reducing the value's certainty. The greater this assurance, the greater the reduc-

---

*The difference from 100.

tion in the value's certainty. It is permissible to consolidate multiple subtractive assignments into a single command. Thus, the command:

```
ECONOMY -= {"poor", "fair" CF 80}
```

could replace the two subtractive assignments in rule R6 without altering the reasoning effect.

The final assignment command in the IF statement of R6's conclusion is additive. It therefore should have the effect of increasing the certainty about the "good" value of ECONOMY. To do so, its certainty factor (20) is combined with the existing certainty (95) for "good" in a confirmative fashion. Because E.CFCO is set to the probability sum method in this example, a certainty of $(95 + 20) - (95 * 20/100) = 96$ results. This certainty can then be combined with the certainty of the rule's premise to determine the intrarule certainty for ECONOMY's "good" value. Unlike the subtractive assignment, as the certainty specified in the additive assignment increases, the resultant certainty also increases, and vice versa.

DEVELOPER AIDS

When developing a rule set that involves fuzzy variables, there are several aids that can facilitate the process. As with certainty factor algebras, the developer should be free to experiment with fuzzy variables interactively, outside of the context of a rule set. For instance, the developer may want to examine the effects of alternative additive or subtractive assignments immediately, without needing to continually revise and recompile a rule set. Another important aid for developer productivity is an automatic input and output facility for entering and displaying values of a fuzzy variable.

Automatic Fuzzy Input and Output

As the developer works at specifying a rule set or interactively experimenting with fuzzy variable manipulations, effort involved in the input and output of fuzzy variable values should be minimized. Being forced to invent elaborate input and output specifications prior to the user interface stage of a development cycle can be quite distracting. Developers need a way to specify intelligible input and output operations for fuzzy variables with minimal effort. Later, the user interface can be made more elaborate and polished.

As an example, Figure 6–2, Chapter 6, used the VALN and CFN functions in an OUTPUT command embedded within a WHILE command:

```
LET I = 1
WHILE I <= NUMVAL(NEWQUOTA) DO
   AT 8+I,5 OUTPUT VALN(NEWQUOTA,I) USING "nnnnn",\
        "with certainty of", CFN(NEWQUOTA,I) USING "nnn"
ENDWHILE
```

to display the values of a fuzzy NEWQUOTA variable, along with their respective certainty factors. Practically the same effect could be achieved by:

```
AT 9,5 OUTPUT NEWQUOTA
```

provided E.OCF is set to TRUE and E.OFUZ is set to, say, 5. The E.OFUZ environment variable causes the inference engine to automatically display up to a certain number of values whenever a fuzzy variable is referenced in an OUTPUT command. In this example, up to five values of NEWQUOTA will be displayed. If NEWQUOTA happens to have only three values, then only those three are output. If it has more than 5, those with the five highest certainties are output.

In effect, the OUTPUT command is automatically reexecuted in succession, until there are no more values of a fuzzy variable or until the E.OFUZ limit is reached. This environment variable can be changed whenever desired. Because E.OCF is TRUE, each output of a NEWQUOTA value is automatically accompanied by its certainty factor. Figure 11–1 shows an example of the effect of the OUTPUT NEWQUOTA command when E.OFUZ is set to 5 and E.OCF is TRUE.

In a similar way, E.IFUZ can be set to indicate how many times each INPUT should be automatically executed in succession. For example, if it is set to 3, then the command:

```
INPUT GROWTH NUM USING "n.nn" WITH "Enter growth rate:"
```

will be executed automatically three times in succession whenever the inference engine encounters it in a rule set. If E.ICF happens to be TRUE, then each of the three growth prompts is automatically accom-

FIGURE 11–1   OUTPUT NEWQUOTA results for E.OCF = TRUE and E.OFUZ = 5

3629.00 with certainty	87
3683.00 with certainty	84
3527.00 with certainty	72
3109.00 with certainty	41
3254.00 with certainty	27

panied by a prompt for entering the growth value's certainty. A developer can stop the successive inputs before the E.IFUZ limit is reached by simply making a null entry (e.g., pressing the return key without typing in a growth rate value).

Interactive Manipulation of Fuzzy Variables

An interactive session should probably begin by setting E.OCF to TRUE and giving E.OFUZ a sufficiently high setting, say 10. This is accomplished by interactively entering the commands:

```
E.OCF = TRUE
E.OFUZ = 10
```

Next, give the variables of interest desired values with desired certainties. For instance, the developer might issue the following two commands:

```
GROWTH += {.04 CF 80, .05 CF 70, .03 CF 50}
UNEMP = .07 CF 90
```

Suppose the developer wants to contrast the effects of the probability sum and maximum methods on the certainties for the GROWTH > = .04 fuzzy expression. Beginning with the maximum method the commands would be:

```
E.CFCO = "M"
?GROWTH >= .04
```

The corresponding response is:

```
TRUE with certainty  80
FALSE with certainty  50
```

Now, trying the probability sum method, the developer would enter:

```
E.CFCO = "P"
?GROWTH >= .04
```

The corresponding response is:

```
TRUE with certainty  94
FALSE with certainty  50
```

Suppose the developer now wants to contrast the effects of the product and minimum methods on the fuzzy expression GROWTH > = .04

AND UNEMP < .076. Beginning with the product, the entries would be:

```
E.CFJO = "P"
?GROWTH >= .04 AND UNEMP < .076
```

The corresponding response is:

```
TRUE with certainty  84
FALSE with certainty  50
```

Now trying the minimum method, the developer would enter:

```
E.CFJO = "M"
?GROWTH >= .04 AND UNEMP < .076
```

The corresponding response is:

```
TRUE with certainty  90
FALSE with certainty  50
```

Interactive explorations such as these are not only a good way to test out the results that would be attained for specific expressions in a rule set, but they are also useful in helping the developer become acclimated to thinking about fuzzy variables.

For instance, suppose Jack wonders what will happen if he takes the square root of a fuzzy variable. He can find out interactively by inventing a fuzzy variable called, say, K, and then using the built-in square root function by entering:

```
K = 44 CF 60
?SQRT(K)
```

The corresponding response is:

```
6.63 with certainty  60
```

Now he enters:

```
K += {28 CF 70,20 CF 80}
?SQRT(K)
```

and the response is:

```
4.47 with certainty  80
5.29 with certainty  70
6.63 with certainty  60
```

What happens if a fuzzy variable is multiplied by another variable? To find out, Jack creates a new variable named C and multiplies it by K:

```
C = 18 CF 45
?C * K
```

and the response (remembering that E.CFJO = "M") is:

```
360.00 with certainty  45
504.00 with certainty  45
792.00 with certainty  45
```

But what if the joint certainty method is changed to the product? Jack enters:

```
E.CFJO = "P"
?C * K
```

and the response is:

```
360.00 with certainty  36
504.00 with certainty  31
792.00 with certainty  27
```

Is it possible to multiply two fuzzy variables together? If so, what is the result? To find out, Jack first adds another value to the C variable:

```
C += 10 CF 75
?K * C
```

and the response is:

```
200.00 with certainty  60
280.00 with certainty  52
440.00 with certainty  45
360.00 with certainty  36
```

The 200 comes from multiplying C's 10 by K's 20, the 280 from multiplying C's 10 by K's 28, and so on.

But why are there only four products shown, when there are six possibilities? The answer is that Guru places a cap on the number of values it will keep track of for a fuzzy expression. Its default is four. Thus, it normally keeps track of the four values with the highest certainty. If more values are desired, the E.NUMV environment variable can be set accordingly. Jack tries setting it to 10:

```
E.NUMV = 10
?C * K
```

and the response is:

```
200.00 with certainty  60
280.00 with certainty  52
440.00 with certainty  45
360.00 with certainty  36
504.00 with certainty  31
792.00 with certainty  27
```

All six values in the Cartesian product of the fuzzy variable's values are now displayed. The E.NUMV environment variable also controls the maximum number of values a fuzzy variable can have during a consultation. It should be set accordingly in a rule set's initialization sequence. The rationale for sometimes having a lower limit is that only those few values with highest certainties may be of interest. It is possible for a developer to specify different limits for different variables in a rule set's variable descriptions [1].

CONCLUSION

Though they are not essential in all expert systems, fuzzy variables can be extremely valuable when representing reasoning knowledge. Without them, certain kinds of problem areas become difficult, if not infeasible, to handle via a rule set. As discussed in this chapter, an inference engine should support both additive and subtractive assignments. It should allow the developer to easily reference individual values (and their certainties) of a fuzzy variable within a rule set, program, spreadsheet, or interactively. An inference engine should be able to evaluate expressions that involve fuzzy variables. These fuzzy expressions can be designed into rule premises and conclusions. In an integrated environment, they can also exist in procedural models, spreadsheets, and interactive sessions. This, of course, opens up many novel and interesting possibilities for programmers and spreadsheet template builders.

EXERCISES

1. What is a fuzzy variable?
2. If X = {2 CF 20,1 CF 60} and Y = {3 CF 70,6 CF 80}, what are the values of the fuzzy expression X*Y? What are the certainties of those values (a) if the minimum and maximum methods are used, and (b) if the product and probability sum methods are used?
3. Discuss the implications of being able to process fuzzy variables within a procedural model.

4. What kinds of functions should an inference engine support for manipulating fuzzy variables?

5. Why is it advantageous to be able to manipulate fuzzy variables interactively?

6. How do E.IFUZ and E.OFUZ help minimize developer effort?

References

1   *Guru Reference Manual*, vol. 1. Lafayette, Ind.: MDBS, Inc. 1985.

2   Zadeh, L.A. "Fuzzy Sets." *Information and Control* 8, 1965.

3   Zadeh, L.A. "The Role of Fuzzy Logic in the Management of Uncertainty in Expert Systems." *Fuzzy Sets and Systems* 11, 1983.

Part IV

WHAT TO LOOK FOR: TODAY AND TOMORROW

The choices here remind me of shopping for an inference engine.

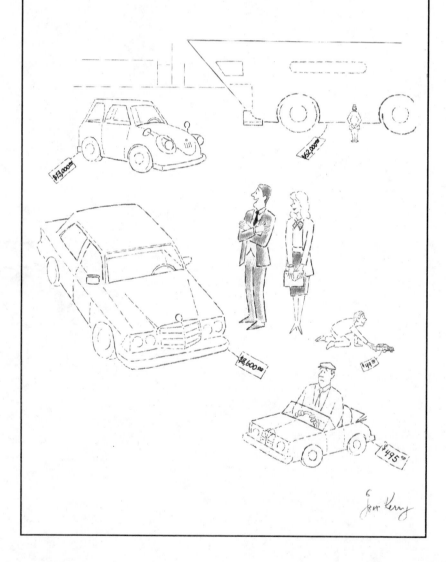

Chapter Twelve

Guidelines for Selecting an Expert System Development Tool

The preceding chapters have acquainted you with today's possibilities for business expert systems. The extent to which these possibilities can be turned into realities depends very much on the tool that is chosen for expert system development. Various tools will not be able to support various expert system capabilities presented in earlier chapters. Some of these capabilities may not be needed for the business applications you presently have in mind. It is important to identify the capabilities that you do (or will) need and then select a tool that supports them.

This chapter provides a fairly extensive set of guidelines that should be considered when selecting an expert system development tool. These guidelines can serve as a checklist, reminding you of capabilities you may want to have. Alongside each selection criterion in the guidelines, you will see a blank space. As you compare and contrast alternative tools, you may want to fill in the blanks to see how well a tool meets the criterion or to see how different tools stack up against each other. Some blanks are followed by parenthetical indications of how well the Guru system fares for those criteria[2].* These provide a useful standard or reference point for assessing other tools of interest to you. Blanks that are not followed by such indications refer to features that exist in Guru. These features may well be of interest in deciding what software to use for building and consulting your own business expert systems.

---

*The indications shown here are software design specifications. Hardware and operating system characteristics may impose more limited practical constraints on the use of a development tool.

Tool comparison charts routinely appear in popular computer magazines and newspapers. These are typically quite superficial due to space limitations in those publications. They frequently ignore major issues and give undue prominence to relatively minor considerations. They lack the details that are so important for clearly distinguishing among different tools' capabilities. For instance, they typically have only one or two entries for certainty factors, indicating whether or not certainty factors are supported. Of course, two tools that "support" certainty factors can have widely different approaches to doing so. One may be primitive, while the other is very extensive and flexible. Yet, comparison charts rarely give any hint of this.

In contrast, this chapter's guidelines for tool selection go into considerable detail. They are organized into several major sections: rule set characteristics, rule set development, consultation, business computing, vendor support, performance, and price. Each criterion is accompanied by a brief explanation of why it is pertinent to the task of selecting a development tool.

RULE SET CHARACTERISTICS

The flexibility and power provided for capturing reasoning knowledge within a rule set are of crucial importance. Flexibility is concerned with the wealth or breadth of capabilities available for characterizing reasoning knowledge. Are the capabilities extensive or does a tool support only an impoverished, narrow assortment of features for specifying knowledge in a rule set? Power is concerned with how much leverage a tool gives to a rule set developer. Can a complex or extensive piece of knowledge be represented in a straightforward manner, with minimal effort? Together, flexibility and power determine how natural and convenient a tool is to use. Not only do these have an impact on a developer's productivity, but they also govern what kinds of expert systems are feasible (technically and economically) with a development tool.

Although limited flexibility and power may be sufficient for a developer's first attempts at expert system construction, tool limitations are ill advised for the long run. As developer experience expands and more ambitious expert systems are undertaken, a limited tool becomes increasingly difficult to use—until a dead end is reached. At such a point, the developer needs to begin again, learning the conventions of a more powerful and flexible tool. Thus, it is vital that a tool provide developers with a growth path, allowing them to start out simply and progress at their own paces, ignoring advanced features until they are needed. Some of the rule set features listed below may not be of immediate applicability to beginners, but all are of interest for developing heavy-duty business expert systems.

Rules

How many rules can a rule set have? _____ (no limit)
> This is an important consideration if a developer intends to build large rule sets or expand rule set sizes over the lifetimes of expert systems.

How many conditions can be specified in the premise of a rule? _____ (no limit)
> A particular fragment of reasoning knowledge may require many conditions. Placing an arbitrary cap on the number of conditions (or characters) that can exist in a premise results in a dead end for the developer.

What kinds of operators are allowed in premise conditions? _____ (numerous)
> Basic conditional operators that should be supported include:
>
> = (equality). _____
> < > (inequality). _____
> > (greater than). _____
> > = (greater than or equal). _____
> < (less than). _____
> < = (less than or equal). _____
> IN (class inclusion). _____

What kinds of expressions can be specified in a premise condition? _____ (numerous)
> The possibilities for logical, string, and (especially) numeric expressions greatly influence a tool's value for building business expert systems. Features that should be considered include:
> Kinds of variables that can be directly referenced:
> > Rule set variables. _____
> > Multivalued (fuzzy) rule set variables. _____
> > Individual values of fuzzy variables. _____
> > Data base fields. _____
> > Spreadsheet cells. _____
> > Program variables. _____
> > Array elements. _____
> > Statistical variables. _____
> > Environmental/utility variables. _____
> These variables can be used in numeric expressions involving:
> > Arithmetic operators for:
> > > Addition. _____
> > > Subtraction. _____
> > > Multiplication. _____
> > > Division. _____
> > > Exponentiation. _____
> > > Modulus. _____
> > > Precedence via parentheses. _____

Built-in numeric functions for:
Logarithms. _____
Date processing. _____
Trigonometric operations. _____
Certainty factor access. _____
Remote communications. _____
Menu option access. _____
Random number generation. _____
Total number of built-in numeric functions. _____ (48)
These variables can be used in text string expressions involving:
String operator for concatenation. _____
Built-in text string functions for:
Case conversion. _____
Trimming blanks. _____
Substring extraction. _____
Pattern match and replacement. _____
Date processing. _____
Total number of built-in text string functions. _____ (18)
These variables can be used in logical expressions involving:
Numeric and string expressions. _____
Wildcard symbol matching. _____
Wildcard string matching. _____
Character class matching. _____
Logical operators for:
Conjunction. _____
Disjunction. _____
Exclusive disjunction. _____
Negation. _____
Built-in logical functions for:
Variable type testing. _____
Known testing. _____
Usage testing. _____
Total number of built-in logical functions. _____ (15)

What kinds of Boolean operators can be specified between conditions in a premise? _____ (several)

Basic Boolean operators that should be supported are:
AND. _____
OR. _____
XOR. _____
NOT. _____

How many actions can be specified in the conclusion of a rule? _____ (no limit)

If the premise of a rule is satisfied, there could be many actions that should be taken. Placing an arbitrary cap on the number of actions (or characters) that can exist in a conclusion can be unwieldy and cause an increase in the number of rules that are required.

What kinds of actions can be included in the conclusion of a rule? _____ (numerous)

> The variety and extent of possible actions is perhaps the most telling factor in assessing a development tool's flexibility and power. The most significant kinds of actions for constructing business expert systems include:
>> Assignment commands. _____
>> Line-oriented input. _____
>> Line-oriented output. _____
>> Expert system consultation. _____
>> Spreadsheet processing. _____
>> Relational data base management. _____
>> SQL inquiries. _____
>> Customized report generation. _____
>> Statistical analysis. _____
>> Business graphics generation. _____
>> Remote communications. _____
>> Procedural modeling. _____
>> Dynamic redefinition of function keys. _____
>> Forms management. _____
>> Menu processing. _____
>> Execution of external programs. _____
>> Postrelational data base access. _____
>> Text processing. _____

Can macro references be included in the premise or conclusion of a rule? _____

> Each macro allows a single word to be used in place of a lengthy sequence of symbols. This saves many keystrokes for frequently needed symbol sequences.

Are rule preactions supported? _____

> A rule's preactions allow the developer to prescribe actions that will be taken as soon as the rule is selected for consideration, prior to testing its premise. This is a convenient localized way to establish the value of some variable that is referenced in the premise. In general, every kind of action that is allowed in a rule's conclusion should also be allowed in its preactions.

How many distinct rule priority levels are supported? _____ (101)

> The ability to give rules different priorities allows a developer to prioritize the order in which candidate rules will be considered during a consultation.

How many distinct cost levels are supported? _____ (101)

> The ability to ascribe different costs to the actions of rules allows a developer to cause the inference engine to consider least-cost candidate rules before those having more expensive actions.

What is the maximum number of characters permitted in each rule's comment? _____ (no limit)

Allowing a developer to comment on each rule is a valuable convenience for ongoing maintenance of a rule set. A rule set manager should be able to display this rule documentation while that rule is being viewed or modified.

What is the maximum number of characters allowed in a rule's reason? _____ (no limit)

An arbitrary cap on how long a reason can be restricts the explanation ability of expert systems that are built with the tool.

Can different premise-testing strategies be specified for different rules? _____

A strategy that is appropriate for testing one rule's premise may not be desirable for other premises. The ability to specify a testing strategy for each rule allows a developer to tune the consultation performance that can be achieved with the rule set.

Variables

How many variables can a rule set reference? _____ (no limit)

Even if an unlimited number of rules is allowed in a rule set, a cap on the number of variables can place major restrictions on rule set development.

What is the maximum number of characters allowed for a variable's label? _____ (48)

Labels are used by an inference engine to explain its line of reasoning. To an expert system user, labels are normally more descriptive than variable names.

How many actions can be specified for finding the value of a variable? _____ (no limit)

As an alternative or complement to determining an unknown variable's value via reverse reasoning, the developer can specify a sequence of actions. The ability to specify multiple actions gives a developer more flexibility and can result in expert system behavior that is not possible if only a single action is allowed per variable.

What kinds of actions can be specified for finding the value of a variable? _____ (numerous)

The degree to which a tool goes beyond line-oriented input actions greatly influences the sophistication of resultant expert systems. The capacity to find a value through a series of user interactions or without any user interaction at all is a definite plus. Some of the basic kinds of actions that might be expected to help find a variable's value include:

Line-oriented input. _____
Line-oriented output. _____
Menu processing. _____
Forms management. _____
Assignment commands. _____
Numeric calculations. _____
Text string manipulations. _____
Expert system consultation. _____
Spreadsheet processing. _____
Record-at-a-time data base retrieval. _____
SQL inquiries. _____
Statistical analyses. _____
Procedural modeling. _____
Remote communications. _____
Business graphics generation. _____
Customized report generation. _____
Execution of external programs. _____

For each variable, can the developer specify whether its find actions are to occur before or after reverse reasoning is attempted? _____

Within a consultation, it may be desirable for the inference engine to treat some variables in one way and the others in another way. This is an example of a highly refined control over expert system reasoning behavior.

How many distinct certainty factor algebras are available for each variable? _____ (16)

The ability to specify different certainty factor computations for different variables is another instance of highly refined control over reasoning behavior. In some applications it may be acceptable for all variable certainty factor computations to be based on the same algebra. In others, close emulation of a human expert may require the simultaneous use of different certainty factor algebras for different variables. Tools that do not allow a developer to select such algebras on a variable-by-variable basis are quite inflexible, providing only one rigid way for trying to emulate human reasoning about uncertainty. On the other hand, if a tool providing, say, 10 algebras is used to build a rule set involving 20 variables, then 10^{20} different possibilities are available for emulating an expert's reasoning about uncertain variable values!

For each variable, can the developer specify how rigorous the inference engine should be when attempting to infer the variable's value? _____

Here again is an example of very refined control over expert system reasoning behavior. Within a consultation it may be desirable for the inference engine to consider all candidate rules for one variable. However, a minimal consideration of candidate rules may be desired when trying to infer the value of another variable. For yet another variable some compromise between these two extremes may be preferred. By changing the rigor choices for individual variables, a developer can modify the behavior that occurs during a consultation.

For each fuzzy variable, can a developer specify a limit on how many values it can have? _____

This is an important efficiency control. When a fuzzy variable's values result from a computation involving multiple fuzzy variables, the number of resulting values can become very large. With a limit control, those values with relatively low certainties can be excluded from subsequent processing, thereby reducing the work for the inference engine.

Initialization

How many actions can be specified in a rule set's initialization sequence? _____ (no limit)

The developer of a rule set should be free to declare or expand a sequence of actions that the inference engine will carry out at the start of a consultation.

What kinds of actions are permitted in an initialization sequence? _____ (numerous)

These may or may not involve user interaction. Some kinds of actions that might be expected include:
Line-oriented input and output. _____
Menu processing. _____
Forms management. _____
Assignment commands. _____
Procedural modeling. _____
Spreadsheet processing. _____
Data base retrieval. _____
Expert system consultation. _____
Statistical analysis. _____
Remote communications. _____
Business graphics generation. _____
Execution of external programs. _____

Security

Can the developer build security controls into a rule set? _____

When a consultation is requested, the inference engine automatically checks the rule set's security controls to determine whether the current user is authorized to use the rule set. Only authorized users are allowed to make use of the reasoning knowledge embodied in a rule set.

Window

What characteristics can be specified for the window that will contain inference engine explanations during a consultation? _____ (several)

Because it prevents full-screen scrolling, a window-oriented explanation is particularly useful when a rule set contains forms management actions. Window characteristics that might be specified by a developer include:

Window position. _____
Window size. _____
Foreground/background colors. _____

Completion

How many actions can be specified in a rule set's completion sequence? _____ (no limit)

The ability to declare and expand a sequence of actions to complete a consultation is very important. Ideally, there should be no arbitrary cap on how many completion actions are permitted for a rule set.

What kinds of actions are permitted in a completion sequence? _____ (numerous)

These actions can be used to customize the way in which consultation results are presented to a user. They can also be used to process consultation results in other ways, out of the user's view. Some of the kinds of actions that might be expected include:

Line-oriented input and output. _____
Forms management. _____
Assignment commands. _____
Data base storage and update. _____
Expert system consultation. _____
Spreadsheet processing. _____
Business graphics generation. _____
Text processing. _____
Remote communications. _____
Statistical analyses. _____
SQL inquiry. _____
Customized report generation. _____
Procedural modeling. _____
Execution of external programs. _____

RULE SET DEVELOPMENT

Beyond the rule set characteristics that can be employed in developing an expert system, a tool's support of the development process itself should not be overlooked. There are two aspects to this development process. One involves the activity of managing the rule set—specifying and revising it. This is accomplished with a development tool's software for rule set management. Second is the activity of testing a rule set to determine whether the expert system behaves as desired. This is accomplished with the tool's inference engine.

A rule set manager should facilitate rapid, convenient rule set construction and revision. In addition to its role as part of an expert system, a tool's inference engine should also furnish facilities to assist developers as they test rule sets. The biggest payoff in developer productivity comes from flexible, powerful, natural methods for representing reasoning knowledge in a rule set. Good rule set development software adds to this productivity. Weak software facilities for rule set construction and testing can severely detract from even the most advanced rule set characteristics.

Rule Set Management

Is the rule set manager an integral part of the consultation environment or is it a separate program? _____ (integral)
  Integration means that the developer does not have to switch among separate programs during the development and testing of a rule set.

Is rule set management accomplished via a text-processing approach or a menu-guided approach? _____ (either)
  Text processing requires a knowledge of rule set syntax, but should allow very flexible rule set viewing and editing. Menu guidance may offer less viewing or editing flexibility, but does not require as much knowledge of rule set syntax.

Is on-line help available during the management of a rule set? _____
  On-line help increases developer productivity by reducing the dependency on paper reference documentation.

While working on a rule set, is the developer free to intermix the activities of adding, deleting, modifying, and viewing rule set contents as needed? _____
  Such freedom greatly enhances developer productivity.

Does the rule set manager provide a broad assortment of control functions for working on rule set contents? _____
  It should be possible to accomplish each control function with a single keystroke. Regardless of whether a text processor or menu-guided manager is being used, basic control functions should allow a developer to easily:
  Move the cursor one line up or down. _____
  Move the cursor one character left or right. _____

Move the cursor one word left or right. _____
Move the cursor to the start or end of a line. _____
Choose between character insertion and replacement editing. _____

Delete the character indicated by the cursor. _____
Delete a character via a destructive backspace. _____
Restart the entry of a line. _____
Delete a line. _____
Restore a formerly deleted line. _____
Insert a new line. _____
Split a line into two lines. _____
Join two lines into a single line. _____

Does a text-processing rule set manager support block manipulations? _____

This allows a developer to quickly move or copy selected blocks of text within a rule set. For instance, the developer may need to enter a new rule that is similar to an existing rule. If the rule is sizable, it is faster to create the new rule by making a copy of the existing rule and editing it with control functions than it is to type in the entire new rule from scratch.

Does a menu-guided rule set manager support automatic rule initialization? _____

This feature allows a developer to use a copy of the most recently accessed rule as a starting point for a new rule that is being created. The developer can edit that copy if desired, rather than typing in the entire new rule from scratch.

Is the rule set manager's pattern-searching ability extensive? _____

Oftentimes a developer may need to view or modify all occurrences of some particular pattern of characters in the rule set. The ability of a rule set manager to focus exclusively on the pattern of interest is valuable. It is far more convenient than forcing the developer to exhaustively look through the entire rule set contents in search of occurrences of the pattern. Useful pattern searching features include:

Search patterns with wildcard string matches (e.g., "K*P" finds any pattern beginning with K and ending with P). _____
Search patterns with wildcard symbol matches (e.g., "V\$n" finds any three-character pattern beginning with V and ending with n). _____

Search patterns with character class symbol matches (e.g., "V[aio]n" finds Van, Vin, and Von patterns. _____
Search in forward and reverse directions. _____
Search with and without regard to case differences. _____
Anchored text searching (e.g., pattern is anchored to the left text margin). _____
Selective text searching within a specified series of lines. _____

Selective context searching (e.g., pattern is recognized only in a rule's conclusion). _____

Automatic text substitution of a desired replacement pattern for each found occurrence of the search pattern. _____

Can the rule set manager print out the current rule set contents after any change and then immediately carry out further changes? _____

This ability allows the developer to keep a paper record of variations of a rule set.

Can the rule set manager save the current rule set contents on a disk file after any change, immediately make further changes, save the revised rule set on disk, and so on? _____

This ability gives the developer a convenient way of generating multiple variations of the same rule set.

Is the rule set manager able to compile a source version of a rule set? _____

Compilation should result in faster consultations and increased rule set security.

During compilation, does the rule set manager analyze the rule set for correctness, consistency, and completeness? _____

Such analysis can be a big time saver for the developer by highlighting potential flaws in a rule set before it is even tested. Informative warning messages should be displayed as potential problems are encountered. The number of different warning messages that a rule set manager can produce is a fair indicator of how extensive the analysis is.

Can compilation warning messages be captured on both disk and printer as well as scrolling on the console screen? _____

Preserving the descriptive warning messages facilitates subsequent rule set revision.

Rule Set Testing

Can the consultation environment be used for testing the efficacy of a rule set? _____

To maximize developer productivity, the rule set manager should be available as an integral part of the environment. A developer should not have to switch among different programs for rule set construction, revision, and testing.

Can any action included in a rule set be executed independently of a consultation session? _____

The ability to directly execute any action in an interactive way speeds up the rule set testing. The effects of any action can be isolated and examined before it is incorporated into a rule set, without involving revision or recompilation of the rule set.

Can the reasoning behavior for a rule set be controlled and tuned by environment settings, without requiring revision and recompilation of the rule set? _____

In order to fully test a rule set, it may be worthwhile to observe and compare the effects of different reasoning assumptions (e.g., consultation rigor or selection order) for the same collection of rules. This kind of testing activity is much more rapid if such assumptions can be altered by simply changing an environment setting outside of the rule set itself. Basic environment settings for testing include the choice of a:
Rule selection order. _____
Premise-testing strategy. _____
Consultation's rigor. _____
Timing strategy for finding an unknown variable's value. _____
Certainty factor algebra for conjunctions. _____
Certainty factor algebra for disjunctions. _____
Default certainty factor algebra for variables. _____
Threshold of the unknown. _____

Is there an inference tracing facility built into the inference engine, allowing the developer to see a step-by-step account of the reasoning as it happens? _____

Such a facility is indispensable when the developer wants to see the sequence of inference engine actions and assess the relative speed of each action.

Can the level of detail presented during a trace be controlled by the developer? _____

This may range from no tracing to very elaborate tracing that reports on the progress of finding each unknown variable, the selection of each rule for consideration, and each rule firing.

Can the developer build his or her own tracing messages into a rule set? _____

In this way, a developer can cause a specialized trace to occur, presenting developer-prescribed trace messages at any desired junctures in a consultation test. These junctures include:
Any point in an initialization sequence. _____
Immediately prior to any premise evaluation attempt. _____
Before or after any action that occurs during a rule's firing. _____
During the attempt to find an unknown variable's value. _____
Any point in a completion sequence. _____

Is there a way to "comment out" (i.e., disable) any undesired portion of a rule set for a given consultation test? _____

For instance, a developer may want to study the effects of having the inference engine temporarily ignore a particular rule, a certain condition in some premise, a certain action in some conclusion, and so on, during a consultation test.

Can testing be isolated on any desired variable? _____

This expedites the testing activity by allowing a developer to focus on the treatment of a particular variable, without requiring a comprehensive consultation.

Can any rule be picked as the starting point for a test? _____

This expedites the testing activity by allowing a developer to focus on the potential firing of a particular rule, without requiring a comprehensive consultation.

Is there a way to automate the testing of a rule set? Can the developer enter a single command to cause repeated consultations, each solving one of a group of previously saved problem descriptions? _____

This ability can help speed up and standardize rule set testing.

Is the inference engine able to produce a printed record of all interaction that occurs during a consultation test? _____

For a lengthy consultation, this helps the developer assess the effects of the test.

CONSULTATION

The power and flexibility that a tool offers for representing reasoning knowledge are primary determiners of what is possible during an expert system consultation. Of equal importance are the abilities that an inference engine has for operating on a rule set. A rudimentary inference engine is capable of processing a given rule set in only one way. The technique it uses for reasoning is always the same, regardless of the rule set being processed. At the opposite extreme are sophisticated inference engines capable of many different reasoning techniques. These adaptable engines can be set, tuned, or directed to reason with rule sets in many different ways. Such flexibility is a contributor to inference engine generality, because all applications are not the same and all human experts being emulated do not necessarily reason in the same way.

In addition to the versatility of inference engine characteristics, the invocation method and environment should be examined when evaluating a tool's consultation capabilities. A variety of methods for starting consultations is advantageous to both the users and developers of expert systems. Similarly, a rich consultation environment is generally preferable to a bare bones environment.

Inference Engine Characteristics

Can the inference engine reason in a forward direction? _____

Forward reasoning ("forward chaining") is generally preferable in situations where all (or most) of a rule set's rules must be considered, where there are few unknown variables, or where there is no single goal. In the latter case, the consultation determines all the implications of a problem, rather than pursuing a specific goal. An example would be a consultation that aims to determine a broad financial plan rather than determining how much to invest in a specific stock.

Can the forward reasoning process be easily tailored without programming or altering the inference engine itself? _____

Built-in adaptability is a definite asset for an inference engine, allowing it to be more general in terms of the breadth of problems handled. The inference engine should provide various "switches" that can be set to give it the desired behavior during forward reasoning. These include:

Choice of the rule selection order. _____
Availability of a number of distinct rule selection orders. _____ (82)
Selection of a default premise-testing strategy. _____
Indication of how rigorous the reasoning should be. _____

Can forward reasoning be requested for a prescribed sequence of rules?

_____

Sometimes it may be desirable to limit a consultation to a certain subset of a rule set's rules. The specific rules to be fired and the order of their firing may even be known in advance. A user may want to repeat the reasoning steps employed in a previous consultation. In each case, consultation speed is increased if the inference engine can make use of such preknowledge.

Is the inference engine able to reason in a reverse direction? _____

Reverse reasoning ("backward chaining") is generally preferable in situations where a substantial portion of rules may be irrelevant to the problem at hand, where there are relatively large numbers of unknown variables, or where there is a specific goal to be pursued.

Can the inference engine accept any unknown variable in a rule set as its goal, for purposes of reverse reasoning? _____

This kind of inference engine flexibility means that very focused consultations are possible. Any consultation can be restricted to any variable of interest, rather than using a rule set's default goal.

Can the reverse reasoning process be easily tailored without programming or altering the inference engine itself? _____

Built-in adaptability is a definite asset for an inference engine, allowing it to be more general in terms of the breadth of problems handled. The inference engine should provide various "switches" that can be set to give it the desired behavior during reverse reasoning. These include:

Selecting a default timing approach for finding variable values. _____

Choosing a rule selection order. _____
Supporting a number of distinct selection orders. _____ (82)
Selecting a default premise-testing strategy. _____
Indicating how rigorous the reasoning should be. _____

Are mixed reasoning methods supported? _____

Mixed reasoning allows some portions of a consultation to proceed in a forward fashion, while others proceed in a reverse manner. This may result in a faster overall consultation than using strictly one reasoning direction.

How many levels of consultation nesting are supported? _____ (50)

The ability of a single inference engine to permit one consultation to be nested within another is valuable. It is one way to overcome a practical limit on the number of rules per rule set. It also provides an easy way to accomplish mixed reasoning. The maximum levels of consultation nesting should not be overly restrictive.

Does the inference engine have built-in mechanisms for reasoning with uncertainty? _____

A generalized inference engine is able to handle the same kinds of uncertainties as a human expert. A developer does not have to program it to accommodate uncertainties. An inference engine should be expected to handle certainty measurements from a variety of sources, including:
The expert system user. _____
Initialization actions. _____
Rule preactions. _____
Actions in the conclusions of fired rules. _____
Variable description actions. _____

How many distinct levels of certainty does the inference engine support? _____ (101)

If there are only a few (e.g., 10) gradations between the highest and lowest levels of certainty, the inference engine's ability to reason about uncertainty is impaired. There should be sufficient distinct levels of certainty for representing and modeling a human expert's uncertainties.

How many different uncertainty thresholds does the inference engine support? _____ (100)

The uncertainty threshold used during a consultation indicates the point at which a certainty factor becomes too low to allow a variable's value to be considered as being known. Depending on the nature of a problem, a low, medium, or high threshold may be desired. An inference engine should be able to work with any one of many possible threshold settings.

Does the inference engine automatically compute certainty factors for the following:

Numeric expressions? _____
String expressions? _____
Logical expressions (e.g., a premise)? _____
Numeric variables? _____
String variables? _____
Logical variables? _____
Each value of a fuzzy variable? _____

Versatility of this kind is important for developing extensive business expert systems. Business applications frequently involve uncertainties about numbers and text strings.

How many methods are built into the inference engine for computing joint certainty factors of expressions? _____ (4)

Values of numeric expressions, string expressions, and conjunctive logical expressions will have certainty factors if terms in those expressions have certainty factors. A flexible inference engine will provide a switch for choosing the algebra to be used for such joint certainty factor computations. Typical choices include:

Minimum. _____
Product. _____
Average of minimum and product. _____
Balance between minimum and product. _____

How many methods are built into the inference engine for computing confirmative certainty factors of disjunctive logical expressions? _____ (4)

Two conditions connected by the OR operator in a premise form a disjunction. A flexible inference engine will provide a switch for choosing the algebra to be used for computing the confirmative certainty factors of disjunctive expressions. Typical choices include:

Maximum. _____
Probability sum. _____
Average of maximum and probability sum. _____
Balance between maximum and probability sum. _____

How many default methods are built into the inference engine for computing the certainty factors of variable values? _____ (16)

An inference engine may not support different certainty algebras for different variables in a rule set. Alternatively, a developer may not choose to prescribe certainty algebras for individual variables. Nevertheless, there should still be a switch for choosing a default certainty algebra for variables in a consultation. An inference engine that has several built-in methods offers more latitude in emulating human reasoning than one that does not.

Can the inference engine base its certainty factor computation for a variable value on both the certainties within a rule and those across rules? _____

If a variable's value is set by the action of some rule, then its certainty factor should be based on certainties in the rule's premise and relevant action. If multiple rules resulting in the same value have fired, then the value's certainty factor should be based on its derived certainties for all of those rules.

What is the maximum number of values that the inference engine can accommodate for each fuzzy variable? _____ (255)

A fuzzy variable can simultaneously have more than one value, each with its own certainty factor. An inference engine should be able to handle a reasonably large number of values for each fuzzy variable.

Can the inference engine make numeric and string calculations for expressions involving fuzzy variables? _____

Beyond allowing constant values to be assigned to a fuzzy variable, a versatile inference engine will be able to evaluate expressions involving fuzzy variables. For instance, the inference engine is able to calculate the fuzzy sum of two fuzzy variables in the course of a consultation. This is a powerful feature to have in situations that involve fuzzy variable manipulation.

Will the inference engine protect rule sets from unauthorized consultation attempts? _____

The inference engine should refuse to reason if a user attempts to consult a rule set without having proper access privileges. Advice offered by an expert system can be very valuable and should be protected from disclosure to unauthorized persons.

Does the inference engine automatically remember the entire sequence of rule firings that occur during the reasoning portion of a consultation? _____

Such an ability means that a consultation can be rapidly rerun. It also enables a developer to design the completion actions to make use of this remembered sequence (e.g., to produce a customized explanation).

Can a user interrupt the inference engine in the midst of a consultation, for an explanation of why a question is being asked? _____

In the course of a consultation, an inference engine may prompt the user for additional input. Before responding, the user should have an opportunity to get an explanation of why this input is needed. This temporary interruption should be easy to make (e.g., by pressing a single key).

After a consultation ends, can the inference engine explain how and why it reasoned as it did? _____

Because an explanation ability is essential for an expert system, the inference engine must be able to explain itself. Built-in explanation facilities should include the ability to examine:

What rules fired to produce the value(s) of any selected variable. _____

What variable values allowed the premise of any selected rule to become true. _____

Explanations in varying levels of detail. _____

Can the inference engine operate on everyday business computers such as IBM microcomputers (or compatibles) and DEC's VAX computers? _____

An inability to do so forces users to work with unfamiliar hardware and operating systems. It can also significantly increase the initial and operating costs of resulting expert systems.

What is the minimum amount of memory required for inference engine operation? _____ (512K)

A development tool with meager or modest capabilities should not require more main memory than a more sophisticated tool. In practice, however, a very large memory requirement is not always a good indicator of sophisticated capabilities. If a machine has more than the minimum required memory, the inference engine should be able to take advantage of that added memory.

Inference Engine Invocation

Are multiple methods available for interactively invoking the inference engine? _____

Potential expert system users span a spectrum from computer novices and casual users to experienced and frequent users. Different modes of interaction are particularly well suited to different segments along this spectrum. Inference engine accessibility is enhanced to the extent that it can be invoked in various modes including:

    The selection of menu options. _____
    Natural language requests. _____
    Command language statements. _____
    Customized interfaces built by a developer. _____

Can the inference engine be invoked in a noninteractive manner? _____

This allows a consultation to be started without any direct initiative by a human user. It may be that there is no human user of the consultation results or, if there is a user, then he or she may be unaware that expert system consultations are taking place. This can be accomplished to the extent that a consultation command can be embedded in a:

    Rule set's initialization actions. _____
    Rule's conclusion actions. _____
    Variable description's find actions. _____
    Rule set's conclusion actions. _____
    Program (e.g., a procedural model). _____
    Spreadsheet cell's definition. _____
    Piece of text for print-time execution. _____
    Macro definition. _____
    Function key definition. _____
    Data base for subsequent retrieval and execution. _____

Can a consultation command cause the inference engine to skip a rule set's initialization actions? _____

In some situations, successive or iterative invocation of a single rule set may be desired. Only the first of these consultations should carry out the initialization actions, if a cumulative effect of the consultations is desired. In order for each consultation to build upon the result of the prior consultation, reinitialization should not take place.

Inference Engine Environment

How many environment controls (switches) are provided for customizing the realm within which reasoning occurs? _____ (110)

A rich assortment of these controls allows the inference engine environment to be easily tailored to a particular user's needs. No programming effort is required and the inference engine software is itself unaffected. A sampling of possibilities includes environment controls for:

    Screen foreground and background colors. _____
    Direction of spreadsheet computation. _____
    Suppressing the displays of various computed statistics. _____
    Baud rate used during remote communications. _____
    Automatic data source transpose during graph generation. _____
    Number of digits displayed to the right of a decimal point. _____
    Character used to denote a decimal point. _____

Date format assumed for date processing (e.g., month/day/year versus /day/month/year). _____
Echoing console input to a printer or disk file. _____
Positioning of diagnostic messages on the screen. _____
Suppressing background grids for graphic displays. _____
Getting automatic context-sensitive help. _____
Ignoring case differences when comparing string values. _____
Ignoring macro expansion capabilities. _____
Automatic certainty factor prompting for user input. _____
Automatic certainty factor display for each output. _____
Delimiter assumed when importing data from an external file. _____
Type of parity checking used during communications. _____
File transfer protocol (e.g., Kermit, XMODEM) assumed. _____
Communications buffer sizes. _____
Routing output to the screen, printer, and/or disk file. _____
Printer characteristics (e.g., page depth, margin, width). _____
Suppressing displays of retrieved data. _____
Synchronous cell movements within windows. _____
Automatic graphics axis scaling. _____

Can environment controls be set by an expert system user prior to consultation? _____

The user might directly switch a control from its default setting to another setting. Alternatively, the developer may build a custom interface that asks a user about what environmental characteristics are desired. The corresponding settings are then made by the customized interface software.

Can environment control settings be specified within a rule set? _____

Such an ability allows the developer to fully control the nature of the environment for consultations involving a rule set. The desired settings are made in the initialization actions and can be restored to their former states in the rule set's completion actions.

Does the inference engine environment allow consultation commands to be freely intermixed with other commands of interest to a business user? _____

This allows expert system consultation to be treated as a standard business-processing activity. It can be exercised at any time, without having to leave one program (e.g., for spreadsheet or data base processing) and to enter another before a consultation can occur. The convenience of a single program that provides a unified AI environment for business computing should not be overlooked.

Can the most recently issued command be recalled with a single keystroke? _____

By pressing a single key, the most recent command reappears on the console screen for editing and reexecution. This saves considerable typing time in cases where you want to correct an error in your last command or execute a slightly modified version of a command.

Is it possible to import data from external sources for use within the inference engine's AI environment? _____

Data values existing on some other computer or produced by some other software could be useful within inference engine's environment. The environment should allow contents of ASCII, DIF, and other kinds of files to be easily imported.

Is it possible to export data from the inference engine's AI environment for use by external software? _____

Data export involves the conversion of some collection of data into a file whose format is acceptable to an external program. Common formats for data export include:
BASIC compatible. _____
ASCII. _____
DIF. _____
Customized formats. _____

BUSINESS-COMPUTING CAPABILITIES

The synergistic blending of business-computing capabilities with expert system technology is crucial for convenient construction of business expert systems. As indicated earlier in this chapter, the ability to specify various business-computing actions *within* a rule set should be considered when selecting a tool. These could be actions that the inference engine takes during the initialization, rule firing, variable value determination, or completion phases of a consultation. Also deserving consideration is the variety of business-computing activities that can be *intermixed* with consultation requests in the environment provided for tool operation. Thus a particular kind of activity (e.g., spreadsheet analysis) can be used for various purposes both inside and outside of a rule set specification.

Previous guidelines have focused on the *existence* of a variety of business-computing capabilities for certain purposes. However, the *extensiveness* of each such capability must also be considered. For instance, two expert system development tools may each have a graphics capability. The graphics capability of one may be minimal—at the level of 1–2–3 graphics, for example. The other tool may provide a full-scale graphics capability—at the level of a stand-alone package such as CHART-MASTER. Every business computing capability existing in an AI environment should be assessed from the standpoint of its extensiveness. Ideally, an expert system development tool should support business-computing capabilities that are at least on a par with their stand-alone counterparts. In this way, an expert system development tool can avoid the criticism that is so often leveled at ordinary integrated packages like Symphony and Framework—one or two strong capabilities coupled with many weak ones.

A detailed examination of all interesting features of each kind of business-computing capability could easily add more than 50 pages to this book. Rather than attempting to be so exhaustive, a few features of each are highlighted here. These have been chosen to identify some of the most important basics. Also included are some advanced features that are indicators of how extensive a capability is.

Data Base Management

Is a relational data base management capability provided? _____

The relational approach to data base management is useful for relatively modest data-handling needs, where there are a few simple relationships among various kinds of data and where top efficiency is not required. Though it has today become commonplace to equate file management with relational data base management, the two are quite different [1]. If documentation equates the term *data base* with *file* or refers to files of data, then the software is most probably file management software. Some relational data base features to consider include:

Tables per data base (max). _____ (no limit)
Tables simultaneously in use (max). _____ (no limit)
Records per table (max). _____ (2 billion)
Fields per data base (max). _____ (no limit)
Fields per table (max). _____ (255)
Characters per field (max). _____ (65,535)
Indexes per table (max). _____ (no limit)
Fields per index key (max). _____ (255)
Customized field types. _____
Virtual fields. _____
Interactive table definition. _____
Interactive table redefinition. _____
Interactive record creation. _____
Batch record creation. _____
Interactive browsing. _____
Read/write security down to the field level. _____
Automatic data encryption. _____
Tables that can be "joined" in a single operation (max). _____ (no limit)
Dynamic sorting by "join" or "project" operation. _____
"Project" or "join" operation can be conditioned by field values.
_____
Expressions and built-in functions allowed in all operations. _____
Data base can be accessed from a programming language (e.g., C).
_____

Is a more advanced, postrelational data base management capability available? _____

> When data-handling needs go beyond the simple relational capability, a more powerful and flexible approach to data base management is valuable. This occurs in situations where there are many kinds of data to be managed, the data interrrelationships are numerous and intricate, there are very large volumes of data values, and very rapid access speeds are desired. Such a capability is of primary interest to professional software developers and is normally beyond the skills of novice computer users. The postrelational (alias extended-network) approach should not be confused with the old CODASYL-network or hierarchical approaches. It overcomes the data structuring and manipulation drawbacks of the older approaches [1].

Can multiple users simultaneously share the contents of the same data base? _____

> The ability of multiple expert systems to concurrently share a common body of environmental knowledge contributes to consistent, efficient advice. As with any good data base management system:
> Locking mechanisms should be furnished for preserving data integrity.
> _____
>
> Individual record locking should be allowed for efficiency. _____

Ad Hoc Inquiry

Is the standard SQL query facility provided for selective data retrieval?
_____

> SQL queries provide a high-level way for selectively extracting data values from a relational data base. Although such a facility is not a required part of a relational data base management system, it is much more convenient than relational algebra (i.e., join, project, etc. operations) for retrieving data from tables. Query features to consider include:
> Tables that can be accessed by a single query (max). _____ (no limit)
> Query output for computed expressions involving multiple fields.
> _____
> Conditions per query (max). _____ (no limit)
> All relational operators (including IN) supported for conditions.
> _____
> Retrieval scope can be specified. _____
> Character class, wildcard symbol, and wildcard string searches.
> _____
> Automatic suppression of duplicate output rows. _____
> Dynamic output editing for fields and computed values. _____
> Multitable query using indexes. _____
> Dynamic sorting of query output in ascending and/or descending direction. _____
> Levels of control break grouping (max). _____ (no limit)

Statistical Analysis

Can basic statistics be generated with a single command? _____

It is not uncommon for decision making to involve at least some basic statistical analyses (e.g., sum, average, standard deviation). The purpose is to summarize the nature and relationships of large numbers of data values, particularly those existing in a data base. The statistics capability might include the following features:

Different kinds of basic statistics supported. _____ (7)

Statistics based on related data in multiple tables. _____

Statistics for computational expression involving multiple fields, cells, and so on. _____

Conditional statistics based on any relational operators. _____

Statistical results automatically preserved in statistical variables. _____

Is a programming facility provided for building customized statistical models that go beyond the basic statistics? _____

Some applications may require the use of specialized statistical analyses.

Spreadsheet Analysis

Does the AI environment provide a spreadsheet-processing capability? _____

Spreadsheet processing is very important in many decision support applications. A spreadsheet is by no means a substitute for a data base, even though there is a tendency in some quarters to consume large numbers of cells with data values. The power of a spreadsheet depends on how much can be done with an individual cell. If a cell can be defined as nothing more than a data value or a formula, then the spreadsheet lacks the power of those that allow cells to be defined in terms of data base retrieval, statistical analysis, or entire procedural models. A sampling of features that should be considered when assessing the spreadsheet capability existing in an AI environment include:

Cells per spreadsheet (max) _____ (65,535)

Windows per spreadsheet (max). _____ (255)

Absolute and relative copy operations within and across spreadsheets. _____

Column and row insertion and deletion. _____

Variable width columns. _____

Locking of vertical and horizontal borders in windows. _____

Cell block names. _____

Editing controls for individual cells or cell blocks. _____

Cell formulas based on fields, statistical variables, program variables, and so on, in addition to cells. _____

Cell defined as a procedural model. _____

Cell defined as a data base access. _____

Spreadsheets can share common models and data bases. _____

Cell creation from SQL query results. _____
Cell definition can be changed while spreadsheet not displayed.
_____

Reevaluation while spreadsheet not displayed. _____
Window color and intensity controls. _____
Automatic cell highlighting (reverse video, blinking, color change, etc.) based on current cell value. _____
Read and write security checking for individual cell definitions.
_____

Graphics

Is a business graphics capability furnished in the AI environment?
_____

The ability to view business data in a graphical way is valuable in many decision-making situations. Not only should this capability offer a good assortment of graph types, it should also allow data to be graphed from a variety of data sources. Features to be considered when examining the graphics capability of an AI environment include:
Multicolor graphs. _____
Bar graphs (flat, 3-D, stacked, percentage). _____
Area graphs (cumulative, percentage). _____
Pie graphs (labeled, percentage, exploded). _____
Scatter graphs. _____
Line graphs. _____
High-low-close graphs. _____
Function plots (linear, polynomial, logarithmic, exponential, trigonometric). _____ (all)
Pictograms. _____
Automatic and customized ranges and scaling. _____
Customizable area, line, mark, and color patterns. _____
Superimposed graphs. _____
Text placement on graphs. _____
Control over legend position and content. _____
Split screen graphing. _____
Data points per graph (max). _____ (no limit)
Slices per pie (max). _____ (no limit)
Lines, bars, areas per graph (max). _____ (no limit)
Graphics data source (spreadsheet, program array, data base query results, statistics results). _____ (all)
Dynamic sorting of data source contents for graph generation.
_____

Multiple data sources for a single graphing operation. _____
Dynamic transpose of data source contents. _____
Graph rotation for plotter output. _____
Graph preservation for "slide show" presentation. _____
Immediate printing of graphics screen image. _____

Text Processing

Is there a general-purpose text-processing capability? _____

Although decision makers normally do not need elaborate word processing systems, a general-purpose text-processing capability can be useful for preparing procedural models, rule sets, letters, memos, reports, forms, and so on. Text-processing features to consider include:

Characters per line (max). _____ (255)
Lines per piece of text (max). _____ (10,000)
Automatic word wrap, if desired. _____
Automatic line numbering, if desired. _____
Text color controls. _____
Number of *single* keystroke-editing operations. _____(22)
Block processing. _____
Wildcard and anchored search and replacement. _____
Direct insertion of new text from another source (external file, query result, computation, statistics result, spreadsheet, procedure execution). _____(all)
Delayed insertion of new text at print-time from another source (external file, query, computation, statistics, spreadsheet, graphics, procedure execution). _____(all)
Mail-merge from multiple tables with a single command. _____
Conditional and sorted mail-merge. _____
Automatic text file backups. _____
Number of formatting controls (margins, headers, footers, etc.) _____ (40)

Forms Management

Is a forms management capability provided in the AI environment? _____

This capability allows visual forms to be invented, preserved, revised, and used. A form is presentation knowledge that prescribes a particular customized way of displaying or collecting knowledge. Forms could be used for screen input and/or output. They could also be used for printer output. Features to look for in a forms management capability include:

Interactive on-screen forms painting. _____
Multicolor form design. _____
Free-form layout of elements within a form. _____
Each element in a form can have its own special visual effects (reverse video, blinking, etc.). _____
Form-at-a-time processing operations. _____ (7)
Automatic editing of data values displayed for form elements. _____
Interactive record creation through customized forms. _____
Interactive record browsing through customized forms. _____
Spreadsheet input and output via forms. _____
Procedural model input and output via forms. _____

Consultation input and output via forms. _____
Dynamic form positioning. _____
Forms per console screen (max). _____ (no limit)
Overlapping forms allowed on the screen. _____

Customized Report Generation

Is a capability furnished for generating customized reports? _____

An ad hoc query capability such as that of SQL provides a way for getting desired reports from a data base—on a spur of the moment basis. Control over the layouts of these ad hoc reports is limited, and this is often fine. However, sometimes reports need to have elaborate layouts. This is especially true for a routine type of report that is needed on a regular or repeated basis. It is also true for reports that need to be formally presented to others. A customized report generation capability should be assessed in terms of features such as:

Interactive, on-screen design of report templates. _____
Multicolor reports. _____
Support of report header and footer. _____
Support of page headers and footers. _____
Automatic page numbering at any desired position. _____
Levels of control break grouping per report (max). _____ (26)
Support of group headers and footers. _____
Free-form design and placement of any header or footer. _____
Report can contain data values from a data base, spreadsheet, statistical variables, program variables, dynamic computations. _____
Multitable access via a single report generation command. _____
Dynamic sorting of report details. _____
Conditional report generation supporting all relational operators. _____

Optional suppression of report details for aggregate statistical reporting. _____

Remote Communications

Does the AI environment offer a remote communications capability? _____

The ability to communicate with computers (or their users) at distant sites is an important aspect of business computing. A sampling of features to consider when investigating an AI environment's communication capability includes:

Dial, hang up, login, and logout operations. _____
Text and nontext file transfer. _____
Support of XMODEM and Kermit protocols. _____
Terminal emulation. _____
File capture and transmit directives during terminal emulation. _____
Directive for local machine to execute a command during terminal emulation. _____

Handshaking support. _____
Split-screen dialog with remote computer's user. _____
Supports raw character, line, and block communications. _____
Baud rate—bits transmitted per second (max). _____ (19,200)
Different types of parity checking supported. _____ (5)
Stop bits and bits-per-byte settings. _____
Controllable communications buffer sizes. _____
Buffer threshold settings. _____
Settings for communication timing and retry behavior. _____
Customizable to a variety of modems. _____

Procedural Modeling

Is a complete structured programming language provided for procedural modeling? _____

A spreadsheet provides one way of representing procedural knowledge, While it is convenient for some kinds of modeling, it is inconvenient or even infeasible for others. This is because ordinary spreadsheets (e.g., 1–2–3) provide little in the way of control logic. From a modeling perspective, a spreadsheet is little more than a sequence of assignment statements. Though it usually requires more skill, a structured programming language is a far more versatile method for specifying procedural models. When considering the programming capability offered by an AI environment, the following kinds of features should be examined:

Number of program variables per program. _____ (no limit)
Program can reference field, cell, statistical, and rule set variables. _____

Multidimensional arrays. _____
Number of built-in functions. _____ (77)
Supports standard computations ($+, -, *, /, **$). _____
Assignment statements for both single-valued and fuzzy variables. _____

Assignment statements with certainty factor specifications. _____

Assignment of definitions to spreadsheet cells. _____
Line-oriented input and output. _____
Form-oriented input and output. _____
Built-in diagnostic status variable. _____
Command length in characters (max). _____ (no limit)
If-then-else control structures. _____
While-do control structures. _____
Test-case control structures. _____
Parameterized program invocation. _____
Parameters per program (max). _____ (26)
Levels of program nesting (max). _____ (no limit)
Program variables, forms, and macros can be global or local. _____

Program can include commands for processing of data bases, spreadsheets, consultations, communications, statistical data, and graphics. _____
Programs can be organized into libraries. _____

Can external programs be run from within the AI environment? _____

In addition to its own integral programming language, an AI environment should be able to execute programs from other sources (e.g., from other software vendors). These may be specialized models or general-purpose software tools.

VENDOR SUPPORT

Before selecting a tool for developing business expert systems, it is worthwhile to investigate the tool's vendor. Beyond providing software, in what ways will the vendor support your efforts at constructing business expert systems? There are at least three areas to explore when gauging the degree of vendor support. One involves the vendor's history or track record. Second is the documentation available for the tool. Third are vendor services, which may range from telephone support to actually developing expert systems for you.

Vendor History

How many years has the vendor been involved in the design and manufacture of software? _____ (7 in 1986)

Longevity is indicative of a company that has been at least reasonably responsive to customer needs.

Is the vendor's principal activity one of providing software to the business community? _____

Experience in business computing is a good sign that the vendor's AI tools are likely to have been designed to support business users.

Does the vendor have an ongoing history of introducing software innovations? _____ (yes*)

If so, it is more likely that the tool (and its subsequent enhancements) will be close to state of the art. The "me too" software companies are typically a step behind. A proven in-house research and development

---

*First viable DBMS for microcomputers, first implementation of the post-relational data model, first multiuser micro DBMS, first integration of spreadsheet and DBMS, first micro implementation of SQL inquiry, first DBMS to run in both PC-DOS and UNIX environments, among others.

staff is a good indicator that you will benefit from vendor innovations on a continuing basis.

Does the vendor have a track record of continuing to enhance a software product after its initial release? _____

Technology does not stand still. It is important to deal with a vendor that realizes this. By seriously listening to customer feedback and "wish lists," a vendor can augment its own internal research efforts. The result is a product that continues to evolve over the years to meet evolving customer needs. This product evolution should, of course, progress in an upward compatible fashion.

Documentation

Is on-line documentation built into the tool itself? _____

A valuable productivity aid is the ability to obtain an on-screen description that helps in using a given aspect of the tool or its environment. These help descriptions should be organized by topic, so the developer can quickly focus on the pertinent description.

How many lines of help descriptions are available? _____ (20,000)

Meager help descriptions are of meager value. Extensive descriptions are of extensive value, provided they are organized for rapid focusing on a desired topic.

Is context-sensitive help available? _____

This means that the software tool will use the present processing context to automatically determine what help description to display on the screen. The developer does not need to explicitly identify the topic of interest.

How many pages of reference documentation are provided? _____ (1,000)

As with all nontrivial software, an expert system development tool should be accompanied by a reference manual. It should be a complete and well-organized document that provides precise, in-depth explanations of every command and facility offered by the development tool. It should have adequate cross-references and indexing. Reference documentation explains what the tool does, what actions a developer can take when working with the tool, and how the tool will behave in response to each developer action. Reference documentation should not be cluttered with tutorial passages. Instructions about how to apply a tool's capabilities in solving various problems belong in an instruction manual—not a reference manual. The size of a reference document is an indicator of how comprehensive it is, as well as how extensive the tool is.

Does the reference document clearly differentiate between explanations intended for beginning developers and those intended only for advanced developers? _____

> Well-organized documentation provides a growth path from basic to advanced topics. It should alert the reader to which passages are directed at advanced developers.

Does the vendor provide instructional documentation? _____ (no [3])

> In addition to a reference manual, sufficient instructional documentation should be furnished with the tool. An instruction manual introduces the reader to the tool's basic purpose and capabilities. It should provide extensive examples showing how those capabilities can be applied to various common situations. Its examples should illustrate common flows or patterns of processing by showing typical series of command invocations or menu-option selections. Unlike a reference manual, an instruction manual should not be expected to cover every possible detail of the tool's behavior. An effective instruction manual brings its reader up to a point where he or she is able to look up topics in the reference manual if more in-depth explanation is desired. Although an instruction manual is of minimal interest to experienced developers, it is very important to others, until they join the ranks of the experienced.

Are sample business expert systems provided by the vendor? _____

> By providing samples, the vendor can give you a good idea of some of the tool's capabilities. These can be very good tutorial devices. The rule sets of these business expert systems may well suggest ideas for constructing your own rule sets with the development tool.

Are the tool and its uses described in detail in books by independent publishers? _____

> Additional instructional materials may be useful complements to (or substitutes for) the vendor's own instruction manual.

Vendor Services

Is "no charge" telephone support available? _____

> If you have a question about some aspect of the tool's operation, it is helpful to be able to discuss it with a qualified vendor representative.

Is a priority support service available? _____

> For fastest access to the vendor's support staff, you may prefer to pay for priority support.

Does the vendor offer open training courses for first-hand instruction in the tools usage? _____ Does the vendor offer tailored, on-site training courses? _____

A training course can accelerate the learning process by providing intensive instruction in a short period of time.

Are special versions of the development tool available for training purposes? _____

A pared-down version of the tool can be an effective training aid, allowing corporate trainees or university students to inexpensively gain hands-on experience in expert system construction and consultation.

Does the vendor offer professional consulting services? _____

Expert system developers can sometimes benefit from the advice of professionals who are well versed in using the vendor's tool.

Does the vendor offer professional application development services?
_____

Organizations needing application systems, including those involving expert system technology, do not always have the personnel or time to do the development work themselves. In such situations, it is advantageous if the customer can draw on an experienced staff of developers. A vendor history of delivering extensive application systems to large corporate and government clients is also a good indication in the effectiveness of the vendor's tools.

PERFORMANCE

Once you have identified well-supported tools that are technically capable of building the kinds of business expert systems that you need, their respective performance traits deserve some study. Inference engine performance depends on a wide variety of factors. First, there is the machine and operating system with which the inference engine is being used. A second factor is the programming language used to implement the inference engine. In general, a noncompiled language (e.g., variants of LISP or PROLOG) yields a slower inference engine than a compiled language. Among compiled languages there are also differences. For instance, implementing an inference engine with the C language (as in the case of Guru) should result in faster consultation processing than a FORTRAN implementation.

A third factor affecting inference engine performance is the quality of rule set design. Two different formulations of the same reasoning knowledge can result in significant performance differences for the same inference engine. For instance, a rule set design that consists of 200 rules is very likely to require more processing time than an equivalent rule set of 50 rules. What is or is not a good rule set design from a performance viewpoint depends on the nature of the inference engine. A rule set design that yields acceptable performance for one inference engine may be suboptimal or even unacceptable for another inference engine— even though the two inference engines are implemented with the same programming language and are running with the same hardware and operating systems.

The rule set characteristics discussed earlier in this chapter can have a large impact on inference engine performance, because they determine what rule set design alternatives are available to a developer. As the flexibility, power, and naturalness offered for representing reasoning knowledge increase, they tend to result in rule sets that are more concise and streamlined. "Rube Goldberg" rule sets involving roundabout ways to specify knowledge can be avoided. An inference engine's performance is enhanced if it does not need to take numerous, lengthy detours to accomplish various reasoning tasks during a consultation.

Another important factor related to performance involves the reasoning controls that are built into an inference engine. Many have been identified earlier in this chapter. These controls allow a developer to govern the inference engine's strategy for reasoning about a particular problem. Depending on the nature of the problem and the design of the rule set, one strategy may result in a faster consultation than another strategy. By giving a developer easily modifiable controls, a tool lets the developer assess the relative performances of alternative strategies. Thus, the developer can tune the performance of an inference engine for a specific rule set or a specific problem. If versatile tuning controls are absent from a tool, then the developer's influence over inference engine speed is correspondingly limited.

Performance is also affected by the quality of the rule set compiler. If there is no compiler, then it is unrealistic to expect top performance from the inference engine. All compilers are not created equal. Some may generate compiled rule sets that can be processed very efficiently, while the compiled rule sets of others may lead to relatively slow inference engine processing.

As the foregoing factors suggest, making sweeping generalizations about the performance of one inference engine relative to another may not always be possible. One should be wary about drawing unwarranted generalizations from comparative benchmark testing. Benchmark results should always be accompanied by a clear explanation of the situation used for testing, the rule set designs employed, and the host hardware/operating system. Provided rule sets are designed fairly and tuning controls are set fairly, the benchmark tests will give a good idea of which inference engine performs fastest in a *specific* situation. In another situation a different inference engine may be faster.

One of the best ways to get a quick feel for an inference engine's speed is to turn on its inference tracing mechanism. Because this provides an on-screen, blow-by-blow account of the inference engine's processing activities, you will be able to see how fast it can select a rule, process a rule, or find the value of an unknown variable. Try this for the sample expert systems provided by the vendor and you will begin to get an idea about whether the inference engine's processing rate is fast enough for your needs.

In addition to inference engine performance, the speed of the rule set manager should be considered. Overly slow processing during the development and maintenance of a rule set can be very disconcerting to a developer. Rule set compilation should also be a reasonably fast activity. By segmenting reasoning knowledge into distinct rule set modules during initial development work, you may be able to reduce rule set maintenance and compilation times. This is because you are able to focus on a small collection of rules at any given time.

PRICING

Software for developing expert systems ranges from hobbyist tools costing as much as a few hundred dollars to more serious tools costing thousands or even tens of thousands of dollars. The first point to keep in mind when considering prices is that price is not always a good indicator of a tool's power or flexibility. Even though one tool may cost several thousand dollars less than another, it may actually be able to do more. Of course, there is little sense in purchasing a tool that cannot handle your business expert system needs today and tomorrow—no matter what its price may be.

Unless you have access to developers who work for free, a tool's price usually reflects only a small portion of the cost of expert system development. Labor and associated overhead costs quickly dwarf the several thousand dollars spent on a tool, particularly if the tool is repeatedly used for expert system development. This is why it is so important to select a very flexible and powerful tool whose conveniences maximize developer productivity while minimizing the development costs and ongoing maintenance costs.

Convenience, as discussed in this chapter, has a much deeper meaning than superficial marketing hype like "user friendly." It is commonplace these days to see software described as "user friendly" if it has a menu interface and can be mastered by a novice within a few minutes (or least no more than a few hours). Of course, such a naive simpleminded view entirely ignores the fact that there are many kinds of soft-

This tool sure is user friendly. It takes no skill or thought at all.

ware users in the world. So-called "user friendly" software is fine for novice and casual users, but can be downright unfriendly for those who have progressed beyond the initial stage of computer familiarity. To a user who is able to directly state a command, wading through a bunch of menus to make the same request is very cumbersome and time consuming (if it is even possible). To a user whose software needs grow and expand with experience, "user friendly" software offers no appreciable growth path. Instead, it offers plenty of mental exercise in trying to figure out ingenious ways for accomplishing more advanced tasks with novice-level capabilities.

When seriously considering expert system development tools, one should look beyond surface "user friendly" claims. The important question *is not*, How quickly can you get to know all aspects of the software? The important question *is*, How easy is it to live with the software on a continuing basis? This convenience is very much determined by a tool's flexibility and power. The tool should be flexible enough to accommodate your growing needs, expectations, and skills. It should allow you to start out simply (with a menu interface, if you like) and grow into its more powerful and extensive capabilities at your own pace. The ongoing convenience that results from flexibility and power translates into high productivity. A tool's cost must be examined in light of the degree of productivity it engenders.

Those who develop business expert systems for resale or other distribution should check on the availability and pricing of run-time versions of the inference engine. For large organizations, the vendor's site licensing policies and prices will also be of interest.

CONCLUSION

This chapter has provided a fairly detailed set of guidelines to oberve when selecting a tool for business expert system development. The selected tool should give a developer extensive flexibility and power for representing reasoning knowledge within a rule set. It should provide facile facilities for rule set development. The inference engine should be sufficiently general, offer a reasonable array of reasoning controls, and operate within a rich AI environment for business computing. The traditional business computing capabilities provided in this environment should be reasonably extensive. The tool should be fully supported, perform adequately, and help minimize cost (and time) required for business expert system development.

An AI environment for business computing should allow you to *create* an expert, *consult* an expert and *be* an expert. By *creating* an expert, your expertise about using knowledge is embodied in a computer-based system. By *consulting* an expert, you can actively employ the reasoning expertise of others to process various kinds of knowledge, for the purpose of deriving new knowledge (i.e., advice). By *being* an expert, you directly exercise your own reasoning capabilities in the course of working with knowledge held in data bases, spreadsheets, models, text, graphic images, and so forth. An AI environment that allows a person to play any or all of these three roles can form the basis for tomorrow's knowledge-based organizations.

EXERCISES

1. Identify the main categories of criteria that should be used when evaluating a business expert system development tool.
2. What factors determine how natural and convenient a tool is to use?
3. What is a growth path and why is it important?
4. With respect to tool evaluation, what are the two major aspects of rule set development?
5. Beyond the existence of a particular business-computing capability in an AI environment, what else about that ability should be considered?
6. Identify several aspects of vendor support.
7. What kinds of factors influence the performance of an expert system?
8. Why are benchmark tests not necessarily good indicators of performance?
9. Explain why the following statement is meaningless: "Software package X is user friendly."
10. Use the documentation of an expert system development tool to see how it fares with respect to the selection criteria identified in this chapter.
11. Can you suggest additional criteria for evaluating a shell's or an integrated AI environment's applicability for constructing and using business expert systems, decision support systems, and artificially intelligent application systems?

References

1 Bonczek, R. H.; C. W. Holsapple; and A. B. Whinston: *Micro Database Management—Practical Techniques for Application Development.* New York: Academic Press, 1984.
2 *Guru Reference Manual*, vols. 1–2. Lafayette, Ind.: MDBS, Inc. 1985.
3 Williamson, M. "In Guru, the Business World Finally Has Its First, True AI-Based Micro Package," *PC Week* 3, nos. 11–14, 1986.

The architecture of organizations sure has changed.

Chapter Thirteen

Knowledge-Based Organizations

Over the past 30 years, advances in computer-based technology have had an important impact on the way in which organizations operate. Over the next 30 years, such advances will revolutionize the way in which we think about organizations. The very nature of organizations is being transformed from an emphasis on working with materials to an emphasis on working with knowledge. Work with material goods will come to be viewed as a secondary or almost incidental aspect of an organization's mission. It will be little more than an automatic consequence of knowledge processing. Furthermore, managing an organization's human and financial resources will also become exercises in knowledge management.

In a most fundamental sense, organizations will increasingly be regarded as joint human-computer knowledge-processing systems. Human participants in these systems, from the most highly skilled to the least skilled positions, can be regarded as knowledge workers. Collectively, they will work with many types of knowledge, in a variety of ways, and with various objectives. Their knowledge management efforts will be aided and supported by computers. Not only will these computer co-workers relieve us of the menial, routine, and repetitive, they will also actively recognize needs, stimulate insights, and offer advice. They will highly leverage an organization's uniquely human skills of intuition, creative imagination, value judgment, the cultivation of effective interpersonal relationships, and so forth.

The potential of such knowledge-based organizations for increased human productivity will be realized to the extent that these organizations are successfully inaugurated and managed. This prospect has impacts on each of the traditional functional areas of management (e.g., marketing or operations) in two significant ways. First, it presents an opportunity to enhance the efficiency and effectiveness of practitioners

301

in each functional area. Second, it presents challenges to investigators in each functional area, for they are now confronted with a new kind of organization. This chapter provides a characterization of knowledge-based organizations that can serve as a foundation for understanding these opportunities and challenges.

KNOWLEDGE WORKERS

Knowledge workers are concerned with procuring, storing, organizing, maintaining, creating, analyzing, presenting, distributing, and applying knowledge in order to meet an organization's goals. Some knowledge workers may be involved with all of these aspects of knowledge management, while others specialize in one or a few of these activities. There are also various types of knowledge to be managed. One type is environmental knowledge, which is knowledge about past, present and/or anticipated states of the organization and its environment. Another is procedural knowledge about how certain tasks can be accomplished. There is derived knowledge, which results from the application of procedural knowledge in analyzing environmental knowledge. Linguistic knowledge is concerned with the syntax and semantics of languages used within the organization. Assimilative knowledge governs the manner in which new knowledge can be acquired. Conversely, presentation knowledge governs the manner in which existing knowledge can be disclosed. Finally there is metaknowledge, which is knowledge about the nature and utilization of knowledge. Reasoning knowledge is a very important kind of metaknowledge.

Figure 13–1 portrays the activities of a knowledge worker with respect to various types of knowledge. Each type of knowledge is susceptible to each of the knowledge management activities. At the same time, one or more of the various types of knowledge are typically used in carrying out a particular activity. For instance, procedural knowledge is the basis for analysis; when environmental knowledge is the subject of analysis, facts or expectations about the organization and its environment may be derived. The maximization of knowledge worker effectiveness and productivity is a paramount issue whose resolution lies in technological advances, appropriate training, and an administrative atmosphere that fosters cooperation among knowledge workers.

Technological Advances

On the technology front, several crucial footholds have already been established beyond the apparently never-ceasing per dollar improvements in hardware speeds and storage capacities. One of these is the technology for intercomputer communications, including local area networks and mainframe-micro linkages. Continued development of this technology is a key for promoting knowledge sharing, cooperative

FIGURE 13-1   Activities of a knowledge worker

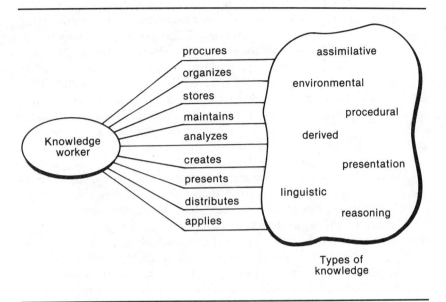

Types of
knowledge

(and consistent) problem solving among knowledge workers, and distributed knowledge processing. The latter two characteristics of a knowledge-based organization are likely to be facilitated by advances in parallel processing and non–von Neumann machine architectures [6].

Another crucial technological element for the realization of knowledge-based organizations is the existence of software tools designed specifically for use by knowledge workers. Each tool brings with it an environment for working with (i.e., managing) knowledge of various kinds. Knowledge workers do not have the technical skills of computer professionals, yet they need tools to support their knowledge management activities. By allowing knowledge workers to directly handle many of their own needs, such tools can enable an organization's computer professionals to concentrate on the most technically demanding tasks such as developing extensive customized software systems. Though the whole area of generic software tools for knowledge workers is still at an early stage, the direction of its evolution should be clear in light of the preceding chapters

Knowledge management software tools can be examined from several interrelated perspectives including capacities, capabilities, and convenience. This software will increasingly be designed so that it is the hardware rather than the software that imposes practical capacity limits. To the extent that the software does impose limits, those limits will tend to be so high that they do not interfere with needs of most demanding knowledge workers. That is, they will not inhibit the convenient exercise of software capabilities.

The capabilities of a knowledge management tool should be assessed in terms of their *breadth* and *depth*. Breadth refers to how many classes of diverse knowledge managmeent tasks the software can perform and/or support: storing procedural knowledge, analyzing environmental knowledge, presenting derived knowledge, consulting reasoning knowledge, and so forth. Depth refers to the extent of the capabilities within each class, ranging from superficial to comprehensive. The guidelines presented in Chapter 12 provide a good way for gauging both the depth and breadth of an AI environment's knowledge management capabilities.

We should expect the capabilities of knowledge management tools to continue to increase in both breadth and depth. That is, they will become increasingly flexible. As in the case of Guru, they will integrate many traditionally separate functionalities in such a way that the total effect is much more than the sum of the individual effects, and the existence of one functionality will in no way constrain the exercise of other functionalities. The result will be a generation of knowledge management tools that enable knowledge workers to work with a single tool for solving a diverse variety of computer-based knowledge management activities.

Such a tool sacrifices nothing relative to the depth of traditional stand-alone software, and actually gains through the synergy of its breadth. It effectively avoids the inconveniences of switching among multiple tools in order to accomplish a task. It furnishes a uniform user interface regardless of the activity being exercised. Perhaps most important is the growth path it offers to knowledge workers. Starting out with the simple aspects of one functionality, workers can grow into its deeper capabilities as needed. The growth path can also progress horizontally into other functionalities supported by the tool. Knowledge workers will be free from dead-end tools and tool fragmentation.

While knowledge management software will enable knowledge workers to solve many of their own needs, it will not be a substitute for the professional application systems developer. Professional developers will support knowledge workers by providing them with customized application systems for record-keeping and decision support. These are systems whose scale, complexity, performance, integrity, or security characteristics would not allow them to be constructed by knowledge workers in a timely, cost-effective manner. The application systems will be driven by expert systems and they will be able to consult expert systems.

Training

Rudimentary computer literacy is, of course, a necessary foundation for knowledge worker training. It is rapidly becoming just as much a basic skill as the traditional reading, writing, and mathematics. But basic computer literacy by itself is insufficient preparation for knowledge workers.

If truly knowledge-based organizations are to be realized, there must be a keen appreciation of the very nature of knowledge. This includes a taxonomy of knowledge types, repertoire of knowledge representation techniques, a familiarity with knowledge-processing methods, and an understanding of knowledge utilization in solving problems in the traditional functional areas of management. This formal study of the fundamentals of knowledge is concerned more with pragmatics than abstract epistemological issues.

The cube in Figure 13–2 is suggestive of the possibilities that can confront knowledge workers in attempting to solve a problem. Some combination of one or more cells must be selected and utilized. The unlabeled axes of the cube are indicative of the need for research into knowledge pragmatics. The beginnings of such investigation can be seen in decision support systems research into the nature of generalized problem processors (recall Chapter 2) and in the AI research efforts that have led to a system like Guru. The unfolding research in this will also draw on work in such fields as psychology, philosophy, linguistics, and decision theory.

As the pragmatics of knowledge are more fully comprehended, they will become an essential aspect of knowledge worker training. They will also stimulate the appearance of new kinds of facilities in knowledge management software tools. Knowledge worker training must obviously encompass the subject of advanced knowledge management

FIGURE 13–2   Knowledge management possibilities

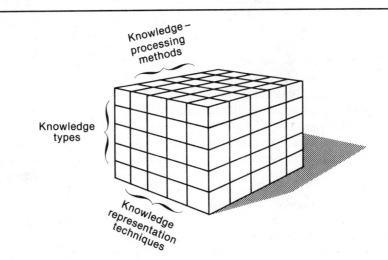

software tools. This includes not only tool characteristics, but also tool selection and effective tool application within each of the functional areas of management.

Cooperation

In addition to technological advances and proper training, cooperation among knowledge workers will be essential to collective knowledge worker effectiveness and productivity with respect to overall organizational goals. This cooperation must be manifest in the sharing of knowledge, in a coordinated reasonable division of labor among the knowledge workers, and in the coordinated timing of knowledge-processing tasks.

The sharing of an organization's knowledge resources among knowledge workers is essential from two standpoints. First, it avoids duplication of effort in knowledge collection and maintenance. Second, it promotes consistent decision making since all knowledge workers have access to the same body of knowledge (or subsets thereof). The shared knowledge may be centralized and/or distributed. In any case, knowledge management software must be capable of ensuring the integrity of shared knowledge, enforcing security restrictions that apply to various classes of knowledge workers, and supporting reasonable access speeds. Furthermore, the knowledge workers must be motivated to conscientiously exercise these software capabilities.

The division of labor among knowledge workers has significant implications for the total productivity of the workers. A division along traditional functional lines will probably continue to be prominent. However, interdisciplinary knowledge workers will become increasingly apparent in knowledge-based organizations. These are functional generalists rather than functional specialists. Division of labor will also come to be viewed from the complementary, yet very different, perspective suggested by Figure 13–2. Knowledge workers will specialize in handling certain types of knowledge, in utilizing certain knowledge representation techniques, and in exercising particular knowledge-processing methods. That is, different classes of knowledge workers will be experts in working with a certain cell or group of cells in the knowledge cube presented in Figure 13–2.

The streamlined coordination of knowledge-processing tasks is of obvious importance. This coordination must be predicated on a valid (and perhaps dynamically changing) prioritization of problems. The assignment of tasks to workers must, of course, match task requirements with knowledge worker skills. The scheduling or timing of knowledge-processing tasks for solving these problems should be designed to avoid knowledge worker contention for the same resource and to promote parallel knowledge worker activity in the solving of each high-priority problem. Automatic triggering mechanisms will exist to notify each knowledge worker involved in solving a problem when progress has reached the point where that worker can begin to take action.

INFRASTRUCTURE

Having focused on the characteristics of the knowledge workers who will populate tomorrow's knowledge-based organizations, we can now step back to view the overall landscape of such an organization. The dominant features of this landscape are local workstations, support centers, communications paths, and distributed knowledge store-houses.

A local workstation is the immediate computer-based extension to a knowledge worker's own innate knowledge management capabilities. The type of knowledge management software that resides at a particular workstation depends on the nature of the knowledge worker. It may be a customized application system built with Guru or it may be Guru itself. In any case, the workstation software will increasingly be based on technical advances in the fields of decision support systems, software integration, and artificial intelligence.

Communication paths enable workstations, and hence knowledge workers, to interact with each other. They also allow a workstation to request and receive knowledge management assistance from other workstations or from various support centers. Thus, a communications capability is a crucial aspect of the workstation software.

A support center is a computer that is not under the immediate control of a knowledge worker but that can provide services to a cluster of workstations. Typically these centers are equipped to carry out processing that would be inefficient or infeasible for a particular workstation or some group of workstations. A local workstation's use of a support center (or communications with other workstations, for that matter) may be entirely invisible to the knowledge worker who operates that workstation.

A support center may also serve as a mechanism for coordinating the activities of multiple workstations. For instance, in the course of solving a decision problem, a knowledge worker may identify various subproblems whose solutions require the expertise of other knowledge workers or of expert systems. Requests to solve these subproblems are initiated (either explicitly or implicitly) at the local workstation and routed along communications paths to other workstations where the subproblems are to be resolved. A support center can serve as a clearinghouse for such communications, coordinating the assignments, timings, and responses of requested knowledge-processing tasks in accordance with the organization's priorities and objectives. In addition to its service work, a support center may carry out certain kinds of processing that are so highly structured and predictable that no knowledge worker discretion or interaction is needed.

The storehouses of knowledge available to knowledge workers may be distributed throughout an organization. Potentially large volumes of knowledge could be stored at each individual workstation. Knowledge can also be stored at support centers. Wherever it is, knowledge can be shared by all knowledge workers having security clearance to use it. Its location is generally influenced by its magnitude, its combined storage-access cost, who its primary users are, and who is responsible for creating and maintaining it. A knowledge storehouse may even exist outside of the organization proper.

This framework for topographical features—local workstations, support centers, communications paths, and knowledge storehouses—provides a basis for studying and designing the infrastructure of knowledge-based organizations. Clearly, there are many possible ways to configure these features. Figure 13–3 is suggestive of some of the possibilities. The formal study of knowledge-based organizations that emerges over the next few years will be concerned with the classification and evaluation of various archetypal infrastructures for uniting an organization's knowledge workers.

Beyond structural variations, there will also be alternatives for the constitution of each infrastructure component. Some local workstations may be mere terminals connected to a support center. Others will be micro- or minicomputers with their own indigenous processors and large local storage capacities. In addition to common present-day input approaches, knowledge workers will have workstations capable of accepting instructions vocally and optically. Vocal and optical workstation responses will complement the more traditional presentation methods. Some workstations will have a broad knowledge management orientation. Others will have a deep orientation, specializing in a particular kind of knowledge processing. In both cases, artificial intelligence and decision support system techniques such as those described in this book will have major impacts on the knowledge management software's facilities.

Support centers will range from micro to mainframe computers, the choice being made among technically adequate alternatives on economic grounds. Microcomputers will make up a significant proportion of support centers. The choice of communications technology will be very much influenced by desired infrastructure coordination protocols and by the nature of what is being communicated. Both magnetic and optical mechanisms for knowledge storage will be prominent and will be increasingly integrated. Knowledge representation techniques that closely mirror real-world entities, attributes, and relationships will become a significant factor in the construction of knowledge storehouses.

FIGURE 13-3   Sample infrastructure for a knowledge-based organization

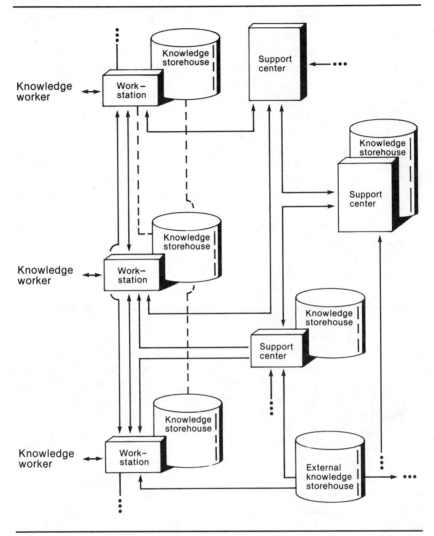

MANAGEMENT OF A KNOWLEDGE-BASED ORGANIZATION

The management of a knowledge-based organization begins with careful planning of its design and construction. Where such a plan is absent, the result will likely be a haphazard organization emerging out of a series of uncoordinated and ad hoc responses to short-term knowlegeprocessing needs. This haphazardness is characterized by redundant effort, inconsistency, inefficiency, and managerial control difficulties. All of these traits tend to place an organization at a serious disadvantage relative to its well-planned competitors.

A plan for increasing, utilizing, and preserving an organization's knowledge resources should have long-term, strategic aspects that provide a framework for developing operational plans. The prospects of ongoing technological advances, increasing knowledge worker expertise, and new environmental challenges suggest that planned flexibility will be very important. This flexibility can take many forms, such as selecting workstation software that supports growth in knowledge worker expertise, choosing workstation and support center hardware standards that are extensible, adopting communication path technology that maximizes communications options, and selecting software that can effectively handle both large and complex knowledge storehouses.

Companies and in-house groups specializing in the customized design and building of infrastructures for knowledge-based organizations will become increasingly prominent. These will be very much analogous to the traditional architectural and construction industries that create and remodel manufacturing, warehouse, and transportation facilities. However, they will be concerned with the creation and remodeling of knowledge processing, knowledge storage, and communication facilities. Just as their traditional counterparts, these new-age architects and builders will employ a variety of tools, techniques, prefabricated components, and subcontracted work efforts in devising the blueprints and building the customized infrastructure for a knowledge-based organization. All of this occurs within the scope of an organization's strategic plan for knowledge management.

Although entirely prefabricated infrastructures may be installed in some cases, customized infrastructures will be very prominent. Their typically higher initial cost is more than offset by the ongoing productivity advantages they can offer. A customized infrastructure is specially tailored to fit the organization's idiosyncrasies and to ergonomically conform to knowledge worker needs. Clearly, the creators of an organization's knowledge management infrastructure must be highly skilled in technical, organizational, economic, and ergonomic considerations.

Technically, they must have expertise at least comparable to today's computer professionals. Using ergonomic principles, they will design and build customized software for knowledge workers to use via local workstations. This customized software handles knowledge-processing activities that are beyond the ability of individual knowledge workers to directly accomplish with available knowledge management tools. Creators of the infrastructure will also specify the structural, security, and integrity characteristics of knowledge storehouses and may even be responsible for furnishing the initial contents (e.g., procedural models, rule sets, and forms) of these repositories.

Comprehension of an organization's existing or planned control structure must be coupled with an appreciation of economical technical options to arrive at a workable configuration of workstations, support centers, knowledge storehouses, and communications paths. The configuration must be not only technically workable, but also organizationally workable from such standpoints as knowledge worker coordination, consistency with knowledge worker incentives, consistency with organizational priorities, maximizing collective productivity, and so forth. Increasingly, the creation or modification of a knowledge-processing infrastructure will be considered to be inseparable from the creation or modification of an organization. The two issues are so inextricably interrelated that they will come to be regarded as practically identical for future knowledge-based organizations.

Once in place, the knowledge-processing infrastructure must be effectively managed. Via each of its workstations, this infrastructure is an extension of or enhancement to a knowledge worker's own innate knowledge-processing abilities. Managing the infrastructure and managing those who use its knowledge resources are inseparable issues for purposes of effective organizational functioning. Coordination and control are the keynotes of this managerial effort whose goal is to maximize the decision-making effectiveness of the organization subject to constraints imposed by its human, material, capital, and knowledge resources.

Global administration and maintenance of the infrastructure and the knowledge it holds will draw heavily on the technical expertise of computer professionals. Local management of the knowledge resources will be carried out by knowledge workers by means of the software available via their workstations. Knowledge-processing activities will be managed by the combined actions of knowledge workers and software. In the course of arriving at a problem's solution, a knowledge worker may request the assistance of other knowledge workers and/or various expert systems.

These specialized knowledge-processing requests may be explicitly stated by the knowledge worker through the local workstation. Alternatively, a request may be generated by the workstation itself (or one of its support centers) as it endeavors to carry out some knowledge-processing task instigated by the knowledge worker. In the latter case, the knowledge worker may even be unaware that the workstation is consulting other knowledge workers or expert systems as it performs its task.

Thus, a knowledge worker will be capable not only of explicitly or implicitly issuing requests, but also of receiving requests for assistance. As far as possible, workstation and support center software should manage these requests in a manner consistent with the organization's goals and priorities. That is, knowledge workers should be relieved from the burden of managing requests. When a request is made that is not directed at a specific knowledge worker, the software will route the request to one of the knowledge workers or expert systems capable of responding to that request. The selection of target processors for undirected tasks will be determined on the basis of relative load factors, relative costs, and response time objectives. This selection process presupposes that the software is capable of understanding the nature of each request in order to identify the set of targets that are feasible in terms of their capacity to respond to the request. Of course, this understanding might be accomplished by an expert system.

The requests for assistance that are pending or in process at a given workstation will be managed by software. This includes both the automatic scheduling of request processing and the preprocessing of requests as they arrive. Before a knowledge worker begins to process a request, it will have been preprocessed in a variety of ways. Its appropriateness for this knowledge worker is automatically checked. The request is examined to detect any ambiguities, inconsistencies, or incompleteness that may exist in it. These are automatically clarified by conversing with the work station (or perhaps knowledge worker) that initiated the request, resulting in a new statement of the problem to be processed.

The workstation preprocessor then undertakes a preliminary analysis of the problem posed by the request to determine whether the workstation itself can generate a solution without knowledge worker effort. If knowledge worker effort is required, then the preprocessing software automatically does as much as it can to lay the groundwork for the actual processing to be carried out by the knowledge worker. This could include a broad range of activities such as gathering needed knowledge from various storehouses, conducting basic analyses whose results will be needed by the knowledge worker, reducing the problem into subproblems and initiating assistance requests for each, and so forth.

To summarize, a workstation's preprocessor organizes, schedules, and lays the foundation for a knowledge worker's problem-solving sessions. Here is yet another place to apply expert system technology. The preprocessor may itself be an expert system. In the course of a problem-solving session, the knowledge worker employs knowledge management tools and/or customized knowledge management software to solve the problem(s) inherent in a request that has been received. The emphasis is on enhancing knowledge worker productivity by obviating the routine and repetitive, providing greater processing speed and accuracy, stimulating insights, furnishing advice, and fostering a synergy based on cooperation. In these ways, a workstation and the infrastructure that it opens into constitute a significant extension to an individual's knowledge management capabilities.

REALIZATION OF KNOWLEDGE-BASED ORGANIZATIONS

Clearly, software based on emerging developments in the fields of artificial intelligence [5], decision support systems [1,2], and software integration [3,4] will play a crucial role in the design, construction, and on-going management of knowledge-based organizations. Furthermore, we expect that results in areas such as social choice theory, cognitive psychology, and communications theory will be applicable to this new kind of organization. However, the remainder of this chapter will concentrate on the contributions that traditional functional areas of management can make to the realization of effective knowledge-based organizations.

At a fundamental economic level, practical ways of measuring knowledge and assessing the value of knowledge are needed. These would be based on an understanding of knowledge types and representation techniques. Knowledge measurement and valuation can provide an objective basis for tracking knowledge worker productivity, evaluating alternative knowledge-processing methods and infrastructure designs, deciding whether to "make or buy" some piece of knowledge, pricing (internal and/or external) knowledge that is to be distributed, studying economies of scale, the general accounting of knowledge assets, and so on.

Classical economics can contribute to the development of incentive allocation schemes for ensuring that both technology and human expertise are harnessed to meet the organization's objectives. Such schemes are of obvious importance for promoting knowledge worker cooperation and effective utilization of the infrastructure's computer power. Thus, when a knowledge worker receives a request, there must be some incentive for acting on that request in accordance with the request's priority. Furthermore, the fact that the action has taken place must be tracked. Conversely, when a request is issued, the cost of fulfilling that request should be apparent to discourage injudicious use of scarce knowledge-processing resources. There must be economic incentives to prevent a knowledge "worker" from passing along all work to other knowledge workers without having added any value.

Understanding the pertinence of economies of scale for knowledge management is another important issue. Compared to a small organization, a large-scale organization may be able to spread the cost of manufacturing a particular parcel of knowledge across many more knowledge-processing tasks that will use it. Because of its larger internal market, the large organization may be able to exploit the knowledge in many more ways, giving the large organization a competitive advantage over smaller organizations. However, this also suggests interesting opportunities for knowledge service organizations that specialize in the generation and external marketing of knolwedge (e.g., rule sets or models) to relatively small organizations. Such a service organization together with its clients may collectively achieve economies of scale that rival (or perhaps) surpass those of a large organization.

The issue of budgets for knowledge processing deserves investigation from such standpoints as appropriate aggregation, automated tracking, variance approval mechanisms, and knowledge worker evaluation. Knowledge-based organizations will routinely choose among alternative investments aimed at augmenting their knowledge assets. This will involve financial analysis that can determine present values for various bodies of knowledge. Prospective mergers will be formally examined in terms of knowledge resources and the potential for exploiting complementary infrastructures and knowledge.

It will be vital for a knowledge-based organization to maintain an account of the present state of its knowledge resources as a basis for control and analysis. Balance sheets specifically citing knowledge assets will permit an analysis of trends in knowledge formation and provide a basis for understanding how well the organization is poised to cope with anticipated growth and needs. Some kinds of knowledge are consumed in the production of new knowledge and have no independent existence after being used in a particular knowledge-processing task. More durable kinds of knowledge can be used repeatedly in a variety of processing tasks. However, a specific parcel of durable knowledge typically becomes less useful or obsolete over some period of time. Thus, issues related to knowledge aging, depreciation, and replacement must be addressed. Yet another important aspect of knowledge accounting is the auditing of knowledge assets and inventories.

To the extent that an organization markets the knowledge it creates, there must be a means for fairly capturing the costs of producing that knowledge. This provides a basis for knowledge pricing. Though the sale of knowledge will involve new media and techniques for knowledge delivery, it will have many similarities to today's publishing industry. However, the emphasis will increasingly be on the sale of knowledge (be it environmental, procedural, reasoning, etc.) rather than the sale of an object that conveys that knowledge. It is important that the knowledge be immediately processible in a variety of ways via the purchaser's workstation and/or support centers. For instance, the knowledge (e.g., rule sets) may be packaged in such a way that it can be immediately deposited in a workstation's knowledge storehouse, where it is directly susceptible to processing with a standard tool (e.g., Guru).

As suggested in the prior section, operations management of a knowledge-based organization is not at all trivial. Experts in this area will be heavily involved in the design of the infrastructure. They will be responsible for devising the protocols and parameters for the software that coordinates knowledge worker activities. These activities may very well take place in the context of a nonstop organization that provides very flexible conditions (times, locations) for knowledge workers. Critical path project management techniques may be employed for complex problems that involve the participation of many knowledge workers. Scheduling an organization's knowledge-processing activities may come to be viewed from a job shop perspective, in which each job is a problem whose completion (i.e., solution) is accomplished through the coordinated actions of multiple specialized knowledge workers. We should expect to see certain material requirements planning principles and quality control techniques adapted to the manufacture of knowledge and decisions (i.e., problem solutions). Operations research models based on simulation or optimization have the potential for extensive application in these various aspects of managing a knowledge-based organization.

Mechanisms for guaranteeing the security of knowledge are vital from the accounting, operations, and legal standpoints. Knowledge workers must be automatically prohibited from making unauthorized alterations to knowledge. Also, the infrastructure must be able to prohibit the disclosure of various subsets of its global knowledge resources to knowledge workers who do not have the authority to view it. The security mechanisms built into the infrastructure should support situations where a knowledge worker needs to use some parcel of knowledge without being able to either view it or alter it.

We envision the emergence of a new functional area of management: knowledge management systems (KMS). It will have close interdisciplinary links with the traditional areas, along the lines just described. It will subsume and reorient such areas as management information systems (MIS) and decision support systems (DSS). KMS will be concerned with the study of infrastructures for knowledge-based organizations. It will take advantage of past work on such topics as data base management, artificial intelligence, generalized problem processors, and linguistic analysis. It will devise a taxonomy of knowledge and create new approaches to knowledge representation and processing. The KMS field will both stimulate and assimilate technological advances in software and hardware.

The foregoing considerations are important for the realization of viable knowledge-based organizations. They are, of course, suggestive rather than exhaustive. As such, they are indicative of research directions for the functional areas of management. In some cases, this research will involve the adaptation or extension of existing concepts and methods to the new organizational context. In other cases, it will lead to the development of fundamentally new concepts and methods. Results of these research efforts, coupled with continuing technological advances, will define the possible constitutions for future knowledge-based organizations and will significantly impact the future curriculum of management schools.

CONCLUSION

We are rapidly entering an era that will be dominated by knowledge-based organizations. Each such organization will be populated by a society of knowledge workers who are interconnected by a computer-based infrastructure. Each knowledge worker will be an expert in carrying out certain kinds of knowledge management activities. The worker's knowledge-processing efforts will be supported by a workstation equipped with an AI environment for business computing, customized knowledge-processing software, and perhaps some problem preprocessing rule sets. The workstation also serves as the knowledge worker's entry point into the infrastructure's knowledge storehouses, support center capabilities, and other workstations.

The design, construction, and ongoing management of an effective infrastructure presents challenges to each of the traditional functional areas of management. Each area can make important contributions to the realization of viable knowledge-based organizations. The focal point for study and research into these such organizations will be a new area, referred to as knowledge management systems (KMS), which transcends the more narrow interests of fields such as MIS and DSS. Its mission involves the identification and creation of concepts, methods, and tools for maximizing the global knowledge worker productivity in an organization.

EXERCISES

1. What are the four major kinds of resources that exist within an organization?
2. Identify the main types of knowledge that need to be managed within an organization.
3. What is meant by knowledge management?
4. Software tools for knowledge management can be examined from what perspectives?
5. Explain the distinction between the breadth and depth of a knowledge management tool's capabilities.
6. Describe the infrastructure of a knowledge-based organization.
7. What roles can expert systems play in the realization of knowledge-based organizations?

References

1 Bonczek, R. H.; C. W. Holsapple; and A. B. Whinston. *Foundations of Decision Support Systems.* New York: Academic Press, 1981.

2 _____. "Developments in Decision Support Systems." In *Advances in Computers*, Vol. 23, ed. M. Yovits. New York: Academic Press, 1984.

3 Holsapple, C. W., and A. B. Whinston. "Software Tools for Knowledge Fusion." *Computerworld* (In Depth), April 1983.

4 _____. "Aspects of Integrated Software." *Proceedings of the 1984 National Computer Conference*, 1984.

5 _____. "Management Support through Artificial Intelligence." *Human Systems Management* 5, 1985, pp. 163–71.

6 West, S. "Beyond the One-Track Mind." *Science 85*, November 1985.

Appendix

Other Knowledge Representation Methods

Rules provide a very natural, convenient, nonprocedural way of representing reasoning knowledge. But this is knowledge for reasoning about what? The answer is that it is for reasoning about the use of other knowledge. This other knowledge could be environmental (descriptive of the current state of the world), procedural (stating the steps needed to accomplish a task), presentational (concerning the appearance of responses), assimilative (specifying integrity requirements), linguistic (characterizing the meanings of requests), reasoning, and so on. Of these, the ability to reference descriptive, environmental knowledge in a rule is essential. Development tools may not support the representation and processing of some of the other kinds of knowledge, but they must offer some approach to representing and processing knowledge that describes the current state of the world.

As we have seen, a development tool may furnish numerous methods for representing environmental knowledge, including data bases, spreadsheets, text, arrays, and variables. All of these methods are familiar to the business-computing community and their popularity is a testimony to their value. Clearly, these methods are essential to any tool seriously concerned with the construction of diverse business expert systems. However, a development tool could support other approaches to representing environmental knowledge. These additional methods arose in the AI field. They have not been generally recognized or important in the field of business computing. It is not necessary to comprehend them in order to build a business expert system. They are, nevertheless, interesting and worth understanding because they have been adopted by some development tools.

Here, we focus on two nonbusiness approaches for handling environmental knowledge: semantic nets and frames. Many of the aspects of these approaches are actually quite similar to aspects of familiar business-computing approaches to knowledge representation. Several of these correspondences are noted in the discussion that follows. In a sense, because of terminological differences, you may already be acquainted with notions of semantic nets or frames without knowing it.

REPRESENTING THE STATE OF THE WORLD

As it reasons about a problem, an inference engine must be able to track the state of the world. Any application world can be viewed in terms of various concepts and their interrelationships [1]. In the quota world, for example, there are concepts such as product name, quarter number, rep name, this year's sales, this year's quota, local advertising amount, and so forth. At a more concrete level there are concepts such as romance, 2, Toby, 13750, 12560, and 2820. Broadly speaking, there are two kinds of relationships that can exist among concepts: definitional and associative [1].

One concept can define or more closely specify the meaning of another. For instance, product name and romance have a definitional relationship in which the latter is one way of defining the former. In a definitional relationship, one concept is an instance, an occurrence, a value of a more abstract concept. Toby is an instance of rep name, 13750 is an occurrence of this year's sales, 2 is one of the possible values of quarter number. Conversely, concepts that are legitimate definitions, instances, or values of the product name concept include romance, scifi, and computer, but not Toby or 13750.

Product name and this year's sales are two concepts that are related, but the relationship is not definitional. Neither is an instance of the other. Nevertheless, they are associated with each other in the sense that any instance of this year's sales (e.g., 13750) has been produced for a particular product (e.g., romance). The concept of this year's sales is similarly associated with the quarter number and rep name concepts. A sales amount is made by a certain rep in a certain quarter.

Consider the concepts of product name, product ID, and commission rate (for a product). These three concepts are associated with each other in the sense that they are all attributes of a broader concept, namely the concept of a product. That is, the concept of a product is an aggregate of three other concepts. Similarly, an instance of the product concept is an aggregate of three values (e.g., romance, ROM, and .03), one for each of the three associated concepts that make up the notion of a product. A concept that is an aggregate of these concepts is sometimes called an entity or an object. The concepts of which it is composed are sometimes called attributes. Thus we can say that a product is a type of object or entity whose attributes are its name, ID, and commission rate. There may be many instances of this object, each composed of three values (one value for each of the three attributes). Interestingly, this "object-attribute-value" notion is a way of characterizing records in a Guru table or postrelational data base.

SEMANTIC NETS

Semantic net representation stems from efforts at modeling memory by researchers such as Quillian [6]. Though there is no operational standard for semantic net specification and usage, basic notions that are generally shared by implementations of this technique are examined here. A semantic net is composed of nodes that represent concepts, be they objects or attributes, concrete instances or abstractions. The relationships between concepts are represented by named arcs between the nodes. An arc's name indicates the meaning (i.e., semantics) of the relationship it represents. Definitional relationships are commonly called "is a" relationships. Associative relationships between an attribute and its object are commonly called "has a" relationships. Other associative relationships are typically given names that reflect their respective meanings.

Specification

Figure A–1 shows typical pictorial portrayals of semantic net relationships. Of course, such drawings are not comprehensible to software that processes semantic net contents. Thus a formal language is used to actually specify a semantic net. Such languages can vary widely from one implementation to another. As an example, the knowledge in part *a* of Figure A–1 might be formally specified as:

```
ISA(Toby,rep name)
```

to indicate that Toby is a rep name. This kind of formalization is called a predicate. Similarly, the arcs in parts *b* and *c* could also be formally stated as predicates:

```
HASA(product,product name)
HASA(product,product ID)
HASA(product,commission rate)
MAKES(rep,sales amount)
CONTAINS(quarter,sales amount)
PRODUCES(product,sales amount)
```

Thus, a semantic net is actually specified in terms of a series of statements, such as the predicate statements just shown [7].

Processing

The ways in which semantic net representations are processed vary from one implementation to another. However, the available processing generally allows the net to be created, modified, and traversed. Traversal refers to the ability to move along the net's arcs to find related

FIGURE A-1   Semantic net representations

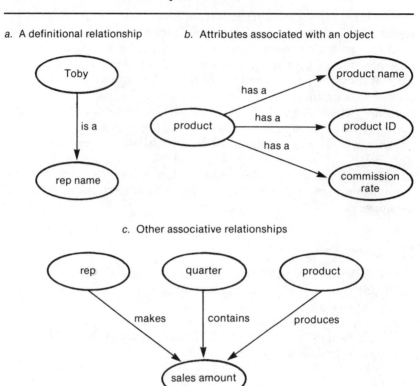

a. A definitional relationship   *b.* Attributes associated with an object

c. Other associative relationships

concepts. For example, in part *a* of Figure A-2, we can begin with Toby and traverse the net to discover that Toby is the name of a rep having a phone of 317–925–8068, who has made a performance of the sales amount 13750 versus the quota amount 12560, in the quarter whose number is 2 for the year 1985, and who has produced this performance for the product whose name is romance. Traversal can normally begin with any node and proceed along arcs in any direction.

Part *b* of Figure A-2 shows another semantic net with the same basic structure. The only difference is that the instances of three attributes (quarter number, sales amount, and quota amount) are not the same as in the semantic net part of *a*. Thus, this net describes Toby's performance for romance in the first, rather than second, quarter. Notice that a large portion of the net will not change regardless of which rep, quarter, or product is involved. Only those nodes at the heads of "is a" arcs vary from one net to another. The other nodes and arcs are structurally static. Interestingly, the constant structural portion of a semantic net can be captured very easily in a standard data base schema. The resultant data base, in essence, contains large numbers of semantic nets, all of which have the same basic structure but which differ in terms of their instances for the attributes.

Specification as a Data Base

Readers familiar with data base management will observe that the schema in part *a* of Figure A–3 is a concise representation of the structurally static portion of the semantic nets like those shown in Figure A–2. This schema is valid for both the CODASYL-network and postrelational data models [2,4]. Each of the four types of objects is represented by a labeled rectangle (i.e., a record type or entity type, in data base jargon). Each of its attributes is named within its rectangle (i.e., fields or data items, in data base terms). The schema says that each rep has a rep name and a phone, each performance has a sales amount and quota amount, and so forth. The MAKES, CONTAINS, and PRODUCES relationships are explicit in the schema. Each arrow in the schema has its customary data base interpretation of depicting a one-to-many relationship between instances of two types of entities (i.e., a 1:N set, in data base terminology). Thus, the schema says that a rep can make many performances, but no performance is made by more than one rep.

The actual data base organized according to this schema is able to accommodate masses of semantic networks like the two shown in Figure A–2. For example, there are 18 nodes in the two semantic nets that contain values of attributes. All of these and their interrelationships are concisely captured in the six related data base records depicted in part *b* of Figure A–3. There is no value redundancy in this data base. Data base access languages permit the traversal of relationships among records in such a data base to find related concepts. In the case of Guru, this (along with record creation, connection, and alteration) is accomplished with a postrelational data manipulation language whose commands can be used as actions within a rule set. When desired records are encountered during traversal, their values can be retrieved into Guru's working variables, arrays, spreadsheet cells, or data tables as a basis for inference. In contrast, some semantic net implementations are not intended for storing large volumes of descriptive knowledge in auxiliary memory.

In the case of the ADVISOR rule set, whose descriptive knowledge needs are typical of many business applications, Jack got along very nicely without any notion of semantic nets. Though a weak point of the relational data model is its lack of semantic representation, Jack's THISYR table (see Figure 5–4, Chapter 5) was quite adequate for representing the descriptive knowledge about rep performance. In applications where there are more concepts with more intricate interrelationships, a semantic net representation (e.g., in an integral postrelational data base) may be preferable.

FIGURE A–2 Semantic nets for performances in distinct quarters

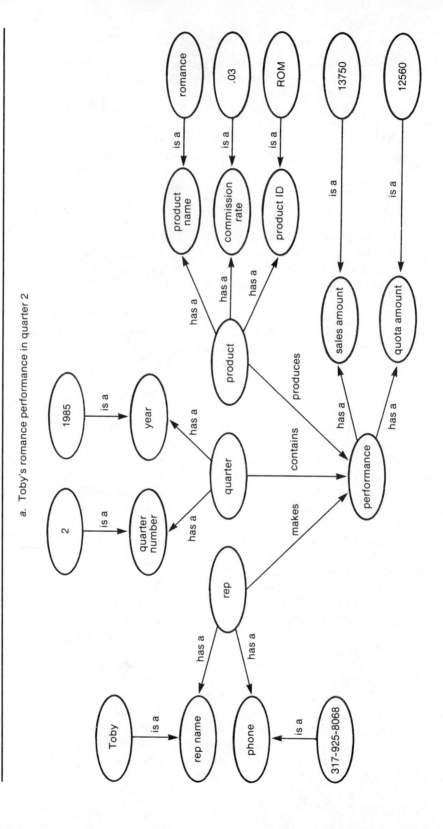

a. Toby's romance performance in quarter 2

b. Toby's romance performance in quarter 1

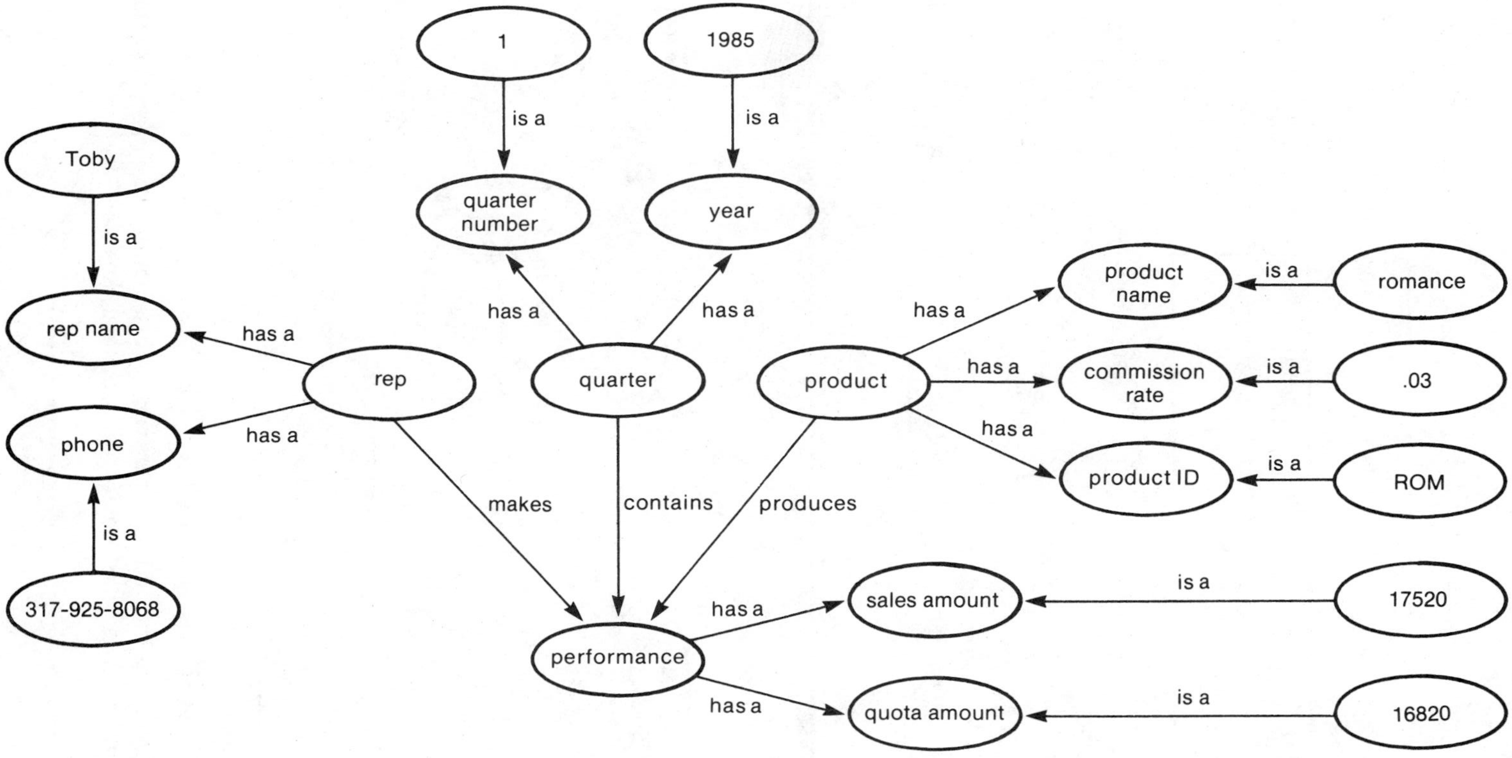

FIGURE A-3   Semantic nets in a data base

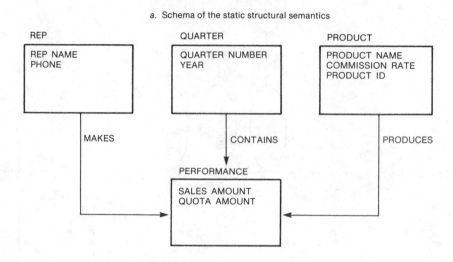

a. Schema of the static structural semantics

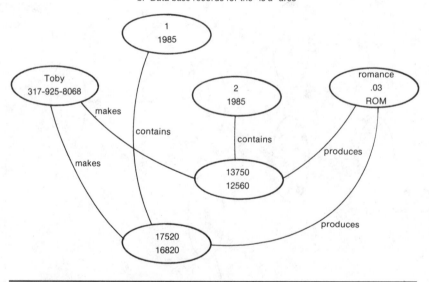

b. Data base records for the "is a" arcs

Retrieval Versus Inference

Sometimes the activity of traversing a semantic net to retrieve related data values is called "inference." Consider the rule:

```
IF:REPNAME="Toby" & QTRNUM="2" & PRODID="ROM"
THEN:SALES=13750 ;QUOTA=12560
```

It could be argued that this captures some of the same knowledge represented in Figures A–2a or A–3b. If ADVISOR contained a rule of this kind for every record in the THISYR table, it would not need to use the THISYR table. Nor would there be any need for semantic nets like those of Figures A–2 or A–3. Thus, traversal to retrieve related values from a net would be replaced by customary inference. In this sense, traversal of a semantic net, or retrieval from a data table for that matter, can be regarded as a sort of pseudo inference. Though it is conceptually equivalent to inference, it is quite different operationally [1]. Retrieval of desired sales and quota amounts will be significantly faster than inference based on rules such as the one shown above. It also takes less effort by the rule set developer and allows the descriptive knowledge to be easily used for other purposes beyond the scope of reasoning about new quotas.

In general, it is a poor practice to try to represent descriptive knowledge (e.g., about a rep's performance) as if it were reasoning knowledge. A human expert would not reason that if the rep name is Toby, the quarter is 2, and the product ID is ROM, then the sales must be 13750 against a quota of 12560. The human expert would simply look up (i.e., retrieve) the pertinent sales and quota amounts in a filing folder, a report, a computerized data base, or some other source.

Conversely, it would be a poor practice to try to represent reasoning knowledge as if it were descriptive knowledge. This would involve an enumeration of all possible new quota problems and their solutions. Each enumerated case would be stored as descriptive knowledge in a table or a semantic net. A quota advice problem would then be solved not by actual inference, but by finding the matching case and retrieving its new quota value. For nontrivial problems, enumeration and retrieval is impractical. Think about what it would entail as an alternative to inference with the ADVISOR rule set. Representing and processing reasoning knowledge as rules is far more efficient and effective than trying to generate and use all possible pieces of advice that would result from those rules.

FRAMES

Frame representation of knowledge originated with Minsky's pattern recognition and analysis research [5]. Since then, various frame formalisms have been proposed. Though there is no universally adopted standard for frame specification and processing, we shall examine here some of the more interesting aspects that might be encountered in a frame representation supported by an expert system development tool. It should be noted that variations exist not only in features and usage, but also in the terminology used to discuss frames. For instance, frames themselves are sometimes called "units," "concepts," or "flavors."

Slots

A frame is used to represent a type of object, entity, or class. The frame's name is indicative of the object being represented. A frame is composed of slots. Each slot corresponds to an attribute that is possessed by the type of object that a frame represents. A slot's name is normally descriptive of the attribute that it represents. Recall the THISYR table introduced in Chapter 5 (see Figure 5–3). That table's structure could be represented as a frame named THISYR and having five slots named REPNAME, PRODNAME, QTRNUM, QUOTA, and SALES. In this example, the THISYR frame represents a type of abstract entity or object, namely this year's results. An instance of a frame consists of specific data values for the frame's slots. Thus, a record in the THISYR table (see Figure 5–4) corresponds to an instance of the THISYR frame.

Just as a table field has various characteristics, so does a frame slot. As with a Guru field, a slot typically has a type (e.g., string, integer, numeric, logical) that specifies what kind of data values it can have, a size indicating how large its values can be, and a label commenting on the nature of the slot. Unlike a Guru field, slots typically do not have pictures or security access codes.

Sometimes, a data base management system (e.g., Guru's) supports virtual fields. These are fields for which no data values are actually stored. Instead, when the field is defined, instructions are specified that indicate how a value is to be determined whenever it is needed for a particular record. For instance, the THISYR table might be altered to have a virtual field named ROOTDIF that is the square root of the smaller of zero and the difference between quota and sales. Its definition would be:

```
SQRT(MIN(0,QUOTA-SALES))
```

Elements in forms and report templates can be specified in exactly the same manner, allowing their values to also be dynamically computed on a when-needed basis. Similarly, frame implementations may allow instructions to be attached to a slot. The THISYR frame could have a slot named ROOTDIF with an attached procedure (e.g., written in LISP) that makes the same kind of computation. When the value of ROOTDIF is needed for frame instantiation, it is calculated by executing the procedure.

Procedural Attachment

Allowing a slot value to be specified in terms of a procedure (or even a rule set consultation) goes a step beyond the usual notion of a virtual field, form element, or template element whose value is specified in terms of an expression. Interestingly, a slot is, in this sense, equivalent to the notion of a cell in a Guru spreadsheet. Remember that, unlike conventional spreadsheet software, Guru's integration allows any cell to be defined in terms of a procedure, a rule set consultation, a data base retrieval, and so on. A cell, say #D8, could be given the name ROOT-DIF by the command:

```
MACRO ROOTDIF #D8
```

Though a procedure is unnecessary in this example, if more intricate processing were required for #D8, this cell could be defined in terms of a Guru (rather than a LISP) procedure involving any of the customary control structures such as those for conditional iteration, case processing, and conditional branching. Whenever the cell's value is needed, it is dynamically calculated by executing the procedure that has been attached as its definition. A collection of related cells in a spreadsheet can thus be regarded as slots of a frame.

Various frame implementations may support differing approaches to procedural attachment. For instance, a procedure may be attached to a frame (rather than a slot) and stored as the value of a special type of slot.* A procedure stored in this way can be invoked by a command designating the slot that holds it, plus any arguments needed by the procedure. In frame parlance, such a procedure is sometimes called a "method" or "operator" and using a command to cause its execution is thought of as "sending a message" to the frame. Because a frame represents an object, frames are usually regarded as an object-oriented approach to knowledge representation and processing.

As noted in Chapter 8, many other depictions of objects are possible: tables, records, spreadsheets, forms, graphs, and so forth. In the Guru system, these are predefined classes of objects and there are many built-in methods attached to each kind of object. These built-in methods constitute a large portion of the Guru software. They are indigenous, object code procedures that do not need to be programmed by a developer. Nor do they need to be explicitly attached to objects. Attachment is automatic. Some methods may be attached to (i.e., meaningful for) diverse types of objects, while other methods are pertinent to only a specific kind of object.

For example, OBTAIN is a method that always exists for each tabular object (i.e., for each table). Invoking OBTAIN for a particular table is in essence sending a message to that table indicating that a particular procedure is to be executed. In the case of sending such a message to the

---

*This is comparable to the idea of storing procedural models in a data base [3,9].

THISYR table, the arguments needed by the OBTAIN method might be the three conditions specified in the message:

```
OBTAIN RECORD FROM THISYR FOR REPNAME=REP & PRODNAME=PROD & QTRNUM=QTR
```

One object can "send a message" to another object. The message indicates which of the recipient's methods should be used. For instance, the preceding message to obtain a record may have been sent by a rule set (another kind of object), which in turn has received a message to carry out its CONSULT method from another object such as a cell, piece of text, or procedural model.

As shown in the foregoing chapters, there is no need to have "slots" in each object for holding all of the possible methods that could be requested for that object. A developer does not need to devise procedures for carrying out commonplace operations for an object. On the other hand, if specialized processing is needed for an object, the developer can specify procedures in Guru's innate programming language or in the C programming language. They need not be explicitly bound to particular types of objects. Notice that procedures themselves can be treated as objects and that PERFORM is a built-in method that is applicable to all custom-built procedures. Customized procedures can be stored in libraries, spreadsheets, rule sets, and so forth.

Another variation of procedural attachment that may be found in a frame implementation is the attachment of a procedure to a slot with the stipulation that it should behave as a *demon.* Computer scientists have long used the term *demon* to refer to processing that is automatically activated when a certain event takes place. In Guru for example, a developer can specify special presentation styles for cells that are contingent on any of a variety of events having taken place. Thus, when a certain cell's value falls below some level, it (and/or other cells) might turn red and begin blinking. In the case of frames, a slot's demon procedure might be executed whenever the slot's value is viewed or altered. The procedure could serve any of a variety of purposes such as logging the activity for a slot's value, checking on the validity of the value, updating another slot that might serve to hold the certainty factor for the present slot, or changing other slot values to be consistent with the present slot's new value.

Inheritance

Frame implementations typically provide a way for representing definitional relationships between objects (i.e., frames). These are the "is a" relationships discussed earlier with respect to semantic nets. Representation of associative relationships such as MAKES, CONTAINS, and

PRODUCES in Figures A–2 and A–3 are generally not supported. The result is a hierarchy of frames that represents a taxonomy or classification scheme.

For instance, the general class of employees could be thought of as being composed of three subclasses: hourly employees, salaried employees, and commissioned employees. There is an "is a" relationship between employees and each of its subclasses (e.g., salaried employee "is a" employee). Each subclass is itself defined in terms of individual employees. Toby is a commissioned employee, which is an employee. All attributes existing for the general class of employees should pertain to all commissioned employees and all attributes existing for commissioned employees pertain to Toby. Thus, Toby *inherits* the properties of the employee concept.

Clearly, this taxonomic inheritance can be depicted in a semantic net. It can also be represented by means of links between frames. When the EMPLOYEE frame is defined, it would be specified as being linked to the SAL, HRLY, and COMM frames. When the COMM frame is defined, it could be specified as being linked to frames for each of the commissioned employees. Such links might be pictorially visualized as shown in Figure A–4a. Some frame systems make a distinction between two kinds of "is a" links. There are those that connect a subclass (e.g., COMM) to a broader class (e.g., EMPLOYEE) and those that connect a frame that is not a class (e.g., TOBY) to one that does represent a class (e.g., COMM). The former could be termed subclass links, while the latter could be called terminal links.

Each frame in Figure A–4a will have slots. As shown there, the slots of a frame in an "is a" hierarchy fall into two categories: those that are inherited by the frame's subclass or terminal frames and those that are not. The former are sometimes called member slots and the latter called own slots. The EMPLOYEE frame has two member slots (NAME and ADDR) that will serve as attributes for each of its subclass frames. The SAL frame has a slot named HIGH, which is its own attribute indicating the highest salary for the class of salaried employees. This frame also has three member slots that are attributes for each of its members. Two of these (NAME and ADDR) are inherited from the EMPLOYEE frame. The three member slots of SAL are inherited as own slots by each of the terminal frames linked to SAL. Similar member slots are specified for COMM, except the monthly salary attribute is replaced by the commission base attribute. Hourly employees have slots for hourly and overtime rates.

Readers familiar with data base management should note that the postrelational schema shown in Figure A–4b is logically equivalent to the frame taxonomy. It uses a forked 1:1 set (named ISA) between record types rather than subclass links between frames. Record occurrences in the data base for this schema are used in place of terminal links

FIGURE A–4   Representing a taxonomy

a. As a picture of a frame hierarchy

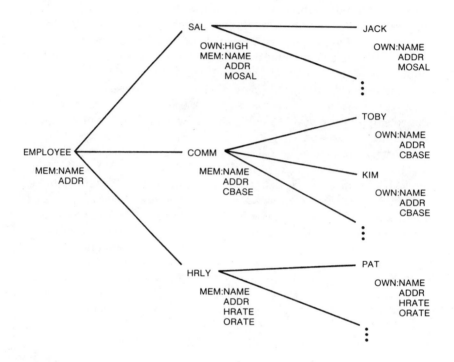

b. In a data base schema

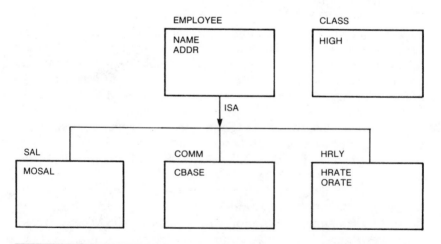

between frames. Because there can be only one instance of a nonterminal frame's own slots, these can be handled as fields in a record type such as CLASS. Such a schema can easily support the representation of thousands or tens of thousands of employees in such a way that information about any of them can be accessed very rapidly.

Similarly, a frame implementation typically provides processing commands for adding slot values to a frame hierarchy and for retrieving those values by navigating through the links. As in the case of semantic net processing, retrieval through a frame structure might be regarded as a kind of pseudo inference. For instance, the links can be used to discover that Jack is salaried and that salaried persons are employees. Therefore, it is known that Jack is an employee. The same conclusion can be drawn by retrieval from a data base having a schema of Figure A–4b.

Frames to Organize Rules

When an expert system development tool supports a frame approach to representing descriptive knowledge, the rules that are specified can typically draw on data values held in slots. Such a tool may also allow (or in some cases require) that each rule be stored in a frame. A rule set, then, would correspond to a frame representing a class (e.g., the class of ADVISOR rules). Each terminal frame linked to this class would have slots holding a particular rule (e.g., rule R1 "is a" ADVISOR rule). A slot would need to be defined for each of the various attributes a rule can have, such as its name, premise, conclusion, priority, cost, preaction sequence, comment, reason, and so forth. Interestingly, this is exactly what you have already seen in Screen 4 of the color insert.

In Screen 4, the slots named Rule, Priority, Cost, Test, Comment, Ready, If, Then, Reason, Needs, and Changes are highly stylized and very visual. Every rule specified in Guru can be considered to be a frame with values for these slots. Every rule set specified in Guru can be regarded as a superclass frame whose member slots are those just mentioned and whose own slots correspond to rule set attributes such as the default goal, the initialization sequence, and the completion sequence. Another of its slots, the one for variable descriptions, is itself a frame representing the rule set's class of variables. This variable descriptor frame has terminal links to frames for each of the rule set's variable descriptions. Standard slots for these are shown in Screen 8 of the color insert.

The superclass frame for a rule set's rules in Guru automatically has several built-in methods (i.e., procedural attachments). These include BUILD, COMPILE, and CONSULT. Other Guru objects (e.g., a spreadsheet) can "send messages" to an object like the ADVISOR rule set, asking that one of its methods be executed. Conversely, the ADVISOR object's slots (e.g., initialization sequence) can contain procedures, which in turn can send messages to other objects (tables, spreadsheets, other rule sets, and so on) for desired method execution. Other development tools that allow rules to be stored in a frame fashion typically do not support such a rich diversity of built-in objects. With those tools, it is up to the developer to explicitly define such objects and their respective methods.

Thus there is an interesting contrast between low-level, blank-slate tools and higher-level tools with prefabricated object classes and methods. At one extreme, the low-level tools have no built-in objects other than the set of numbers and strings. They have built-in methods for numeric and string operations. All other kinds of objects are built from the ground up. At the other extreme are tools that have anticipated the major kinds of objects that will be needed. These higher-level tools are based on the idea that developers should not be required to reinvent the "wheel" (i.e., the spreadsheet, data base, and so forth). A high-level tool obviously saves a great deal of development effort, provided its built-in object classes are sufficient for a developer's needs. If they are not sufficient, then a developer will need to choose an alternative high-level tool that does support the desired object classes or resort to low-level specification of such classes and their associated methods. As the field matures, we should expect to see tools that fall between the two extremes as well as a trend toward more high-level tools.

Benefits

Proponents of development tools that support frames correctly point out that rules provide a very convenient way for representing reasoning knowledge, but are not good at representing structured descriptive knowledge. They correctly argue that frames provide more versatility than the shells that go no further than the simple idea of representing descriptive knowledge in the guise of variables (often called "attributes") and their values. They try to address the knowledge representation and processing deficiencies of such shells by using frames in addition to rules. This is similar in spirit to the motivation behind AI environments for business computing. The principal difference is that such environments (e.g., Guru) have opted for commonplace business-computing methods of knowledge management, rather than the explicit use of frames (or semantic nets for that matter) that do not conform to the familiar, highly practical ways of thinking about business problems.

Tools that combine frames and rules have been cited as providing three benefits. First, frames furnish a structural language for describing the objects and attributes referred to in rules. Spreadsheets, data bases, forms, text, and all the rest do the same, while providing greater diversity and specialization to the kinds of objects commonly used in business problem solving. Second, frames are said to support a layer of "generic deductive" capability about those objects that need not be represented explicitly as rules (i.e., pseudo inference via retrieval). In problem areas requiring extensive categorization this is beneficial. However, business problems (e.g., setting sales quotas) do not tend to be heavily involved with taxonomy issues. They often involve a much richer array of associative interrelationships among masses of data values that can be handled quite nicely with appropriate data base management techniques. Third, frames can be used as an aid to organizing and managing rules. As was seen in Chapter 4, this can be accomplished (e.g., via Guru's BUILD command) without the developer even being conscious of the notion of a frame.

CONCLUSION

Attempts to augment conventional rule specification with frame or semantic net mechanisms are symptomatic of the need for rich knowledge management capabilities when it comes to developing expert systems. Other mechanisms such as predicate calculus [1] or scripts [8] are also candidates. For the developers of business expert systems, none of these is an adequate substitute for a healthy assortment of business-computing methods for knowledge management. Nevertheless, they may increasingly become available as additional facilities in the repertoire of a development tool. This will depend to a considerable extent on how quickly they can gain acceptance as natural, convenient ways of thinking about business problems. It will also depend on how well they can be extended to handle more real-business-world representation issues. For example, frames might be extended to provide built-in support of large volumes of data values, explicit associative relationships (in addition to taxonomies), certainty factor computations, fuzzy variables (i.e., fuzzy "slots"), and so on. The style used for integrating frame processing with rule processing is also important. Is the integration truly synergistic or must one know about frames in order to make any practical use of rules? Issues such as these must await the results of further research and practical developments.

References

1 Bonczek, R. H.; C. W. Holsapple; and A. B. Whinston. *Foundations of Decision Support Systems.* New York: Academic Press, 1981.

2 _____. *Micro Database Management.* New York: Academic Press, 1984.

3 _____. "Specification of Modeling Knowledge in Decision Support Systems," in *Processes and Tools for Decision Support,* ed. H. G. Sol. Amsterdam: North-Holland, 1983.

4 Holsapple, C. W. "A Perspective on Data Models." *PC Tech Journal* 2, no. 1, 1984.

5 Minsky, M. "A Framework for Representing Knowledge." in *The Psychology of Computer Vision,* ed. P. Winston. New York: McGraw-Hill, 1975.

6 Quillian, M. R. "Semantic Memory." in *Semantic Information Processing,* ed. M. Minsky. Cambridge, Mass.: MIT Press, 1968.

7 Raphael, B. "SIR: A Computer Program for Semantic Information Retrieval." in *Semantic Information Processing,* ed. M. Minsky. Cambridge, Mass.: MIT Press, 1968.

8 Schank, R. C. and R. P. Abelson. *Scripts, Plans, Goals and Understanding.* Hillsdale, New Jersey: Erlbaum, 1977.

9 Stohr, E. A. and Tanniru, M. "A Data Base for Operations Research Models." *International Journal of Policy Analysis Information Systems* 4, no. 1, 1980.

Glossary

AI. Same as *artificial intelligence.*

AI Environment. A piece of software that integrates traditional (e.g., business) computing capabilities with AI technology such as natural language processing and inference. Within this environment, natural language conversation can be used to exercise many of the traditional capabilities (e.g., business graphics, statistics generation), expert systems that employ those capabilities (e.g., spreadsheet analysis, data base management) can be built, and the traditional capabilities (e.g., procedural models, spreadsheets) can themselves carry out expert system consultations. Thus, in a single piece of software, the capabilities of an inference engine, rule set manager, and natural language processor are blended with traditional capabilities.

Array. A named collection of elements arranged into columns and rows, where each element behaves and can be processed like a variable.

Artificial Intelligence (AI). A field of study and application concerned with identifying and using tools and techniques that allow machines to exhibit behavior that would be considered intelligent if it were observed in humans.

Assignment. The act of assigning a new value to a variable.

Assimilative Knowledge. Knowledge that controls what knowledge is acceptable for assimilation into a knowledge system.

Backward Chaining. An approach to rule-based reasoning in which the inference engine endeavors to find a value for an overall goal by recursively finding values for subgoals. At any point in the recursion, the effort of finding a value for the immediate goal involves examining rule conclusions to identify those rules which could possibly establish a value for that goal. An unknown variable in the premise of one of these candidate rules becomes a new subgoal for recursion purposes.

Candidate Rules. A group of rules that the inference engine has determined to be of immediate relevance at the present juncture in a reasoning process. These rules will be considered according to a particular selection order and subject to a prescribed degree of rigor.

Cell. The smallest constituent of a spreadsheet. Visually, a spreadsheet's cells are arranged into rows and columns. Each cell is referenced by the row and column in which it exists. A cell can have a definition which indicates how to compute the value of that cell. Advanced spreadsheets allow cells to be defined in terms of commands in addition to traditional expressions.

Certainty Algebra.   The mathematical conventions that are used to combine two or more certainty factors to yield a single certainty factor.

Certainty Factor.   A numeric measure of the degree of certainty about the *goodness, correctness, likelihood,* and so forth, of a variable value, an expression value (e.g., a premise), or an assignment action.

Comment.   A portion of a rule consisting of internal documentation about that rule.

Competing Rules.   Those candidate rules that have yet to be considered.

Completion Sequence.   A portion of a rule set composed of actions that the inference engine will carry out after all reasoning with the rule set's rules has been completed.

Conclusion.   A portion of a rule composed of series of one or more actions that the inference engine can legitimately carry out if a rule's premise can be established to be true.

Condition.   A logical expression composed of a logical variable, of a logical function, or of two expressions connected by a relational operator such as $>$, $=$, $<=$, IN, and so on. The two participating expressions must be of the same type (e.g., both numeric). In the case of the IN operator, the second expression is typically a collection of expressions.

Confirmative Certainty.   The certainty factor that results from combining two or more certainty factors in such a way that they confirm each other. The resultant confirmative certainty factor is at least as large as the largest contributing certainty factor.

Constant.   A known value that never changes.

Consultation.   The activity of acquiring or producing expert advice or solutions to a problem.

Data Base.   A collection of records of many different types organized according to a single, unified logical structure that allows data redundancy to be controlled. The logical structure must conform to the structuring conventions of one of the five major data models. A file is not a data base.

Data Base Management System.   The software that supports one of the data models. It allows the logical structure of a data base to be defined and allows data to be accessed on the basis of that structure.

Data Model.   Consists of a well-defined set of logical data structuring constructs and conventions, plus one or more access languages capable of manipulating data organized according to its logical structure mechanisms. There are five distinct data models: hierarchical, shallow-network, relational, CODASYL-network, and postrelational.

Decision Support System.   A computer-based system composed of a language system, knowledge system, and problem processing system whose purpose it is to support decision-making activities.

Dependency Diagram.   A diagram containing nodes for the variables (i.e., factors) that are pertinent to a problem area. The nodes are connected by arrows that portray the dependencies that exist among the variables.

Descriptive Knowledge.   Knowledge about past, present, and hypothetical states of an organization's environment.

Environment Knowledge.   Same as *descriptive knowledge.*

Expert System.   A computer-based system composed of a user interface, an inference engine, and stored expertise (i.e., a rule set, a "knowledge base", or an entire knowledge system). Its purpose is to offer advice or solutions for problems in a particular problem area. The advice is comparable to that which would be offered by a human expert in that problem area.

Expert System Development Tool.   Software used to facilitate the development of expert systems. The three types of tools are programming languages (and their respective interpreter or compiler software), shells, and AI environments.

Expert System Shell.   Same as *shell.*

Expression.   A constant, a variable, a function or a series of constants, variables and/or functions connected by meaningful operators.

Field.   A named category of data. Fields are used in defining the structure of a data base.

Find Actions.   Those actions stated in a variable description that an inference engine can use (e.g., as an alternative to backward chaining) to find the value of that variable when it is unknown.

Firing a Rule.   The activity of carrying out the actions in a rule's conclusion, once it has been established that the rule's premise is true.

Form.   A piece of presentation knowledge that indicates the visual layout of display slots, the source of the value that can appear in each slot, and special attributes for the slot (e.g., reverse video, blinking).

Form Management.   The ability to define forms and to subsequently process an entire form at a time with any one of several commands.

Forward Chaining.   An approach to rule-based reasoning in which the inference engine determines the effect of currently known variable values on unknown variables by firing all rules whose premises can be established as being true.

Forward Reasoning.   Same as *forward chaining.*

Frame.   A representation of an object in terms of slots where there is one slot for each of the object's characteristics. A particular instance of an object consists of a value for each of the frame's slots. The value may be assigned or determined by a procedure attached to the slot. Frames can be related to each other via inheritance slots.

Function.   A named object whose value is determined by performing a particular kind of operation. The function name (e.g., SQRT) indicates the nature of the operation (e.g., finding a square root). A function typically has one or more arguments whose values are operated upon in order to determine the function's value. Each argument is an expression.

Fuzzy Set.   A generalization of the traditional mathematical notion of a set that permits partial membership in a set.

Fuzzy Variable.   A variable that simultaneously has two or more values. The certainty factor of one value may differ from that of another value.

Heuristic.   A rule-of-thumb. The rules in a rule set may be thought of as being heuristics.

Induction.   A process that attempts to derive general rules (or to build a decision tree) based on example problems and their solutions.

Inference Engine.   A piece of software that is able to accept a problem statement from the user, use reasoning knowledge about the problem area in attempting to derive a solution, gather needed problem-specific information (e.g., from the user) in the course of reasoning, explain why it needs this added information, present the solution to the user, and explain the line of reasoning used in reaching the solution.

Initialization Sequence.   A portion of a rule set composed of actions that the inference engine will carry out before considering the rule set's rules.

Joint Certainty.   The certainty factor that results from combining two or more certainty factors in such a way that they detract from each other. The resultant joint certainty factor is no larger than the smallest of the contributing certainty factors.

Knowledge Base.   That part of an expert system containing application-specific reasoning knowledge that the inference engine uses in the course of reasoning about a problem. In expert systems whose reasoning knowledge is represented as rules, the knowledge base is a rule set or rule base. In some expert systems, a knowledge base can also contain initial values for variables. The traditional AI notion of a "knowledge base" is a small, yet interesting and important, aspect of the much more all-encompassing DSS notion of a knowledge system.

Knowledge-Based System.   An AI term that is typically taken to be synonomous with the notion of an expert system. Of course, management information systems and conventional decision support systems are also "knowledge-based" (i.e., concerned with the representation and processing of knowledge).

Knowledge Engineer.   A person (or group) that elicits reasoning knowledge from a human expert in the course of building an expert system. From the broader DSS viewpoint, anyone who is concerned with building any kind of knowledge into a knowledge system can be considered to be a knowledge engineer.

Knowledge System.   That subsystem of a decision support system in which all application-specific knowledge is represented for use by the problem processing system. This includes knowledge of any or all types (e.g., descriptive, procedural, reasoning, etc.) represented in a variety of ways (e.g., as data bases, spreadsheets, procedural models, rule sets, text, graphs, forms, templates, etc.).

Knowledge Worker.   A person who manages various kinds of knowledge in the course of filling some role in an organization.

Language System.   That subsystem of a decision support system that consists of (or characterizes) the class of all acceptable problem statements.

Linguistic Knowledge.   Knowledge about languages used for communication purposes.

LISP.   A programming language that has been used for more than a quarter of a century by computer scientists who work in the AI field. It is oriented toward the processing of symbolic data represented as linked list structures (i.e., LISt Processing). A list structure is processed with various functions such as CAR (returns the first element of a list), CDR (returns all but the first element of a list), and CONS (prefixes one list to another).

Logical Constant. True or false.

Logical Expression. An expression whose value (if it is known) is either true or false.

Logical Function. A function whose value is true or false.

Logical Variable. A variable whose value is presently either true or false.

Management Information System. A computer-based system for keeping current records about some aspect of an organization or its environment.

Menu. A collection of options available for user selection.

Metaknowledge. Knowledge about knowledge.

Modeling Knowledge. Same as *procedural knowledge.*

Natural Language. A kind of user interface that allows the user to carry on a conversation with a computer-based system in much the same way as he or she would converse with another human. The system is able to learn new terms, understand new requests in the context of prior requests, overlook grammatical errors, and carry out actions implied by the conversation.

Nested Integration. The approach to software integration in which all secondary components are constrained to being used within the confines of a single dominant component.

Nonprocedural. Indicates that a procedure (i.e., a definite *sequence* of steps) is not specified. That is, there is no explanation of how to accomplish a task. There is no programming. Reasoning knowledge captured in the guise of a rule set's rules is nonprocedural.

Numeric Constant. A number composed of digits, an optional decimal point, and an optional leading sign (+ or −). An integer constant is a special case of a numeric constant because it contains no decimal point.

Numeric Expression. An expression whose value (if it is known) is a number. The expression can involve numeric constants, numeric variables, and/or numeric functions connected by numeric operators such as $+$, $-$, $*$, $/$, $**$, and MOD (modulus).

Numeric Function. A function that yields a numeric value with respect to its argument(s).

Numeric Variable. A variable whose value is presently a number. An integer variable is a special case of a numeric variable in that its value is an integer.

Object-Oriented Language. A language for representing objects and processing those representations with various methods. The methods available for processing an object (e.g., a spreadsheet cell, a data base record, a graph, a form, a variable, etc.) depend on the nature of that object.

Picture. A sequence of placeholders and possibly some literal symbols that control the appearance of a value as it is being displayed.

Postrelational Data Base. A data base whose records are not restricted to tabular organization and processing. All types of real-world relationships (e.g., 1 to 1, 1 to many, many to many, recursive, forked) can be directly represented in a semantically lucid manner and can be processed with various postrelational access languages. This kind of data base is sometimes called a multiarchical or extended-network data base.

Preactions.   A portion of a rule consisting of actions that the inference engine will carry out before examining the rule's premise.

Premise.   A portion of a rule composed of one or more conditions connected by Boolean operators such as AND, OR, XOR (exclusive OR), and NOT. If a rule's premise can be established as being true, then the rule's conclusion is valid. A premise is an example of a logical expression.

Premise-Testing Strategy.   The strategy that an inference engine uses when trying to establish the truth of a rule's premise.

Presentation Knowledge.   Knowledge that controls the way in which presentations are made.

Problem Processing System.   That subsystem of a decision support system which accepts problems stated in terms of the language system and draws upon the knowledge system in an effort to produce solutions.

Problem Processor.   Same as *problem processing system.*

Procedural.   Indicates that a procedure (i.e., an explicit *sequence* of steps) has been specified. A program has been devised stating, in detail, how to accomplish a task.

Procedural Knowledge.   Knowledge about how to produce a desired result by carrying out a prescribed series of processing steps.

Procedural Model.   A program that represents a piece of procedural knowledge about how to analyze some set of input data. When a procedural model (e.g., for regression analysis) is executed it carries out a prescribed algorithm and reports the results.

Programming Language.   A formal language for representing procedural knowledge.

PROLOG.   A programming language that has been used for more than a decade by computer scientists who work in the AI field. It is oriented toward processing Horn clause axioms (a particular kind of axiom allowed in first-order predicate calculus). These axioms are processed by a resolution theorem prover using the principle of unification.

Reasoning Knowledge.   Knowledge about what circumstances allow particular conclusions to be considered to be valid.

Record.   A group of data values consisting of one value for each of a prescribed set of related fields.

Relational Algebra.   The low-level access language whose commands produce new intermediate tables by operating on one or two existing tables.

Relational Calculus.   The high-level access language whose commands operate on multiple tables simultaneously without requiring any intermediate tables.

Relational Data Base.   A data base whose records are organized into tables that can be processed by either the relational algebra or relational calculus. Relationships between tables are represented by field redundancy.

Relational Operator. The operator in a condition that relates one expression to another (e.g., $>$, $<=$).

Report Generation. The ability to use a single command to generate an entire report patterned according to a template.

Reverse Reasoning. Same as *backward chaining.*

Rigor. An indication of how exhaustive an inference engine is in considering candidate rules. Will all be considered (full rigor) or is it possible for some competing rules to be disregarded?

Rule. A named fragment of reasoning knowledge consisting of a premise and a conclusion. In addition, a rule may have other attributes such as a priority, a cost, a preaction sequence, a premise-testing strategy, a textual description, and an internal comment.

Rule Base. The collection of all rules sets available to an inference engine.

Rule Set. A named collection of rules that represent reasoning knowledge about some problem area. A rule set is used by an inference engine to solve specific problems in that area. In addition to rules, a rule set may also contain an initialization sequence, a completion sequence, and variable descriptions.

Rule Set Developer. A person who uses a rule set development tool to capture an expert's reasoning knowledge in the guise of a rule set.

Rule Set Manager. Software that is used to formally specify, modify, analyze, and compile a rule set.

Selection Order. The order in which the competing rules remaining for a group of candidate rules are to be considered (e.g., based on relative rule priorities, costs, positions, numbers of unknown variables in premises, etc.).

Semantic Net. A graphical representation of binary relationships between objects. Each node in the net represents an object. Two nodes are related by an arrow that points from one to the other. The arrow is labeled to indicate the semantics of the relationship. The postrelational data model's logical structuring facilities have a great deal in common with semantic nets.

Semantics. The meaning of a symbol, expression, or relationship.

Shell. A kind of expert system development tool consisting of two stand-alone pieces of software: a rule set manager and an inference engine capable of reasoning with rule sets built with the rule set manager.

Spreadsheet. A collection of cells whose values can be displayed on the console screen. By changing cell definitions and having all cell values reevaluated, a user can readily observe the effects of those changes.

String Constant. A string of text composed of alphabetic characters, digits, punctuation, and/or other recognizable symbols.

String Expression. An expression whose value (if it is known) is a string of text. The expression can involve string constants, string variables, and/or string functions connected by the string concatenation ($+$) operator.

String Function. A function that yields a text string value with respect to its arguments.

String Variable.   A variable whose value is presently a string of text composed of alphabetic characters, digits, punctuation, and/or other recognizable symbols.

Synergistic Integration.   The approach to software integration in which each component can be used independently or multiple components can be used in tandem to produce an overall effect that is greater than the sum of the individual component effects. There are no clear dividing lines between component capabilities and no component limits the use of any other.

Table.   A named collection of records, each of which is composed of one data value for each of the table's fields. A table is not a file, but may exist in one or more operating system files.

Template.   A piece of presentation knowledge that indicates the visual layout of a report's contents and the sources of values that can appear in particular locations.

Text Processing.   The activity of manipulating (creating, altering, viewing) passages of text. The formatting capabilities of a text processor are not as extensive as those of a word processor.

Unknown Expression.   An expression whose value is not known because the value of at least one of the expression's variables is unknown.

Unknown Threshold.   This is the certainty factor level below which a variable or premise value is considered to be unknown.

Unknown Variable.   A variable whose value is presently unknown.

Variable.   A named object whose value can change. A variable's present value is referenced via the variable name.

Variable Descriptions.   That portion of a rule set consisting of descriptions of the natures of variables used in the rule set's rules. Each variable can be described in terms of such characteristics as its find actions, the timing of those actions, the degree of rigor to be used in establishing its value, the certainty algebra to be used in determining that value's certainty factor, and so on.

Virtual Field.   A field whose values are calculated as needed rather than actually being stored in a data base.

Wildcard Symbol.   A symbol which, when encountered in a text string, is considered to match with any other symbol(s).

Index

This book has been set Compugraphic 8600, in 10 and 9 point Palatino, leaded 2 points. Part and chapter numbers are 14 point Palatino Italic. Part and chapter titles are 24 point Palatino. The overall type area is 26.5 picas by 48 picas.